Musical Form

John Dewey Library
Johnson State College
Johnson, Vermont 05656

Musical Form

Studies in Analysis and Synthesis

ELLIS B. KOHS
University of Southern California

HOUGHTON MIFFLIN COMPANY BOSTON
Atlanta   Dallas   Geneva, Ill.   Hopewell, N.J.   Palo Alto   London

John Dewey Library
Johnson State College
Johnson, Vermont 05656

781.5
K827m
79-3038

Copyright © 1976 by Houghton Mifflin Company. Copyright © 1973 by Ellis B. Kohs. All rights reserved. No part of this work may be reproduced or transmitted in any form or by any means, electronic or mechanical, including photocopying and recording, or by any information storage or retrieval system, without permission in writing from the publisher.

Printed in the U.S.A.

Library of Congress Catalog Card Number: 75-39796
ISBN: 0-395-18613-7

To my mother and father

Contents

Preface xiii
Suggested Supplementary Materials xv
Table of Abbreviations xvii

1 *Structural Principles Common to the Arts*   1

    Repetition, Contrast, Variation, and Balance 1
    Space: Distance, Dimension, and Volume 4
    Tempo 4
    Structure and Ornament 4
    Suggested Exercises 5

2 *The Motive*   7

    Thematic Motives 7
    Accompanimental Motives 12
    Suggested Exercises 14

3 *The Melodic Phrase*   17

    Vocal and Instrumental Melody 17
    Poetry, Prose, and Music 18
    The Sentence and the Musical Phrase 19
    Motivic and Nonmotivic Melodies 21
    The Rhythmic Structure of Phrases 21
    Phrase Length Determinants 22
    Suggested Exercises 24

4 *The Cadence*   25

       Perfect Authentic Cadence 28
       Imperfect Authentic Cadence 31
       Plagal Cadence 32
       Half Cadence 33
       Modal Cadence 34
       Suggested Exercises 35

5 *The Phrase as a Structural Unit*   37

       Phrases of Various Lengths 39
       Nonphrases 45
       Suggested Exercises 46

6 *Extensions of the Phrase*   47

       Extension at the Beginning 47
       Extension in Course 47
       Extension at the End 48
       Extension by Phrase Repetition 50
       Multiple Extension 51
       Suggested Exercises 52

7 *The Period*   55

       Two-Phrase Periods 56
       Three-Phrase Periods 62
       Four-Phrase Periods 65
       Nonperiods 67
       Suggested Exercises 70

8 *Extensions of the Period*   73

       Preliminary Extension 76
       Extension in Course 76
       Precadential Extension 76
       Postcadential Extension 76
       Confirming Extensions vs. Dissolutions 78
       Suggested Exercises 79

9   *Phrase Groups*   81

> The Chain Phrase   81
> The Chain of Phrases   82
> *Suggested Exercises*   86

10 *Polyphonic Devices*   89

> Imitation   89
> Canon   91
> Inversion   91
> Stretto   91
> Diminution   91
> Compression   92
> Augmentation   92
> Expansion   92
> Retrograde   93
> *Suggested Exercises*   94

11 *Small Song Forms: Binary Form*   99

> *Suggested Exercises*   104

12 *Small Song Forms: Ternary Form*   107

> *Suggested Exercises*   110

13 *Small Song Forms: A Miscellany of Special Cases*   111

> Incipient Ternary (Rounded Binary) Form   112
> Extension and Dissolution   116
> *Suggested Exercises*   119

14 *Large (Compound) Song Forms: Song and Trio*   121

> *Suggested Exercises*   127

15 *Homophonic Variations*   129

     Variation Procedure   129
     Variation Form   134
     Suggested Exercises   *142*

16 *Polyphonic Variations: Ostinato, Ground Bass, Passacaglia, Chaconne*   143

     Ostinato   143
     Ground Bass   145
     Passacaglia and Chaconne   148
     Suggested Exercises   *157*

17 *Canon*   159

     Suggested Exercises   *166*

18 *The Invention*   169

     Two-Voice Invention   169
     Three-Voice Invention   172
     Suggested Exercises   *175*

19 *Fugue*   177

     Exposition   178
     Development   181
     Procedures Related to Fugue   187
     Suggested Exercises   *199*

20 *Polyphonic Variations: Chorale Variation*   201

     Cantus Firmus Treatment   203
     Polyphonic Style   207
     Suggested Exercises   *215*

21 Rondo Forms   217

          Rondeau 219
          ABABA-Type Rondo 221
          ABACA-Type Rondo 224
          ABACABA-Type Rondo 229
          Suggested Exercises 247

22 Altered Rondo Forms   249

          Extended Rondo 249
          Compressed Rondo 254
          Rondeau and Rondo in Concerto Movements 257
          Suggested Exercises 260

23 Sonata Form   261

          Introduction 262
          Exposition 263
          Development 265
          Recapitulation 266
          Coda 268
          Some Examples of Sonata Form 269
          Suggested Exercises 289

24 Near-Sonata Forms: Sonatina, Sonata-Rondo   291

          Sonatina 291
          Sonata-Rondo 296
          Sonatina-Rondo in a Concerto Last Movement 300
          Suggested Exercises 302

25 Vocal Forms   303

          Recitative 303
          Arias and Art Songs 306
          Suggested Exercises 321

26 *Works Comprising Several Movements*   *323*

       Two-Movement Works 324
       Three-Movement Works 326
       Four-Movement Works 327
       Works of More Than Four Movements 327
       Suggested Exercises 329

       References *331*
       Index *333*

Preface

This book is designed primarily for the student of music who is preparing for a professional career in that very great and demanding art. It is hoped that students in all fields—performance, music education, music history, theory, composition, conducting, and church music, as well as the inquiring and informed amateur—will find here new avenues of thought and new insights regarding the art and craft of musical composition.

This work attempts to demonstrate my conviction that it is more important to ask relevant and significant questions than it is to establish comfortably easy and oversimplified answers. In the pursuit of this objective, it is essential that the teacher encourage individual initiative and creative thinking in students, and discourage the mistaken assumption that the aim of education is the acquisition of factual knowledge. There is no substitute for direct experience in the arts. Words *about* music must never be mistaken for education *in* music.

Teachers in colleges, conservatories, and universities that operate under the semester system will find that the present text may be used in a single semester course for a rapid survey of the field. Only a few of the exercises will then be assigned, and the emphasis will be on comprehending the text and listening to some of the cited illustrations.

If two semesters are available, the instructor may wish to assign a larger number of exercises. It is not intended that any one student should attempt all the suggested exercises.

If the quarter system is used, it should be possible to cover the text without the written assignments in one quarter, adding a small number of assignments in two quarters, and a larger number of assignments in three quarters.

Most of the chapters include suggested exercises in composition. The easier ones may be assigned to students with some talent in this area. The more difficult ones may be assigned to students in the general class who are majoring in composition, and to those taking courses in composition.

The amateur too may wish to dip into the book here and there as his curiosity leads him, to explore some topic that may arise from his reading about music or from his listening experiences.

The list of suggested supplementary materials is designed to provide a basis for optional intensive study; it is hoped that no student will find it a burden to secure at least one of the suggested items. If only one additional work is used, the Burkhart *Anthol-*

ogy is perhaps the most serviceable. If two, then the anthology and either the Beethoven or the Mozart *Sonatas*. Because frequent reference is made to the Bach, Mozart, Beethoven, and Brahms scores, I have indicated them throughout the text by means of the abbreviations shown on page xv. The more extended list of scores and books that follows is intended to help those who wish to extend their purview still further; these materials should not be regarded as required adjuncts to the text.

The terms and signs pertaining to harmonic analysis are largely in general use. Where there may be some doubt about usage, the terms are explained in a footnote. Teachers wishing to correlate this text with a book on theory or harmony may want to consider using my *Music Theory*, but no such association is necessary.

No one can write a book unaided. The present work owes much to the kindness and generosity of many people who have read portions of the manuscript in various stages of its realization. Among these, I particularly wish to mention Carl Bricken, Ingolf Dahl, Alice Ehlers, William Gardner, Scott Goldthwaite, Joan Meggett, Leonard B. Meyer, William Poland, Halsey Stevens, Dan M. Urquhart, Thomas Warburton, and Robert E. Wolf. Robert U. Nelson and Paul Pisk read the entire manuscript and made many very excellent and helpful suggestions. Richard Appleton untangled a number of knotted thoughts and helped to make the book more readable for the nonprofessional.

Finally, I owe a great debt to the many students at the University of Southern California, without whose challenging presence this book could not have been written; and to my colleagues on the staff of the School of Music, whose constructive criticism has been matched by friendly encouragement and the unintended stimulation of their own high standards and professional excellence.

Ellis B. Kohs

Suggested Supplementary Materials

It is hoped that the student will have access to a music library with a far-ranging collection of scores of all periods and styles. Phonograph records of the works analyzed should be available for audition of those compositions represented here only in notation or in diagram.

One may wish to have a personal copy of the following works, referred to throughout with the abbreviations at the left:

Burkhart, Charles, *Anthology for Musical Analysis.* 2d ed. New York: Holt, Rinehart and Winston, 1972.

BS   Beethoven, Ludwig van, *Sonatas for Pianoforte.*

BW   Brahms, Johannes, *Piano Works,* Vol. 2 (the keyboard works from op. 76 to op. 119).

BWTC   Bach, Johann Sebastian, *The Well-Tempered Clavier,* Vols. 1–2.

MS   Mozart, Wolfgang Amadeus, *Sonatas and Fantasias for Pianoforte.*

The instructor may wish to have the school library make available the following scores to which occasional references are made:

Bach, Johann Sebastian, keyboard works: *Two-part Inventions, Three-part Inventions, French Suites, English Suites,* the *Partitas,* the *Goldberg Variations,* the *Clavierübung,* the several collections of organ chorales, and the *Passacaglia and Fugue* for organ; chamber works: *Sonatas and Partitas for Unaccompanied Violin, Sonatas for Clavier and Violin, The Art of Fugue, Musical Offering;* also, the six *Brandenburg Concertos,* the *Passion According to St. Matthew,* the *Mass in B minor,* and the four *Suites for Orchestra.*

Bartók, Béla, *Piano Concerto no. 3.*

Beethoven, Ludwig van, the nine symphonies, the string quartets, the piano concertos, *Leonore Overture no. 3.*

Berg, Alban, *Concerto for Violin and Orchestra.*

Berlioz, Hector, *Fantastic Symphony, Harold in Italy, The Damnation of Faust.*

Bizet, Georges, *L'arlésienne Suite no. 1.*

Brahms, Johannes, the four symphonies, the three sonatas for violin and piano, *Variations on a Theme by Joseph Haydn,* op. 56a–b.

Chopin, Frédéric, *Ballades.*

Debussy, Claude, *Prélude à l'après-midi d'un faune.*

Dvořák, Antonin, *Symphony in E minor* ("From the New World").

Franck, César, *Symphony in D minor, Sonata in A major for Violin and Piano.*

Haydn, Joseph, *String Quartets,* op. 74, 76.

Kohs, Ellis B., *Three Chorale Variations on Hebrew Hymns, Sonata for Clarinet and Piano.*

Mahler, Gustav, *Symphony no. 4, Symphony no. 9, Das Lied von der Erde.*

Mendelssohn, Felix, *Concerto in E minor for Violin and Orchestra, Songs without Words.*

Mozart, Wolfgang Amadeus, *Symphony in C major* (K. 96), *Symphony in D major* (K. 133), *Symphony in E-flat major* (K. 184), *Symphony in D major* (K. 504), *Symphony in E-flat major* (K. 543), *Symphony in G minor* (K. 550), *Symphony in C major* (K. 551); the string quartets, *The Magic Flute,* Overture to *The Marriage of Figaro.*

Piston, Walter, *Sonata for Violin and Piano.*[1]

Purcell, Henry, *Dido and Aeneas.*

Rameau, Jean-Philippe, *Pièces de Clavecin.*[2]

Scarlatti, Domenico, *Sixty Sonatas* (2 vols).[3]

Schubert, Franz, *Symphony no. 8 in B minor, Symphony no. 9 in C major, Der Erlkönig.*

Schumann, Robert, *Concerto in A minor for Piano and Orchestra.*

Stravinsky, Igor, *Symphony of Psalms, Octet for Wind Instruments, Sonata for Two Pianos.*

Wagner, Richard, Prelude to Act 1 of *Die Meistersinger.*

Wolf, Hugo, *Das verlassene Mägdlein.*

---

[1] Arrow Music Press. New York, 1940.
[2] Bärenreiter edition (ed. Jacobi). Kassel, 1958.
[3] G. Schirmer (ed. Kirkpatrick). New York, 1953.

Table of Abbreviations

Augmented	Aug.
Bracket	⌐¬ or ⌊⌋, generally used to indicate a motive; a series of brackets indicates continued use of the motive. It may also be used to show groupings of other factors, such as harmony.
Cadences:	
Deceptive Cadence	Dec. Cad.
Evaded Cadence	Ev. Cad.
Half Cadence	H.C.
Imperfect Authentic Cadence	I.A.C.
Perfect Authentic Cadence	P.A.C.
Plagal Cadence	Pl. C.
Diminished	Dim.
Enharmonic	Enh.
Extension[1]	Ext.
Hands (in performance):	
left hand	l.h.
right hand	r.h.
Introduction	Intro.
Inverted (or Inversion)	Inv.
Keys (on diagrams):	F minor indicated as f:
indicated by a letter followed by a colon.	A major indicated as A:
Measure, measures	m., mm.
Mode: major indicated by capital letter, minor by lower case (if the word *mode* is lacking).	G major indicated as G: G minor indicated as g:
Modulation	Mod.
Opus	op. 2
Opus/Number	2/1

---

[1] Preliminary and postcadential extensions shown on diagram by horizontal rather than curved line.

Movement	ii
Phrase	Phr.
Antecedent Phrase	Ant. Phr.
Consequent Phrase	Cons. Phr.
Pianoforte	Pf.
Repetition	Rep. (or ·/.)˙
Retransition[2]	Retrans.
Sequence	Seq.
Signs:	
Repetition of the previous unit (may be a phrase, group, or formal division).	·/.
Formal repetition of section enclosed by sign.	‖: :‖
Themes (or Sections):	
Principal Theme (or Section)	P.T. (P.S.)
Second Theme (or Section)	S.T. (S.S.)
Closing Theme (or Section)	C.T. (C.S.)
Third Theme (or Section)	T.T. (T.S.)
Codetta	C^{tta}
Transition[3]	Trans.
Varied (Varied Repetition)	Var. (Var. Rep. or Var. ·/.)
Violin I, Viola, Violoncello	Vl. I, Vla., Vlc.

(See also pp. 194 and 198 for explanation of symbols used in fugue analysis.)

[2] Shown on diagram by a horizontal rather than a curved line.
[3] Shown on diagram by a horizontal rather than a curved line.

Musical Form

Structural Principles Common to the Arts 1

Music was not always an isolated or self-contained cultural phenomenon removed from other means of communication and from other avenues of personal and group experience. It has become separated from such expressions of the human spirit as poetry, dance, theater, and religion only in comparatively recent times. In the cultures of so-called primitive peoples the arts are inseparable; they derive meaning and value from their social function and mutual association. Thus a harvest rite might include a dance accompanied by vocal and instrumental music, a song with supposedly magical words, and specially designed costumes appropriate to the occasion. An inner circle of active participants might be surrounded by an outer circle of observers or more passive participants.

The arts in Western culture have become increasingly more specialized, more highly stylized. They have tended to develop independently, using separate forms. They are no longer part of the rituals of active, everyday group life; rather, they are the object of comparatively passive contemplation by the few who seek them out. Yet, as children display the characteristics of their parents, so today's arts reveal features and structural principles as evidence of their common inheritance and origin. It is the purpose of this chapter to suggest a few of these common principles so that the formal possibilities and the expressive values of music can be viewed in their original, larger perspective.

REPETITION, CONTRAST, VARIATION, AND BALANCE

It is a characteristic of the visual and plastic arts (for example, architecture, painting, sculpture, dance) and the verbal arts (such as theater, prose, poetry), as it is of music, that they always display in their works the qualities of coherence and comprehensibility. Coherence and comprehensibility result from the capacity of the mind (both the artist's and the listener's or viewer's) to organize remembered experience. This ability, of course, varies according to an individual's background, intelligence, and imagination. Among a group of persons listening to the same composition or looking at the same painting, each will react in a manner that is conditioned by his previous exposure to similar stimuli. The printed words you are reading now have no meaning in themselves: the letters are mere shapes, the words are combinations of shapes. The ideas they stimulate are a product of both my thoughts and your previous verbal and nonverbal experiences.

Form is achieved in the arts through the organization of intelligible units in accordance with at least provisionally accepted rules of repetition, contrast, and variation. The elementary forms in Example 1.1 demonstrate some of the ways in which the creative mind functions in assembling a work of art.

Example 1.1   Three-part design with two figures.

XxXxX   oOo   xXxXx

Analysis of this simple design reveals *repetition* of the letter *x* within each of the outer groups and repetition of the letter *o* in the center group. Further repetition may be observed in the same number of letters, five, in the two outer groups. There is also continual alternation of large and small letters throughout the design.

There is *contrast* in both size and shape, in the inferior numerical weight (three) of the middle group, and in the plans of alternation of *X* and *x* in the outer groups. There is *variation,* achieved by retaining the figure within each group but changing the size of adjacent letters. The third group repeats the use of *X* and *x*, but the sequence is different. There is *balance,* a use of symmetry in each group and among the three. The third group, however, is somewhat lighter in weight than the first group because there is one less large *X*.

Example 1.2   Free development of elements.

XXXX. . OOOOOO . oooo

X̄XXXXXXX. ⊠⊠⊠. oXoX

XXXX. . . . . ooOOOOOo

This is a rather complex form. Line 3 is a varied repetition of line 1. Line 2 is a reworking or development of elements derived from line 1. The main figures (or motifs) are *X* and *O*, the latter varied as *o*. The dots, which are nonalphabetical material, provide additional contrast.

In line 1 the number of large *X* figures is the same as the number of small *o* figures, providing both repetition and balance. The *X* and *o* groups enclose a contrasting number of large *O* figures. It may be observed also that *O* is related to *X* on one level of analysis because both are capital letters. On another level capital *O* is related to small *o* because they are the same letter of the alphabet. Thus the *X* group and the *O* group combine to form one large unit (all capitals) while the *O* group and the *o* group combine to form another large unit (all are the fifteenth letter of the alphabet). The *O* group belongs to *both* the large units, and serves as a connecting link. Line 2 uses the same elements as line 1, but these are sometimes embellished by a dash (above, below, or superimposed). *O* is superimposed on *X* three times, to provide additional density and complexity of texture. In line 3 the dots and the circles, which previously had been separated, now combine to form unbroken groups. The overall effect of line 3 is comparative simplicity and unity of design, perhaps even repose, following the more active maneuvers of line 2.

Let us turn from these abstract designs to consider the manner in which some of the principles they illustrate apply to some of the arts. In poetry, for example, repetition may be achieved through the use of such means as rhyme, alliteration, and meter. Contrast may be provided within a given meter by a change in the number of weak pulses between accents or by cross-rhythms created by phrasing, punctuation,[1] or even word meanings.

Dance, since it exists in time as well as in space, forms an obvious parallel to music. A leap in the air is in striking contrast to a static position on both feet, and both are different from the dynamic equilibrium of a stance on one foot. Consecutive leaps in the same direction provide cumulative repetition. Leaps alternately to the left and to the right provide balance and constitute a mirror type of motif variation.

Repetition in architecture may be observed in the rows of similar columns of a Greek temple, and in the symmetrical hierarchy of arches on the facade of a Gothic cathedral. In both instances there is great contrast of vertical and horizontal lines, of volumes and shapes. Variation is found in the employment of the same shapes in different sizes, in different proportions, or in different relationships to one another and to other shapes.

Repetition in music may be achieved in many ways and on many levels. This is illustrated in Example 1.3 with the analysis of the popular French folk song, *Frère Jacques*.

Example 1.3   Repetition in music. *Frère Jacques.*

The motifs, in music usually called *motives,* are labeled x, y, and z. The variants of x are indicated as x^1 and x^2. It should be observed that y is itself a variant of x, since it also involves the interval of a third: x is a filled-in third, y is a leap of a third. Furthermore, x^2 differs from x because it outlines a descending rather than an ascending third, it is embellished by an upper neighboring tone, and because four eighth notes replace the initial two quarter notes.

Repetition is present not only in motive usage but in connection with whole measures. Thus every even-numbered measure is a repetition of the preceding odd-numbered measure, which results in a form one might describe in symbols as *aabbccdd*. It will be observed, finally, that all of line 2 may be regarded as a variation of line 1.

Contrast is provided, of course, by the different pitches, rhythm patterns, and so forth. Note also the balance created by the tendency toward ascending motion in mm. 1–4 and descending motion in mm. 5–8, an arch form that appears very frequently in melodic lines.

[1] See Example 3.1b.

SPACE: DISTANCE, DIMENSION, AND VOLUME

Distance, dimension, and volume obviously are factors that pertain to the spatial arts such as architecture and sculpture. They have their counterparts, however, in the world of music. Everyone senses closeness between tones played on adjacent keys of the piano, for example. Notes at opposite ends of the piano *sound* far apart. This sense of aural distance is psychological and conditioned rather than self-evident or inherent in the tones themselves.

The dimensions of height, width, and thickness seem irrelevant to intangible music, yet familiarity with musical notation (which exists in two-dimensional space) has conditioned most people to think that melodies are somehow horizontal, that chords are vertical, and that density created by simultaneous tones or lines is comparable to thickness. In the latter connection the familiar term *musical texture* suggests an analogue with the warp and woof and the tightness or looseness of weave. The concept of volume refers to occupied space in the visual, tactile world. A cubic foot of iron occupies the same volume as a cubic foot of feathers. The word *volume* in the aural world refers to loudness, which depends upon wave frequency, intensity, and partial (overtone) structure.

TEMPO

As units of space are measured in inches or meters, time is measured in seconds and minutes. Although ordinary, objective time is an absolute, people experience all units of time in a subjective, psychological way that is quite relative. One minute of a Haydn rondo-allegro will appear to have a different duration than a one-minute piece in slow tempo by Webern; the four-plus minutes of uninterrupted Eb harmony at the beginning of Wagner's *Das Rheingold* do not seem of comparable length to a four-minute string quartet movement by Mozart. In the experience of musical tempo one is aware of the possibility of slow, moderate, or fast movement—acceleration and deceleration. Since the clock does not change pace, all these sensations are purely subjective. Consistency, contrast, or variation in tempo are all important factors in the larger aspects of musical form; witness the term *movement*, which indicates a semi-independent temporal division of a composition. A group of movements played in succession may form a symphony, sonata, or suite.

STRUCTURE AND ORNAMENT

The distinction between structure and ornament may be observed in all the arts. In drama and in the novel one may find decorative secondary plots, comic relief, and so forth. In architecture it is not uncommon for a cathedral or temple to be decorated by sculpture. Likewise in music there are distinctions between functional chords and decorative nonharmonic tones, between theme statements and purely connective passage work.

SUGGESTED EXERCISES

1. Submit three or four examples from several arts other than music of the ways in which repetition, contrast, and variation operate to secure form. Identify the examples clearly, and discuss each in detail.

2. Submit three or four short examples of music. Discuss how repetition, contrast, and variation are used to achieve form in each.

3. Write in musical notation the melody of *America* and *The Star Spangled Banner*. Discuss each in terms of the elements of form: (a) repetition, contrast, variation, balance; (b) distance, dimension, volume; (c) tempo; (d) structure and ornament.

The Motive

A *motive* is a short, continuously or frequently recurring musical figure or shape having a distinctive character and a clearly recognizable profile. Each factor in this definition is critical. If the musical idea was more than a very few notes, not frequently or continuously employed, or without distinct profile, the term would not apply.

Motives may be described in terms of their *function,* that is, thematic or accompanimental; or in terms of the prevailing *constant,* for example, rhythm, melody (interval contour), or rhythm and melody combined.[1]

In the following sections, some thematic motives, both rhythmic and melodic, and a few rhythmic and melodic accompanimental motives will be examined.

THEMATIC MOTIVES

Example 2.1   Rhythmic motive. Beethoven, *Symphony no. 5 in C minor,* i, mm. 1–21 (reduced score).

---

[1] Some of Wagner's *leitmotiven* may seem harmonic rather than melodic or rhythmic (see, for example, the famous first two chords of *Tristan und Isolde*), but, in fact, the chords are associated with simultaneous melodic and/or rhythmic elements and sometimes with orchestration as well.

Although the characteristic rhythm (♪ ♫♩ | ♩) appears consistently in these measures, the melodic leap of a third, used at the beginning, does not. The motive must therefore be regarded as essentially rhythmic rather than melodic. Toward the end of the cited passage, there is a change in the *anacrusis* (upbeat) pattern. The *new* melodic shape (see mm. 14–18) is both *imitated* (repeated in another part) and *inverted* (turned upside down).[2] The motive is indicated by a bracket.

A four-note motive (♫♩ | ♪ ♪) pervades the *Intermezzo in F minor*. A few of the many melodic shapes assumed by this rhythmic motive are illustrated below.

Example 2.2   The four-note motive. BW, 118/4.

The rhythmic motive in Example 2.3 ♪ ♫♩ | ♩. or its variant ♪ ♫♩ | ♪♩ is an element that is found in and that helps to relate the transition theme (T.T.), mm. 8–13, the closing theme (C.T.), mm. 21–28, and the codetta (C^tta), mm. 29–31; the melodic shapes of which are otherwise different.

Example 2.3   Motivically related themes. MS, K. 333, ii, mm. 8–10, 21–25, 29–30.

The melodic shape shown in Example 2.4a assumes two rhythmic guises in the course of the movement. In the introduction it appears in slow tempo, with a dotted rhythm (see Example 2.4b), while in the development section, shortly after the cancellation of the key signature, and transposed to E minor, it is in a fast tempo and in even, undotted quarters (see Example 2.4c).

Example 2.4   Motivically related themes. BS, 13, i.

(a)   *(b)* Grave   *(c)* Allegro

[2] See the index for reference to pages where these terms are discussed more fully.

In Example 2.5a the melodic motive of three tones ascending stepwise (C–D–E) found in m. 1 takes on numerous rhythmic and melodic aspects. In addition to pervading the opening theme itself in Example 2.5a, it is an important element in the later themes, Examples 2.5b and 2.5c. (Brackets indicate motivically related units. Dotted lines indicate that the motive has been rearranged in anagram fashion.)

Example 2.5   Motivically related themes. Schubert, *Symphony no. 9 in C major,* i.

(a) Andante

(b) Allegro

(c)

In Example 2.6 the principal themes of the first two movements are related by their joint use of a three-note melodic motive that involves a descending step followed by an ascending fourth.

Example 2.6   Motivically related themes. Franck, *Symphony in D minor.*

(a) Lento

(b) Allegretto

A century before Bach, Frescobaldi developed many of the then new polyphonic forms in a manner that strongly influenced the North German school of composition. At one point in his *Capriccio on La, Sol, Fa, Re, Mi* (that is, A–G–F–D–E), he weaves an intricate contrapuntal texture in which this melodic motive of five tones appears simultaneously in three voices, in combination with a variety of rhythmic patterns.

Example 2.7   Melodic motive in three voices simultaneously. Frescobaldi, *Capriccio on La, Sol, Fa, Re, Mi*, mm. 32–35.[3]

The two-measure motive that appears at the beginning of the movement in Example 2.8a is long enough to be divisible into parts or fragments. These fragments then become significant in themselves through repetition and imitation. The imitative development of one fragment (x) is shown in Example 2.8b. There is a suggestion of motive inversion in Example 2.8c. A hypothetical tonal inversion would read as indicated in Example 2.8d.

Example 2.8   Motive basis of thematic material. BS, 2/1, i.

(a) Basic motive, mm. 1–2.

(b) Development of fragment (x), mm. 11–13.

(c) Suggestion of motive inversion, mm. 21–22.

(d) Hypothetical tonal inversion of basic motive.

[3] In the second statement of the motive A–G–F–D–E in the alto line, the last note, E, is transferred to the soprano line. The G in the soprano line, m. 4, may be regarded as an interpolation which decorates the F♯ in the manner of an appoggiatura.

A three-note motive encompassing the interval of a tritone serves as the basis of the main theme in Example 2.9. Developmental techniques include note repetition and inversion. The rhythmic freedom resulting from the frequent alternation of 2/4 and 5/8 meter is of particular interest.

Example 2.9   The main theme and its motivic basis. Bartók, *Concerto for Orchestra,*[4] iv, mm. 3–11.

Example 2.10   Motivic basis of thematic material. MS, K. 283, i, mm. 16–22 and 43–45.

(a) Mm. 16–22.

(b) Mm. 43–45.

The transition section (mm. 16–22) between the first and second themes is based on a one-measure motive. The motive recurs later (mm. 43–45) with stretto-like over-lapping.[5] The clear relationship between the eighth note and the sixteenth note aspects of the motive is of particular interest here.

[4] *Concerto for Orchestra* by Béla Bartók. Copyright 1946 by Hawkes & Son (London) Ltd.; Renewed 1973. Reprinted by permission of Boosey and Hawkes, Inc.
[5] See page 181 for discussion of *stretto*.

The main thematic idea of the *Rhapsody in G minor* of Brahms is based on a four-note figure. There is a step between the first two notes; the second, third, and fourth form the outline of a triad. Note the use of inversion in two instances, and the 4 + 4 (= 8) measure grouping.

Example 2.11   The main theme and its motivic basis. BW, 79/2, mm. 1–8.

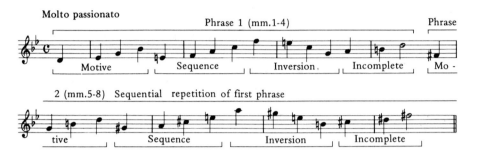

Several of Bach's *Two-* and *Three-Part Inventions* should be carefully examined. The *invention* (see Chapter 18) is a short work in imitative style based on one or two, or sometimes more, motives which are stated at the beginning and then developed throughout with little or no interruption. The themes may be developed in combination or separately, through repetition, sequence, and so forth.

A number of the preludes in BWTC are inventions in style, although not titled as such. See, for example, Volume 1: *Preludes nos. 13, 14,* and *20.* Compare these with *Prelude no. 1* which, although based on a well-defined half-measure motive, is neither polyphonic nor imitative. Therefore it is not an example of invention style, but what some writers call prelude form or style.

ACCOMPANIMENTAL MOTIVES

The theme of the middle section (mm. 59ff) of BS, 2/1, iv is accompanied by a series of chords that employ the following rhythm: ♩ ♩ ♩ ♩ . Similar procedures

are used in BS, 13, i, mm. 51ff and BS, 14/1, i, mm. 1–4.

Example 2.12   Accompanimental motives in BS, 13 and 14/1.

(a) 13, i, mm. 51ff.

(b) 14/1, i, mm. 1–4.

The Alberti bass figure is a device designed to give chords a sense of rhythmic animation. It may be regarded as a type of accompanimental motive. Examples of this are plentiful in MS, since there is hardly one sonata in which the device is not employed. The following examples are typical.

Example 2.13　　Alberti bass figures.

(a) MS, K. 279, i, mm. 5–8.

(b) MS, K. 309, iii, mm. 1–4.

(c) MS, K. 545, ii, mm. 1–4.

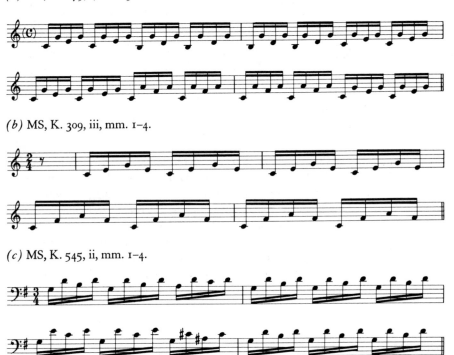

In Example 2.14 the accompaniment figure in the bass consists of a repeated single tone which is a pedal point at the same time. A similar procedure appears in the middle section and the coda of the first movement of Brahms's *Sonata no. 3 in D minor for Violin and Piano.*

Example 2.14   Single tone as pedal point.

(a) BS, 28, i, mm. 1–10.

(b) Brahms, *Sonata no. 3 in D minor for Violin and Piano*, mm. 88–91.

Melodic ostinato figures are not uncommon as accompanimental motives. In Brahms's *Symphony no. 1 in C minor*, iv, mm. 118ff, the second theme is accompanied by a *basso ostinato* of four quarter notes in a descending stepwise progression, fa–mi–re–do (see Example 16.2). Bizet, in the "Carillon" movement of his *L'Arlésienne Suite no. 1*, scores a three-note figure (mi-do-re) for the horns in unison, to suggest the pealing of church bells; it is used throughout the movement, except for the middle section, and is harmonized with great ingenuity (see Example 16.1). See also the illustrations in works by Stravinsky, Brahms, Purcell, and Bach in Examples 16.3, 16.4, 16.5, and 16.6, respectively.

SUGGESTED EXERCISES

1. Identify the motive(s) used in BWTC, Volume 1, *Preludes nos. 13, 14, 19, and 20;* use musical notation. Are they melodic or purely rhythmic? Isolate and describe the constant and the variable factors in the motive repetitions.

2. Locate Alberti bass figures in three different movements of Mozart sonatas other than those mentioned in the text above. Write the figures in musical notation.

3. Carefully examine each movement of BS, 2/2. Identify the motives used, indicating the measure number of the first appearance of each. Identify the motives as either thematic or accompanimental, melodic, or rhythmic. Discuss the constant and the variable factors in each. Note any use of sequence, imitation, or varied repetition.

4. Identify the chief thematic and accompanimental motives in the Brahms *Intermezzo,* BW, 119/2.

5. Trace the development of the three-note melodic motive that opens the Brahms *Ballade,* BW, 118/3.

6. Explain the rhythmic relationships of the phrases that begin in mm. 1, 17, 33, and 41 of MS, K. 545, ii. Explain further the rhythmic parallels to be found between mm. 33–40 and mm. 41–49; to what extent is there melodic parallelism here? Compare further the keys and the cadence formulas.

7. Compose four or five thematic ideas in which motives of various characters and lengths are developed in different ways.

8. Compose four or five accompaniments of different character to any familiar tune, using a different accompanimental motive in each.

The Melodic Phrase 3

Melody may be considered from a historical and anthropological as well as from a purely musical point of view. A comprehensive study of the subject would necessarily include such far-ranging topics as the melodic art of early civilizations and contemporary, so-called primitive societies, Byzantine and Gregorian chant, medieval popular song, the classical traditions of China, India, and other Eastern civilizations, seventeenth-century monody, folk songs of many lands, instrumental and vocal melody of the classical and romantic eras, operatic aria and arioso, declamatory style in opera from Monteverdi through Debussy, Schoenberg's *Sprechgesang,* and so forth. In this review, however, only a few of the more important aspects of the subject will be considered, with reference primarily to music of the eighteenth and nineteenth centuries. It is hoped that this introductory study will suggest the procedures and provide the tools for analyzing melodies of any period, in any style.[1]

VOCAL AND INSTRUMENTAL MELODY

It is customary to distinguish between vocal and instrumental melody. But most instrumental melody shows in some way its derivation from vocal melody which antedates even the earliest musical instruments. Instruments were invented to produce sounds that the human voice could not create. Thus, there are instruments that have the capacity to exceed the range of male and female voices; execute wide leaps that are difficult or impossible for the human voice; produce a variety of tone colors or produce several tones at the same time; and play long lines without the interruption of breath pauses. Vocal melody is generally characterized by a rather limited range, small and relatively infrequent leaps, little color or dynamic contrast, and frequent breathing points.

In prehistory, vocal melody probably developed as a form of emotionally inflected speech. Melody has been associated with words since earliest times, and wordless vocalization has always been a rather rare phenomenon. Thus it is not surprising to find that some of the characteristics of melody are derived from speech, and that some of the melodic forms are related to the forms of prose and poetry.

---

[1] For a discussion of melody, see the article in *Harvard Dictionary of Music,* edited by Willi Apel, 3d ed. (Cambridge: Harvard Univ. Press, 1970).

Music for more than one executant was performed by voices and/or instruments interchangeably before the Renaissance. In this period instruments and performance techniques became more highly developed and distinctive instrumental genres made their first appearance. This was accompanied by the development of a variety of notational styles for keyboard and fretted instruments; these were quite different from the notation for vocal music, which was also used for wind and unfretted stringed instruments.

Cross-fertilization of vocal and instrumental styles which began in the seventeenth century reached a high point in the music of Bach, whose instrumental melodies frequently seem vocal, but whose vocal writing suggests an instrumental style. Mozart's universally applicable melodic style may be observed in such diverse works as operatic arias, violin concertos, and piano sonatas. The florid vocal style of Bellini is echoed in the highly decorative keyboard melodies of Chopin, and Paganini's violin virtuosity is mirrored in the piano pyrotechnics of Liszt.

POETRY, PROSE, AND MUSIC

There is a free-flowing rhythm in prose that is not found in poetry. Poetry employs meter, an underlying pattern of strong and weak pulses over which the text is superimposed. Music may have the free rhythmic flow of prose, or it may be conceived with a metrical foundation. Most music is metrically oriented. Gregorian chant, however, employs the freer rhythms of prose (see Example 3.2a).

The differences between prose rhythm and poetic rhythm may be seen very clearly by comparing the two texts in Example 3.1. Example 3.1a, a prose text, is drawn from Shakespeare's *Macbeth;* 3.1b from the opening of his *Sonnet 65.* Both are extended sentences; both have contrasting short and long clauses, well punctuated by commas. The prose example contains many changes of pace and accent, and the repetition of several words (*her* and *it,* particularly). The four lines from the sonnet are in iambic pentameter; in every line except the first there are rhythms that oppose the underlying meter. The rhyme scheme, the repetition of *nor,* and the internal rhyme of line 4 are unifying factors.

Example 3.1   Prose rhythm vs. poetic rhythm.

(a) Shakespeare, *Macbeth.*

Since his Majesty went into the field I have seen her rise from her bed, throw her nightgown upon her, unlock her closet, take forth paper, fold it, write upon't, read it, afterwards seal it, and again return to bed; yet all the while in a most fast sleep.

(b) Shakespeare, *Sonnet 65.*[2]

Since brass, nor stone, nor earth, nor boundless sea,
But sad mortality o'ersways their power,

[2] Lines 2, 3, and 4 of the text are given a double analysis in which the upper scansion shows the meter, the lower scansion the rhythm.

How with this rage shall beauty hold a plea,
Whose action is no stronger than a flower?

The two settings of "Kyrie eleison" that follow show similar contrast in the handling of rhythm. The plainsong melody, Example 3.2a, is rhythmically free and completely nonmetrical. In the second melody, from Bach's *Mass in B minor,* Example 3.2b, the rhythm is superimposed on a meter of alternating strong and weak pulses. It may be observed that in 3.2a the last three pitches are the same, in mirror image, as the first three; and that in 3.2b the three long notes at the beginning are balanced by the three at the end. Both melodies have an arch shape, and both begin and end on the tonic or key center. Breathing points are indicated by the editorial addition of commas.

Example 3.2   Nonmetrical and metrical rhythm in music.

(a) Gregorian "Kyrie" (excerpt).

Ky - ri - e   e - lei - son.

(b) "Kyrie" theme from Bach's *Mass in B minor.*

Ky - ri - e   e - lei - son, e - le - i - son.

The derivation of musical meter from poetic meter is clearly revealed in the persistence of such concepts as duple and triple meter; strong and weak pulses; the measure, which corresponds to the poetic foot; counterrhythms and accents; and the distinction between half and full closes or *cadences.*[3]

Poetic meter existed for many centuries before it was adapted to musical needs in the Middle Ages. The gradual development of musical notation led to further refinements and complexities that had not been needed in the notation of poetry. Thus music employs special signs to indicate meter, tempo, accent, rhythmic ratios and proportions, measure, and so forth.

THE SENTENCE AND THE MUSICAL PHRASE

Language is not a random flow of undifferentiated words; words must be grouped together to form sentences. The sentence is composed of words that have different functions; some words are nouns, others are verbs, or adjectives. Some of these elements are structurally indispensable, others are optional, decorative, dependent. Every sentence must have a subject and a predicate; an adjective must modify a noun or a pronoun, and may not stand alone.

Music is also a combination of elements that have differentiated functions. Music has its own special kind of grammar and syntax. Successive tones may be grouped to form

[3] See Chapter 4 for a full discussion of cadences.

a *musical phrase* having a sense of completion and unity similar to that found in a verbal sentence. Some tones, like the verbal subject and predicate, are essential to the musical structure; others are decorative. Suspensions, appoggiaturas, neighboring tones and similar decorations cannot stand alone without resolution any more than an adjective may stand without a noun or pronoun. Musical phrases may be simple or complex; a short musical idea may be expanded by a variety of means, such as parenthetical insertions, or extensions at the beginning or the end. The following examples illustrate these parallels.

Example 3.3   Sentences and musical phrases compared.

(*a*) A short, complete statement in words: Rome is the capital of Italy.
In music:

(*b*) The same, with decorative elements added in words: Ancient Rome is the capital of romantic Italy.
In music:

(*c*) Expansion of the same, with internal extension in words: Ancient Rome, the mecca of all tourists, is the capital of romantic Italy.
In music:

(*d*) Two simple statements joined to make a large one in words: Rome is the capital of Italy. It is a fascinating city.
In music:

Rome, the capital of Italy, is a fascinating city.

(e) Terminal extension in words: Rome, mecca of tourists, is the capital of romantic Italy, and cradle of Western civilization.

In music:

(f) Repetition for emphasis in words: Rome, Rome, Rome!—the word alone conjures up images of ancient temples, visions of Renaissance art, and the specter of today's traffic on the Via Veneto.

In music:

MOTIVIC AND NONMOTIVIC MELODIES

In Chapter 2, several instances of melodic phrases in which motives were used as building blocks were examined. Not all melodies are of this type, however. Long, non-motivic melodies are perhaps just as common, and are most frequently found in slow movements of a lyrical or contemplative nature. Illustrations may be found in Examples 5.4, 5.8, 7.5 (mm. 1–8), 7.7 (mm. 1–4), 7.11, and 24.2 (the principal theme).

THE RHYTHMIC STRUCTURE OF PHRASES

It must be recognized that rhythm exists on several hierarchical levels. Thus, in 3/4 meter the first beat is strong, the second and third beats are weak. In a slow tempo, if beats 2–3 are subdivided, all the beats are accented relative to the fractions, thus: ONE-and-TWO-and-THREE-and. In a fast tempo, 3/4 may sound like 12/4 if the measures are in groups of four, and only every fourth downbeat will seem truly accented. Example 3.4 illustrates the manner in which measures are grouped to form pulsation on a larger scale.

Example 3.4   The rhythmic grouping of measures in the phrase.

(a) Iambic grouping ($\smile \prime$) on two levels.

(b) Trochaic grouping (´ ˘) on two levels.[4]

(c) Dactylic grouping (´ ˘ ˘) on one level, anapaestic (˘ ˘ ´) on another.

It follows that melodic phrases should be studied in the light of their manifold rhythmic properties. The barline is frequently irrelevant to the rhythmic structure and may even be misleading, as in the case of the second theme of the third movement of Schumann's *Concerto in A minor for Piano and Orchestra*. It is written in 3/4 but sounds as though it is in 3/2.

Example 3.5   Rhythm of the second theme. Schumann's *Concerto in A minor for Piano and Orchestra*, iii.

PHRASE LENGTH DETERMINANTS

It is frequently difficult to identify melodic phrase endings, or to successfully write them in extended exercises or short compositions. It will be useful, then, to consider briefly some of the ingredients or factors that help to provide the sense of cadence that marks the end of a melodic phrase. These include: (a) a long note, especially one that follows several shorter notes (Example 2.1 is a good illustration; an exception, caused by the word setting, may be found in Example 3.2b—note the quick breath that must be taken before the last quarter note of m. 2); (b) a restful (rather than an active) scale degree; (c) largely stepwise motion to the cadence, followed perhaps by a leap to provide a natural break or cesura; (d) the close of a symmetrical repetition; (e) the need for a breath (in music with text); (f) implicit or explicit harmonic resolution.[5]

A composer may wish the seams or musical joints to be somewhat concealed or inconspicuous. To that end, various devices may be used to continue the motion at a cadence, instead of stopping it,[6] or adjacent phrases may be connected by the device of *elision* or overlapping.[7]

Phrases in polyphonic music frequently are more difficult to identify than phrases in homophonic music because in the former the several melodies tend not to come to a cadence simultaneously. In the latter, however, where there is only a single melodic

---

[4] The larger grouping may also be heard as iambic.

[5] In Example 19.10 compare the implicit imperfect authentic cadence on the first beat of m. 3 with the explicit perfect authentic cadence on the first beat of m. 17.

[6] This is the so-called covered cadence.

[7] See Example 3.6.

line, the supporting harmony moves to a cadence simultaneously with the melody. For illustrations of melodic phrases that do not necessarily coincide with harmonic cadences see:

> Example 17.1g, where the cadences occur as follows: the upper voice in m. 5, the middle voice in m. 6, and the bass voice in m. 8 because of the *canonic imitation*
>
> Example 17.3, where the cadence in the upper voice occurs in m. 4, the lower voice in m. 5
>
> Chapter 17, Exercise 1, where the upper line comes to a cadence in mm. 5, 8, 11, 16, and 22; the middle line in mm. 4, 7, 10, 15, 18, 21
>
> Example 19.3
>
> Example 20.12b

Occasionally phrases will have extensions at the beginning or at the end and it may be difficult to decide whether or not they are integral parts of the phrase. In MS, K. 284, i, for example,[8] m. 22 may be considered as (a) preceding the phrase that appears to begin in m. 23, (b) an anacrusis (upbeat) and therefore a part of the phrase, or (c) an extension of the previous phrase which moved to cadence in m. 21.

Extensions designed to continue the momentum and bridge the gap between phrases are frequently tagged on to the end of a phrase. They may be found in the melody line (see Example 5.7, m. 4), or in the accompaniment (see Example 4.7, m. 187).

The length of a phrase is easily measured if it begins on the first beat of one measure and ends on the last beat of another, as in Examples 7.1a and 7.7. If a phrase ends on the first, second, or third beat of its fourth measure, the phrase is still considered to be four measures long rather than three plus a fraction.

The counting problem is magnified if there is an elision or overlapping of phrases, or if the phrase begins in the second half of a measure and ends in the first half of a later measure. In the first instance, the elided measure should be counted twice, that is, both as m. 4 of the first phrase and as m. 1 of the second phrase, with the result that $4 + 5 = 8$ rather than 9! In the second case, the measures must be considered as units in which the beats are grouped as 3–4 | 1–2 rather than | 1–2–3–4 |. These structures may be diagrammed in the following manner.

Example 3.6   Diagrams of phrases.

(a) Where elision is involved.

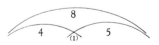

(b) Where a four-measure phrase begins on an upbeat and ends on a downbeat.

[8] Example 5.9.

It follows from the diagrams that the first full or complete measure is considered m. 1.

Another practical problem in measure counting occurs where there are first and second endings. The two endings are alternates and not played in succession; therefore the first and second endings have identical measure numbers. (See Example 21.4, m. 8.)

A double bar occurring in the middle of a measure should not be confused with a regular barline, and does not affect the counting of measures. Such a double bar may be used to make formal sections stand out more clearly (BS, 22, ii, m. 12), to effect a formal repetition (Example 21.1), or may be used at a change of meter, key signature, or tempo (Example 21.6, m. 173).

Cadenzas that ignore the indicated meter create a problem of another kind. In BS, 27/1, iii (Adagio con espressione), m. 26, there is a dotted half note in the left hand properly occupying the full measure, but the right hand is supposed to play notes that add up to 9¾ beats!

Further experience in analysis will disclose additional problems. But it should also provide further know-how in problem solving.

SUGGESTED EXERCISES

1. Identify the melodic phrases in the soprano line of BWTC, Volume 1, *Prelude no. 6*. On what notes do the phrases end? Justify your decisions.

2. Analyze in similar fashion the soprano line in BWTC, Volume 1, *Prelude no. 19*, and *Fugues nos. 2 and 3*.

3. Analyze the rhythmic structure of the opening eight measures of BS, 2/2, ii. Show the rhythm within the measure and the relationship between the weak and the strong measures within the phrase. Analyze in similar fashion the Rondo movement, mm. 1–16, which immediately follows it.

4. Does the first phrase of BS, 2/3, ii end in m. 2, 3, 4, 8, 10 or 11? Give your reasons for accepting the one you choose, and for rejecting each of the others.

5. In the following movement, BS, 2/3, iii, does the first phrase end in m. 3, 4, or 8? Explain.

6. Identify and discuss the opening melodic phrases in BS, 7, i–iv. Identify the factors that may be considered phrase length determinants.

7. In BS, 7, i, is m. 25 a point of cadence? Explain.

8. In MS, K. 310, i, where does one expect the first phrase to end? What does it *not* end in m. 5? What happens in m. 9? In movement iii, how many melodic phrases are there in the section that runs from mm. 1–28? What elements weaken the cadences in these measures?

9. Analyze one movement of a Mozart piano sonata thoroughly; identify all the melodic phrases. Discuss the use of extensions, phrase lengths, cadences, elisions, symmetrical vs. asymmetrical internal structure, repetition, sequence, motive usage, deliberate ambiguities, and so forth.

10. Compose several short passages based on selected materials derived from one or more of the Mozart or Beethoven sonatas. These should illustrate some of the procedures discussed in this chapter. Analyses should accompany each exercise.

The Cadence

A *cadence* is more than a purely harmonic event; it is a composite of rhythmic, melodic, textural, and harmonic factors. Its functions include establishing key centers and defining formal divisions: cadences affect tonality when used at the end of a series of roving modulations, and they frequently prove to be potent as form determinants.

The literature of music abounds with cadences of almost infinite variety. In addition to tonal cadences in the major and minor modes, modal cadences based on the medieval modes can be found in some music. There are weak and strong cadences, and prepared and unprepared cadences. The criteria used to locate, identify, and evaluate cadences are numerous too. Only a few typical examples will be considered here, in order to suggest some helpful analytical procedures.

In general, a cadence may be viewed as a point of rest occurring at the end of a musical phrase. Relative degrees of rest in language are distinguished by such punctuation marks as the comma, colon, semicolon, and period. Similar distinction is made between different degrees of rest in music, but unfortunately there are no conventional signs to indicate them. The feeling of rest, or pause, should not be confused with the absence of sound which is indicated by the notational sign of a rest; such measured silence may occur anywhere, not only at phrase endings.

Most of the generally accepted terms describe cadences only in terms of the harmonic factor; the most important of these terms are listed in Table 4.1. It should be understood, however, that such categorization is a vast oversimplification because of its failure to take other equally important critical elements into account.

Table 4.1 Cadence types, in terms of the harmonic factors.

Term	*Description*
Authentic Cadence	A cadence closing with V–I; both chords are in root position; I must be a triad.
Perfect Authentic Cadence (P.A.C.)	The root of I is doubled in the soprano (highest sounding) line.
Imperfect Authentic Cadence (I.A.C.)	The third or fifth of I is in the soprano (highest sounding) line.
Plagal Cadence (Pl.C.)	A cadence closing with IV–I; both

chords are in root position; I must be a triad. (There are no subtypes.)

Half Cadence (H.C.) — A cadence closing on the V triad (not V⁷) in root position.

Phrygian Cadence[1] — A type of half cadence; used with particular frequency in the baroque era. (See Example 4.14 and the paragraph preceding it.)

Modal Cadence — Modal cadences are generally characterized by the absence of the leading tone and/or the presence of an interval other than the fourth or fifth in the bass progression to the last chord.

Subtypes of modal cadences derive their names not from the chords used, but from the mode employed. The last chord is built on the tonic in each of the illustrations below. The penultimate chord is optional and not a factor in the definition.

Dorian, or transposed Aeolian   Phrygian   Lydian   Mixolydian   Aeolian, or transposed Dorian (if F♯ is used)

At this point it is useful to consider some of the factors that help to make a cadence weak or strong, the factors that define the more particular qualities of different cadences. One or more factors may be applicable in any given cadence; each cadence should be evaluated only after all the pertinent elements have been considered. The following chart lists some of these factors or criteria; in addition, it indicates some of the ways in which they may be employed.

Table 4.2 Factors affecting the weight of a cadence.

Factor	*Helps create a strong cadence if*	*Helps create a weak cadence if*
Rhythm	the last note is long.	the last note is short.
	the last note falls on a strong beat.	the last note falls on a weak beat.
	there was repetition of symmetrical units.	there was no rhythmic repetition or symmetry.
	the motion stops.	the motion continues.

[1] One should distinguish the *tonal* Phrygian cadence (which is understood as ending on V) from the *modal* Phrygian cadence (which ends on the tonic or final of the mode).

Melody	the last note is a restful scale degree (1, 3, 5).	the last note is an active scale degree.
	there was repetition of symmetrical melodic units.	there was no melodic repetition or symmetry.
	the melodic motion stops.	the melodic motion continues.
Harmony	the original key is used.	there is a change of key.
	the last chord is not embellished.	the last chord is embellished.
	the last chord is prepared (for example, by I_6^4–V).	the last chord is unprepared.
	the last chord is I preceded by V.	the last chord is V, or a final I is preceded by a chord other than V.
	final I is in the position of the octave.	final I is in the position of the third or fifth.
	all cadential chords are in root position.	some of the cadential chords are not in root position, or root position is only implied.
	the harmonic motion stops.	the harmonic motion continues.
	there was repetition of nonmodulating symmetrical units.	there was no repetition of nonmodulating units.
	there is an interruption in a series of symmetrical repetitions in a modulating sequence.	there is an uninterrupted series of symmetrical repetitions in a modulating sequence.
	the last chord is extended by repetition, cadence formula is repeated, or there is an extending pedal point.	the last chord is of short duration, and is neither reiterated nor extended in any way.
Register, Tempo, Dynamics, Texture, Orchestration	there is *no* change at the moment of cadence (for example, with the sounding of the last chord).	there *is* a change at the moment of cadence, resulting generally in an evaded cadence.
Mode	there is no change at the moment of cadence.[2]	there is a sudden change of mode at the moment of cadence, resulting generally in an evaded cadence.[2]
Elision (overlap of phrases)	it is absent.	it is present.

It should be observed that the tempo of a composition affects cadential weight. Thus, the greater forward momentum of a fast tempo requires a more extended or more elaborate cadence than is needed to halt the motion of a slow tempo. A simple V–I progression that could be a serviceable cadence in slow tempo might go by unnoticed in fast tempo.

[2] Picardy third excepted.

PERFECT AUTHENTIC CADENCE

The strongest cadence, other factors being equal, is the perfect authentic cadence; it may be strengthened or weakened by various associated factors.

A perfect authentic cadence that is primarily strengthened by its rhythmic position may be observed in Example 4.1. The several factors that create cadential strength include (a) the tonic key; (b) a slowing down or broadening of the harmonic rhythm prior to the cadence; (c) a strong bass progression (4–5–1); and (d) the use of symmetrical four-measure groups, creating accented first measures in mm. 140, 144, and 148; as a result, the final measure (152) is heard as if it too were the first of a four-measure group.

Example 4.1   BS, 2/1, i, diagram of the closing measures.

Look at the cadence at the first double bar of this movement (m. 48). It is weaker than the cadence in m. 152 because it is not in the tonic key; it is decorated by an appoggiatura chord;[3] and it falls on the third rather than the stronger first measure of a four-measure group.

A perfect authentic cadence may be strengthened by extension. This may be accomplished by (a) repetition of the cadential formula, one or a number of times (Example 4.2); (b) prolongation of the root of the cadential chord as a pedal point, perhaps for several measures; (c) a combination of these means (Example 4.3).

Example 4.2   MS, K. 279, iii, mm. 53–56.

Example 4.3   BS, 14/1, ii, mm. 47–59.

[3] An appoggiatura chord embellishes a structural chord much as an appoggiatura embellishes a chord tone. See for instance Example 5.4b, where I_6^4 embellishes V. See also Example 16.4, where a suspended V^7-of-V decorates V.

If the last chord is decorated or embellished by an appoggiatura chord, the cadence is weakened. This may be observed in BS, 2/1, i, mm. 47–48, where the tonic chord is embellished by its dominant, thus:

A♭: $\underline{V^7}$–I. This is a very familiar and frequently employed device, largely ignored by
$\quad$ I

most harmony textbooks. The literature of music contains many examples; a few are listed below.

BS, 2/1, ii, mm. 8, 16, 60	BS, 13, ii, mm. 8, 16
BS, 2/2, ii, m. 8	MS, K. 283, ii, m. 4
BS, 2/2, iii, m. 8	MS, K. 310, ii, mm. 31, 86
BS, 2/2, iv, mm. 8, 16	MS, K. 311, i, mm. 39, 112
BS, 7, ii, m. 8	

Continuing motion in either or both the melody and the accompanimental texture weakens a cadence. In Examples 4.4 a and b the accompaniment continues after the melody has moved to a cadence on the first beat.[4]

Example 4.4   *(a)* MS, K. 279, iii, mm. 9–10.

(b) MS, K. 279, ii, mm. 5–6.

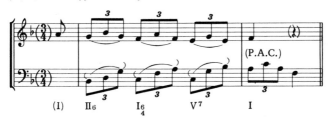

Note that the cadence in Example 4.4b is weaker than the cadence in Example 4.4a because the root of the I chord does not appear in the bass until the second beat, although the *sense* of the harmony is present on the first beat.

In Example 4.5, the deceptive cadence in m. 16 heightens the expectation of and the need for the realized cadence in m. 20. The latter is then further strengthened by the varied repetition of mm. 13–16 in mm. 17–20. But the cadence in m. 20 is also weakened by the continuing eighth note motion in the melody and the continuing texture, motives, and rhythmic motion of the accompaniment.

---

[4] For an illustration of the way continuing motion in the melody weakens a cadence see Example 5.7.

Example 4.5   MS, K. 310, iii, mm. 13–22.

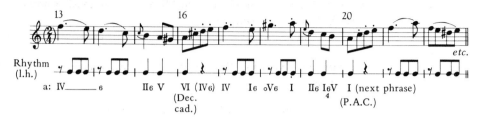

Rhythm (l.h.)

a: IV_____6   II6 V   VI (IV6) IV   I6 ₒV6 I   II6 I6V   I (next phrase)
                        (Dec.   4   (P.A.C.)
                        cad.)

A cadence in a contrasting key is weaker than one in the tonic key, other elements being equal. This may be observed by comparing the cadences at mm. 4 and 8 of Example 4.6. The P.A.C. in m. 8 is strengthened by the fact that it occurs at the end of a symmetrical repetition, both melodic and rhythmic. However, since it involves a modulating sequence, it is also somewhat weakened. Compare it with the cadence in the tonic key at the second double bar.

To help make this point clear, try the following experiment: play the two phrases in reverse order so that the first phrase moves to a cadence in the tonic (D♭) and the second in the key of the dominant (A♭). Symmetrical repetition and modulating sequence are present as in the original, but the second cadence is not in the tonic key and hence weaker than the first. Since the second, consequent, phrase does not now end on a comparatively strong cadence, the effect of the entire eight-measure period is weakened.

Example 4.6   BS, 27/2, ii, mm. 1–8.

D♭: - - - - - to - - - - - - - A♭: (P.A.C.)   [A♭] - - - - - to - - - - - - D♭: (P.A.C.)

Rhythmic delay in the appearance of the expected harmony, and elision with the following phrase weaken the cadence in m. 187 of the next example.

Example 4.7   BS, 14/2, i, mm. 185–88.

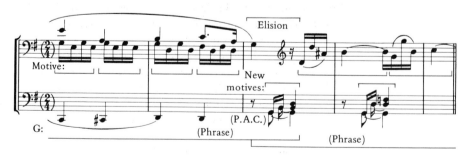

Motive: Elision   New motives:

(P.A.C.)

G: (Phrase)   (Phrase)

A cadence may be weakened by a lack of explicit harmony, as in Example 4.8, m. 8. The preceding measures only suggest the V chord by virtue of its melodic outline.

The cadence is further weakened by continuing eighth note motion in the accompaniment. However, a tonic pedal point following the cadence provides additional strength.

Example 4.8   BS, 10/1, iii, mm. 6–9.

IMPERFECT AUTHENTIC CADENCE

The imperfect authentic cadence (I.A.C.) is somewhat weaker than the P.A.C. It may be strengthened or weakened by the same means as those described in reference to the P.A.C. Thus only two illustrations will be included here.

Continuing motion in both the melody and the accompaniment and elision with the following phrase weaken the I.A.C. in Example 4.9a. The F in the melody line on the first beat of m. 33 is at once the end of the previous phrase and the beginning of the next (elision), weakening the sense of phrase termination. Furthermore, the V chord in m. 32 is not in root position. With so many weakening factors, the very presence of a cadence in m. 33 may be questioned.

Compare it with the later situation, at m. 39 in Example 4.9b. Here there is a slightly stronger I.A.C. in another key. The V chord is stronger than the one in m. 32 because of the use of root position on the fourth beat of m. 38. However, the G♯ on the first beat still seems the real bass tone for the entire measure, particularly in view of the B♭ and A in the bass in m. 37. Since the next melodic phrase begins on the second beat, there is no melodic elision at the cadence; there is an elision in the harmony, however, as in 4.9a, since a:I is both the end of the previous phrase and the beginning of the next.

Example 4.9   BS, 2/3, i.

(a) Mm. 31–33.

(*b*) Mm. 37–39.

a: (I.A.C.?)

PLAGAL CADENCE

The IV–I, plagal, or so-called Amen cadence (Pl.C.) is not often encountered. It is sometimes used as a sort of afterthought or terminal appendage following an authentic cadence in order to conclude a cadential extension. A good example of this is the extended close of the "Hallelujah" chorus of Handel's *Messiah*.

In Example 4.10, the *Romance in F major* by Brahms, the final cadence in mm. 55–56 is a plagal cadence. However, it appears at the end of a tonic pedal point (mm. 54ff) which serves as a codetta or extension of the V–I progression (cadence?) in mm. 53–54. One ought to consider which of these is the "true" cadence and which analysis provides the best sense of balance with the preceding four-measure phrase.

Example 4.10   BW, 118/5, mm. 53–57.

Brahms frequently uses a cadential progression that is a mixture of elements derived from the authentic, the plagal, and the half cadence formulas. He accomplishes this by employing V–I as the understood *root* relationship between the last two chords, using a *bass* line that suggests IV–I, and treating the last chord as V (the dominant) in the larger context. This is illustrated in Example 4.11 where the second chord suggests either A:I, the tonic chord in A major, or a:I with a raised third (a:I#3), the Picardy third in A minor. With the first chord analyzed as dominant of the second chord, the cadence appears to be a P.A.C. in either A major (A:) or A minor (a:). If, however, one considers the tonal center as A but the first chord as a substitute for IV (the subdominant), then a modified plagal cadence may be sensed.

In the light of the larger context, the music is clearly in D minor. The first chord should be analyzed as dominant of the dominant (in this case as $_0V_4^3$ of V), the second chord as V, and the cadence then viewed as a type of half cadence. It is not only important to see the "final solution" of the analytical problem, but also to understand the secondary implications which provide this cadence with its particular quality and flavor.

Example 4.11 Mixture of authentic, plagal, and half cadence elements. BW, 79/2, m. 13 (reduction).

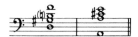

Alternative analyses:

A: $_0V_4^3$ ^{b7} to I (P.A.C. in A major)
a: $_0V_4^3$ to I#3 (P.A.C. in A minor)
A or a: 4 to 1 (bass progression suggests plagal cadence in A major or minor)
d: $_0V_4^3$-of-V to V (half cadence in D minor)

A variant of the formula described above involves the inverted II triad or seventh chord as a substitute for IV in a quasi-plagal cadence. In Example 4.12a the progression of triads found in the closing measures of Brahms's *Intermezzo in F minor* is reduced to simple terms. There is a suggestion of both f:II and f:IV. Example 4.12b involves a seventh chord; since the chord seventh does not resolve, the first chord may be considered (to use William Mitchell's apt term[5]), a "pseudo-seventh chord."

Example 4.12 Substitution of II for IV in a plagal cadence.

(a) Substitution of II₆ for IV. *(b)* Substitution of II⁶₅ for IV.

f: II₆ I#3   f: IV I#3   f: II⁶₅ I

HALF CADENCE

A half cadence (H.C.) is a weak cadence, since the closing V needs resolution. It may be further weakened or strengthened by means such as those discussed in reference to the P.A.C.

[5] See William Mitchell, *Elementary Harmony* 2d ed., (New York; Prentice-Hall, 1948), pp. 173ff.

Example 4.13   Half cadence weakened by an appoggiatura-like I₆ chord. MS, K. 281, iii, mm. 1–4.

B♭:   I₆ V
                                                                                            ⁴

A half cadence may be strengthened by such means as prolongation (extension) of the terminal V chord (BS, 13, i, mm. 27–37), a stopping of the motion through the use of a fermata (BS, 2/1, i, m. 8), or a halt in the flow of the bass line and the harmonic rhythm (BS, 2/3, iii, m. 8).

Example 4.14   The Phrygian cadence.

a: IV₆   V

In the Phrygian cadence, the terminal chord commonly has a V function. The name is derived from the melodic cadences D–E (ascending whole step) and F–E (descending half step) found in the untransposed Phrygian mode. In post-medieval harmonic practice, the ascending whole step is found in an upper voice, not necessarily the top one, simultaneously with the descending half step in the bass line. Illustrations abound in baroque music; see, for example, the final cadences of the slow movements of Bach's *Brandenburg Concertos no. 4 in G major* and *no. 6 in B♭ major,* and the short, two-chord transition that separates the two allegro movements of *no. 3 in G major.* See also the final cadence of the third movement of several of Bach's sonatas for clavier and violin.

MODAL CADENCE

During the latter part of the Middle Ages and throughout the Renaissance, when the modes derived from early medieval monophonic music were still the theoretical foundation of polyphonic music, it was customary for accidentals to be applied at cadences in order to provide a raised seventh degree (leading tone) in the penultimate chord. This alteration of the pure mode at the cadence led the way to the eventual replacement of Dorian and Phrygian by minor modes, and Lydian and Mixolydian by major modes. The modal cadences discussed below are more characteristic of the neo-modal writing of the nineteenth and twentieth centuries than of actual medieval and Renaissance practice, although some recent converts to musical medievalism seem to show greater strictness than the original practitioners in adhering to dogma—a practice that may be due in part to a desire to escape from the cadential patterns of the classic and romantic eras.

Examples of modal cadences abound in the music of those composers who use medieval rather than major and minor modes as a rule—for example, such otherwise quite different composers as Ralph Vaughan Williams and Paul Hindemith. A rare example from the first half of the nineteenth century is quoted in short score in Example 4.15.

Note the use of transposed Aeolian mode and, at the cadence, the lowered leading tone and the stepwise progression in the bass.

Example 4.15   Berlioz, "The Invocation to Nature" from *The Damnation of Faust,* closing measures.

SUGGESTED EXERCISES

1. Locate and identify all the cadences in selected movements of sonatas or string quartets by Mozart or Beethoven. Discuss the elements that contribute weakness or strength to these cadences.

2. Locate the deceptive and evaded cadences in the same movements that were selected for the previous exercise. Indicate their effect on the phrase structure and identify the immediately following realized cadence, if any.

3. Examine selected works of the *ars nova,* Renaissance, and baroque eras. Establish the mode employed. Identify and describe the cadential procedures in each.

4. Discuss in detail the cadences in a selected work in BW with special attention to any irregular or unusual features.

5. Analyze the cadences in the measures indicated below. All the compositions are in BWTC, Volume 1. Identify the cadence types. Discuss the relevant harmonic, melodic, rhythmic, textural, and other associated features in each. Indicate the means used to achieve any pre- or postcadential extensions. List the factors contributing to cadential weakness or strength.

   Prelude no. 1, mm. 11, 19, 35
   Fugue no. 1, mm. 10, 14, 19, 24
   Fugue no. 2, mm. 17, 29
   Prelude no. 7, m. 25

6. What significant events, relative to the cadence, occur in the following measures of BWTC, Volume 1?

   Prelude no. 1, m. 32
   Prelude no. 7, mm. 8–10, 68–70

7. In the following measures there are suggestions of cadence. Why are they not "true" cadences? All examples are from BWTC, Volume 1.

   Prelude no. 2, mm. 28, 34
   Fugue no. 2, mm. 10, 11 (first beat of each)
   Prelude no. 8, mm. 26, 29, 35

8. Identify all the cadences in the following works in BWTC, Volume 1. Discuss each in detail.

    Fugue no. 2
    Prelude no. 6
    Prelude no. 8

9. Examine and compare in detail all the cadences in BS, 2/1. Rewrite three or four of these without changing the style of the work to achieve reasonably valid alternatives.

10. Compose a short work for piano, or small ensemble (in a style to be determined by the instructor). Particular attention should be devoted to the cadences, which should be discussed thoroughly in a companion essay.

The Phrase as a Structural Unit   5

This chapter will be concerned with the phrase as a melodic-harmonic-rhythmic structure primarily as it appears in homophonic forms, and secondarily in polyphonic forms. A structural phrase, like a verbal sentence, is a reasonably self-sufficient and complete unit, comprising melodic material, harmonic movement, and rhythmic span. This sense of the term should not be confused with its use to denote articulation in performance. In Example 5.1, the eight-measure structural phrase consists of one long and several short phrase-members, with phrasing slurs to indicate legato performance and dots to indicate staccato.

Example 5.1   Phrasing slurs within a single structural phrase. BS, 7, iii, mm. 1–8.

In polyphonic music there is a further distinction between a *melodic* phrase and a *structural* phrase. This is characterized by overlapping melodic phrases in different voices which may have independent, nonsimultaneous cadences. Occasionally, they do move to a cadence simultaneously, producing a *harmonic* cadence which closes a structural phrase. See Examples 5.2 and 5.3; the brackets indicate melodic phrases.

Example 5.2   Overlapping melodic phrases in polyphonic texture *without* a harmonic cadence. BWTC, Vol. 1, *Fugue no. 16,* mm. 17–18.

Example 5.3   Overlapping melodic phrases in polyphonic texture *with* a harmonic cadence. BWTC, Vol. 1, *Fugue no. 16*, mm. 23–24.

(g: P.A.C.)

In contrast, the melodic, harmonic, and rhythmic elements of a homophonic phrase usually work together in complementary fashion toward a common objective.

Structural phrases of different lengths and with various types of internal organization may be found in both homophonic and polyphonic music. Slow movements, minuets, and final rondos of multimovement compositions in homophonic forms frequently display themes with a simple, symmetrical phrase structure, reflecting the folk song and the court dance of which they are a stylized outgrowth. First movements frequently have broader and more expansive thematic complexes, freely developing from short motives.

One popular misconception is that phrases are usually four measures long. Indeed, both folk and so-called popular music normally employ four- or eight-measure phrases; the symmetry and balance that this provides is effective for the group or social dancing that the music is intended to accompany. This very severe limitation, however, need not be imposed on music that is designed primarily for listening.

The following illustrated phrases are from two to forty measures in length. In order for a two-measure phrase to have a sense of independence and completeness, the tempo must be quite slow and there should be enough harmonic activity to provide the need to rest. A forty-measure phrase is usually in a fast tempo, and divisible into phrase-members that are separate and distinct in themselves, but lack the sense of completion provided by harmonic cadences.

There is generally a 1:1 correspondence between structural phrases and cadences, as there is with verbal sentences and the punctuation mark of the period. Occasionally, a dependent section within a larger structure (for example, the *B* section of an *ABA* form) may be a *dissolved phrase*. In effect, this is a phrase which ends without a cadential close. The harmonic resolution which occurs in the following phrase is not to be construed as the cadence of the previous phrase, nor is this situation to be confused with the structural elision. The purpose of dissolution is to heighten the continuity and flow between sections; it may be regarded as an alternative to the cadence. One should remember that cadences are structural terminations, not initiatory events; they are constructive in purpose. Dissolutions tear down and weaken the structure, and end without a sense of completion or fulfillment.[1]

---

[1] See further discussion of the dissolved phrase in connection with *ABA* form (Chapter 12).

PHRASES OF VARIOUS LENGTHS

Two-measure phrase (in 4/4 comparable to four measures of 2/4).

Example 5.4

(a) MS, K. 283, ii, mm. 3–4.

(b) MS, K. 570, ii, mm. 1–2.

The following three-measure phrase should be viewed as beginning just *after* the first beat and ending *on* the first beat. Thus the length is exactly three measures.

Example 5.5 BWTC, Vol. 1, *Fugue no. 12*, mm. 4–7.

In Example 5.6, an elision of four-measure phrases makes it seem as though the phrases were three measures long. A distinction is made between the three-measure melodic unit and the four-measure phrase.

Example 5.6 Scarlatti, *Sonata in B♭ major,* K. 544 (Longo 497), mm. 1–8.

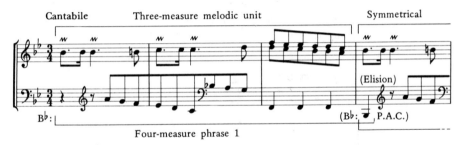

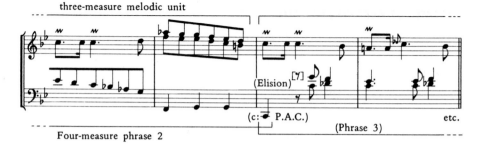

three-measure melodic unit

(Elision)[7]

(c: P.A.C.)

(Phrase 3)

etc.

Four-measure phrase 2

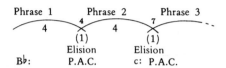

A four-measure phrase may be an indivisible unit; more frequently it is composed of equal members (2 + 2). The asymmetrical 1 + 3 or 3 + 1 is rare (see Example 5.9). In Example 5.7, clearly a 2 + 2 group, the cadence falls on the first beat of the fourth measure; the sixteenth note momentum continues in the upper voice.

Example 5.7   MS. K. 279, iii, mm. 1–4.

Subdivided 2 + 2, the following phrase closes on the second beat. The cadential V is decorated by an appoggiatura-like 6/4 chord.

Example 5.8   BS, 2/1, ii, mm. 1–4.

In Example 5.9, which has a grouping of 1 + 3, the first measure serves as a long anacrusis (upbeat). The continuing momentum after the "cadence" on the third beat of m. 25 leads us without interruption to m. 26 and the next phrase. In the context, one senses a cadence in m. 25, though neither the questionable V nor I are in root position. The extended melodic line, the harmonic activity, and the span of the rhythm all suggest genuine phrase structure here.[2]

[2] Substitute the following cadence in m. 25 and all doubt is removed:

(P.A.C.)

Example 5.9   MS, K. 284, i, mm. 22–25.

The first five-measure phrase in the following illustration serves as a sort of introduction to the movement as a whole. The following two phrases, each also five measures
long, have an interestingly different internal construction. Both seem to be based on
a four-measure idea which has been expanded to five. The added measure (indicated
by a bracket above the staff) appears in a different relative position in each phrase.

Example 5.10   BS, 27/2, i, mm. 1–15 (melody line).

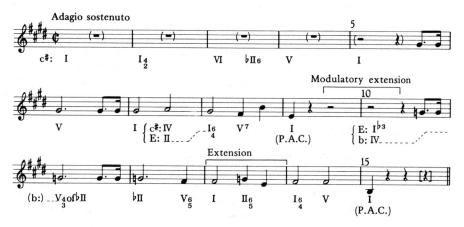

Example 5.11 shows how a phrase may be expanded from four to six measures by the
melodic repetition of two measures. There is a slight change of harmony in the repeated measures.

Example 5.11   MS, K. 279, ii, mm. 1–6.

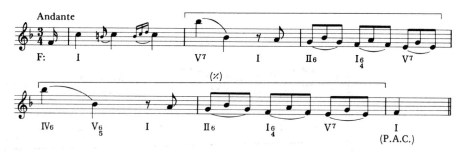

If the final measure of what "should have been" an eight-measure phrase is treated
as the beginning of the following phrase, the result is a seven-measure phrase (Example
5.12). The grouping by twos here makes the music comparable to four measures in

4/2 meter; in the latter situation, the cadence would have fallen on the "normal" first beat of the fourth measure (see brackets). If the elision in the seventh measure is discounted, it may be viewed as a six-measure unit. Thus, three different interpretations may be upheld, each with some degree of merit.

Example 5.12   BS, 2/1, iv, mm. 103–09.

In Example 5.13, a one-measure motive treated sequentially results in expansion to seven measures. Compare mm. 1–4 and 5–8 of this movement.

Example 5.13   BS, 2/2, ii, mm. 13–19.

In Example 5.14a, modified repetition in the second and fifth measures, and harmonic extension of the V chord in m. 6 (shown in small notes, parenthetically), cause the basically four-measure phrase to be expanded to seven. The melody with the extensions removed would appear as in Example 5.14b.

Example 5.14   BW, 79/2, mm. 14–20.

(a) Original melody line (extensions in parentheses).

(b) The same, with extensions removed.

An eight-measure phrase is usually subdivided 4 + 4, as 4 is generally 2 + 2. The relationship to the common four-measure phrase is easily seen if one omits the odd-numbered bar lines (see Example 2.6b). There are other groupings too, such as the 3 + 3 + 2 in the opening theme of Schubert's *Symphony no. 9 in C major* (see Example 2.5a). In the Bartók theme quoted in Example 2.9, the 2 + 2 + 2 formula is camouflaged somewhat by the asymmetrical alternation of 2/4 and 5/8 meter.

For an example of a nine-measure phrase, 4 + 5, not 3 + 3 + 3 as one might expect, see Example 23.5, mm. 1–9. A later statement of the theme in the same example (mm. 53–62) is slightly altered and extended to ten measures, that is, 4 + 6, not 5 + 5.

Very long phrases are most commonly found in a fast tempo, where a sixteen-measure phrase, for example, may be compared to one of eight measures in a slower tempo (see Example 11.1, mm. 9–24). See also the twenty-one-measure phrase that opens Beethoven's *Symphony no. 5 in C minor* (Example 2.1).

The *chain phrase* is a single phrase composed of a thematic complex, rather than a simple idea stated once. It may comprise a group of closely related ideas, repeated or in sequence, or it may be a loose collection of contrasting materials. There is always a clear separation into groups (phrase-members) and a single cadence at the close. In the classic era this form is found most frequently in principal theme statements and in development sections of first movements in sonata form.

The twelve-measure chain phrase in Example 5.15 has three clearly separated phrase members (4 + 4 + 4) with a single cadence at the end of the third member. The use of syncopation helps to relate the second and third members and to separate them from the first. The motivic connection of members 2–3 with the opening member is somewhat tenuous at best; the two-note figure at the beginning, and its variant two measures later, both iambic, may be regarded as present in mm. 6 and 9 in a trochaic transposition (that is, up-*down* changed to *down*-up).

Example 5.15   BS, 10/2, i, mm. 1–12.

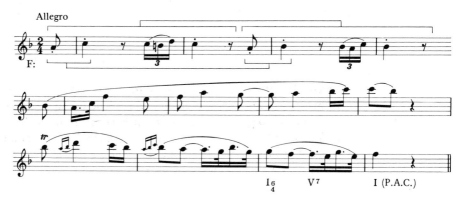

Each of the three sections that make up the twelve-measure chain phrase (4 + 4 + 4) in Example 5.16 has a different texture. This creates more than the usual amount of variety for a single phrase. In the opening member an Alberti bass accompanies the single melody line. The middle member is subdivided (2 + 2) and employs canonic imitation at the octave. The final member, in three-part harmony, is again homophonic in texture.

Example 5.16   MS, K. 332, i, mm. 1–12.

The opening thematic group in Example 5.17 may be seen as coming to a cadence at m. 24. However, the tie over the barline prevents the necessary feeling of repose. Measures 25–32 prolong and strengthen the sense of G:I that was weakened by the tie in m. 24, and lead into a modulatory transition (mm. 33–40) which closes on an unmistakable half cadence. From this point of view, the forty measures constitute a rather complex chain phrase subdivided as indicated below.

Example 5.17   MS, K. 283, iii, mm. 1–40.

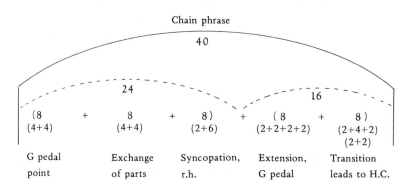

In Example 5.18, the component units are distinguished by radical changes in texture. There is an elision between m.3 and m.4; the accompaniment figure of the second four-measure unit begins in m. 4, but the melody commences only with the upbeat to m. 5. The half cadence at m. 17 (first beat) is prolonged for five measures by harmonic extension. The main body of the phrase is indicated in the diagram by an arch, the postcadential extension by a horizontal line.

Example 5.18   MS, K. 284, i, mm. 1–21.

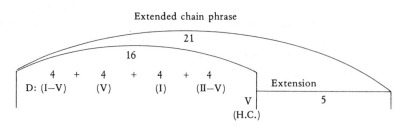

In Example 5.19, there is a rather remarkable grouping of 6 + 4 + 6 rather than 8 + 8. It is more unified in texture and materials than the more symmetrical illustrations cited above. The echo-like repetitions which extend each phrase member are of particular interest.

Example 5.19   MS, K. 331, ii (Trio), mm. 1–16.

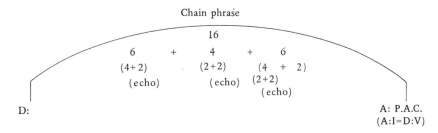

The second theme group (mm. 11–28) of Example 23.2 is an extended chain phrase of eighteen measures, grouped 7 + 8 + 3. The opening group of seven is the second theme proper, the group of eight measures constitutes the closing section, and the closing three measures are a codetta which is little more than a cadential extension.

NONPHRASES

Before leaving the subject of phrases and phrase structure, a word should be said about nonphrases, a convenient term to describe elements that appear to be, but are not, true phrases.

In Example 5.20a, one would expect mm. 13–16 to comprise a four-measure phrase, particularly since this structure is preceded by four-measure phrases (mm. 1–4, 5–8, 9–12). However, the harmony in m. 16 is not I in B♭ but F:IV and therefore too unstable to be suitably cadential. Measure 17 might at first seem to provide a plagal cadence in F, but the melodic balance, the further development of the rhythm, and the harmonic instability all point to the need for continuation to the true cadence in m. 20. Observe also the overall melodic progression from C (the dominant) to F (the tonic). Similarly, in Example 5.20b the apparent cadence in G minor in mm. 4–5 should be viewed as a short-term "tonicization" of d:IV, hence unstable and noncadential.

Example 5.20   (a) MS, K. 330, ii, mm. 13–20.

(*b*) BS, 10/3, ii, opening measures.

SUGGESTED EXERCISES

1. Analyze the following:

   BS, 2/1, ii, mm. 1–8
   BS, 2/1, ii, mm. 17–27
   BS, 2/2, iii, mm. 1–8
   BS, 2/2, iii, Trio, mm. 1–8
   BS, 2/3, i, mm. 1–8
   BS, 2/3, ii, the first phrase. Does it end in m. 3, 4, 8, 10, or 11? Give reasons.
   BS, 2/3, iii, mm. 1–8
   BS, 2/3, iii, Trio, mm. 1–8, 9–16. Compare with mm. 33–40.

2. Identify and discuss the first phrase in each of the following movements. Indicate the type and location of the cadence and the inner structure of each:

   MS, K. 281, i, ii, iii
   MS, K. 282, i, ii
   MS, K. 284, ii, iii
   MS, K. 309, i, ii, iii
   BW *(Intermezzi)* 116/2, 117/1, 118/1–2, 116/4
   BW *(Capricci)* 116/3 and /7
   BW *(Ballade)* 118/3

3. Using any four or five of the phrases described in this chapter as structural models, compose original phrases using completely different materials. These compositions for solo instrument or small ensemble, vocal or instrumental, should be written for class members and performed during a class period. Merits and weaknesses should be frankly discussed.

4. Using materials derived from any one of the phrases described in the text, compose three or four original phrases with different inner structures. You may wish to use the materials of one phrase and apply it to the structure of another. Each example should be concerned with a different technical problem. Follow the procedure outlined in Exercise 3.

Extensions of the Phrase

It has been suggested that a musical phrase may be expanded in numerous ways. In this chapter the subject will be pursued a little further, demonstrating specific techniques in greater detail.

An *extension* is an appendage that may be attached to the beginning or end of a phrase, or may be inserted in the course of the phrase. It customarily creates asymmetry and imbalance in order to realize esthetic objectives that symmetry and balance are incapable of achieving. Its additive, decorative function is seen at once if one imagines the extension removed, leaving exposed the symmetrical, balanced structure of the unadorned "basic" phrase.

EXTENSION AT THE BEGINNING

Extension at the beginning of a phrase is sometimes accomplished by a postponement of the entrance of the melodic line until the accompaniment pattern has been established (Example 6.1). Or it can be achieved by delaying the accompaniment until the melody has completed an introductory anacrusis. In example 5.19, for example, the first measure of the melody appears before the accompaniment, and has the character of an anacrusis and an extension.

Example 6.1 Two-measure accompaniment preceding entrance of melody (m. 35). MS, K. 309, i, mm. 33–36.

EXTENSION IN COURSE

Extension in the course of a phrase may be compared to a parenthetical insertion which can be removed without damage to the sense or structure of a verbal sentence.

The extension is usually accomplished by exact or varied repetition of an immediately preceding portion of the phrase. In some cases this may suggest an echo effect.[1] The repetition may involve changes of dynamics, register, or orchestration.

The following seven-measure phrase is an expansion from a five-measure phrase: the first two measures are repeated, with one tone altered. The grouping is 2 + (2 +)3, or 2 + (⅟. +)3, the interpolation shown in parentheses.

Example 6.2   MS, K. 282, iii, mm. 9–15.

In Example 6.3 a six-measure phrase has been expanded to eight. (This also could have been contracted to four by the omission of the present mm. 3–6, with a normal and "balanced" I–II–I₆–V–I harmonic structure as a result.) The extra length is created by the modified repetition of mm. 3–4 in mm. 5–6. It is instructive to compare this phrase with the one in mm. 37–42; they are the same in every respect, except that in the latter case the extension is missing.

Example 6.3   MS, K. 280, ii, mm. 1–8.

Additional illustrations of extensions in the course of the phrase may be found in Examples 5.10, 5.14, and 5.19.

EXTENSION AT THE END

There are two general classes of closing or terminal extension; they are distinguished by their position relative to the cadence.

[1] See Example 5.19.

Precadential extensions are most commonly caused by deceptive or evaded cadences; they postpone the realized cadence and thus prolong the phrase (see Example 5.10).

Postcadential extensions are usually associated with prolongation of the closing harmony by means of repetition or pedal point (see Examples 4.2, 4.3, and 5.18). If the cadential formula is repeated a number of times for emphasis, the end of the extension should not be analyzed to include another cadence since such analysis would imply the presence of another phrase.

The listener expects the phrase in Example 6.4 to be eight measures long, to end in m. 16, and thus balance the opening phrase (mm. 1–8). Three measures (mm. 16–18) are inserted following the evaded cadence on the first beat of m. 16. The evasion is caused by the abrupt leap and the lack of resolution in the melody. If mm. 16–18 were removed, a symmetrically balanced eight-measure phrase would result. It should be observed that the extension employs material related to the preceding measures and repeats the II₆–I₆–V formula which is the preparation for the cadence, this time fully realized in m. 19.

Example 6.4   MS, K. 309, iii, mm. 9–19.

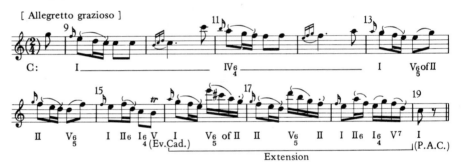

The phrase in Example 6.5 is five measures long, 3 + 2, unlike the preceding parallel phrase, which is 2 + 2. Preparation for a P.A.C. in m. 7 is thwarted by the deceptive resolution V–VI. A second attempt proves successful, and the phrase closes in m. 9. The extension uses materials derived from the previous measures.

Example 6.5   BS, 10/3, iv, mm. 5–9.

Use of postcadential extensions may be found in the following examples. An emphasis on tonic harmony in the postcadential extension may be observed in Example 8.6. Extension involving repetition of the cadential harmonic formula appears in Example 8.4. A postcadential extension that changes function and dissolves into a transition is illustrated in Example 8.6. In Example 23.5, the cadence in m. 29 is extended to m. 31 by means of the sustained tone in the melody line and repetition of the accompaniment figures without any change of harmony.

EXTENSION BY PHRASE REPETITION

Music may be extended by exact or varied repetition of a complete phrase. The usual means of variation include (a) addition of melodic embellishments such as appoggiaturas and neighboring tones; (b) exchange of materials between upper and lower voices; (c) slight changes in the structure of the melody or harmony; or (d) contrast in register or dynamics.

Example 6.6 Exact repetition. BS, 10/2, ii, mm. 1–8.

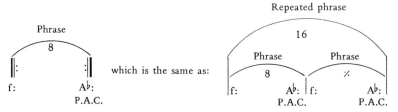

Varied repetition is employed later in the same movement (mm. 125–140); syncopation and a few nonharmonic tones, such as suspensions, and échappées, are used as melodic embellishments. It is also used in BS, 28, i, mm. 1–20; the opening ten-measure phrase is repeated an octave higher.

Example 6.7 Varied repetition. BS, 10/2, ii, mm. 125–40.

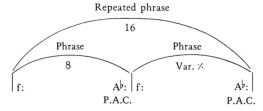

In Example 6.8, variation in the second phrase, essentially a repetition of the first, is achieved by an exchange of upper and lower parts, a few changes in the harmony and melody line, and the dissolution of the second cadence through evasion.

Example 6.8 MS, K. 283, iii, mm. 74–89.

MULTIPLE EXTENSION

A phrase may be prolonged by more than a single extension, as demonstrated by the following illustrations. In Example 6.9 the first half of the phrase is stated and repeated in variation; the second half is then stated and similarly repeated. This is as different from repetition of the whole phrase as *aabb* is different from *abab*. Thus there are two extensions, one in the course of the phrase, the other terminal, precadential.

Example 6.9   MS, K. 283, ii, mm. 9–14.

Example 6.10 is quite interesting. The first "phrase" is deprived of its cadence by a cesura in the voice leading (evaded cadence). The "phrase" is then repeated from the beginning, but in its course dissolves into a modulating transition which leads to the next large division of the movement. Since there is only one true cadence in these measures, perhaps the entire section should be regarded not as a repeated phrase plus extension, but as an extended chain phrase. There are two extensions, the modified repetition of the first "phrase" or member, and the postcadential extension following the second.

Example 6.10   MS, K. 310, i, mm. 1–22.

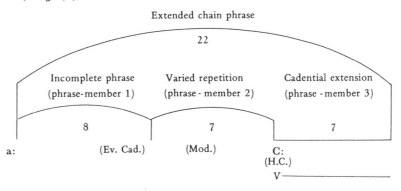

In Example 6.11 there is a varied complex of extensions. A preliminary extension appears as a sort of introduction, before the first phrase begins. There are also internal

John Dewey Library
Johnson State College
Johnson, Vermont 05656

and terminal extensions, as the analysis indicates. If the music is performed with the extensions (indicated by dotted line) omitted, no essential part of the structure is missing; satisfying and well-balanced four- and six-measure phrases will result.

Example 6.11   Mendelssohn, *Songs without Words, no. 1*, 19/1, mm. 1–15.

SUGGESTED EXERCISES

1. Analyze thoroughly the second theme of BS, 27/2, iii, mm. 21–43, a chain phrase with several extensions. Locate each extension, describe the means used, and describe each according to type. Diagram your analysis, using the above examples as models.
2. Analyze in similar fashion BS, 27/2, iii, mm. 71–87. Compare the techniques used here with those found in mm. 21–43.
3. Locate and describe the extensions in the following passages:

   MS, K. 282, ii, mm. 1–12
   MS, K. 283, i, mm. 43–53
   MS, K. 279, ii, mm. 1–6
   MS, K. 533/494, iii, mm. 1–6
   BS, 14/1, ii, mm. 41–62. Compare with mm. 33–40.
   BS, 28, i, mm. 40–62
   BS, 7, ii, mm. 9–14
   BS, 7, iii, mm. 9–24. Compare with mm. 1–8.
   BW, *Intermezzo in A minor*, 116/2, mm. 1–4, 5–9
   BW, *Intermezzo in A minor*, 76/7, mm. 1–8

4. In the *Rhapsody in Eb major* by Brahms (BW, 119/4), the measures are grouped in fives (5 + 5 + 5 and so forth). Are these 3 + 2, 2 + 3, 4 + 1, or some other ar-

rangement? Is it possible to view each group as a 4 that has been extended by one measure, and if so in which measure and by what means?

5. The opening eight measures of the *Romance in F major* by Brahms (BW, 118/5), constitute two four-measure phrases. There is similar material in the last ten measures of the work. How are the latter measures divided (4 + 6, 5 + 5, 6 + 4)? Is there evidence of extension? If so, where and by what means?

6. Using the structure of any of the extended phrases described in this chapter as models, compose original phrases with completely different materials. The composition exercises should be performed in class and be subject to general critical discussion.

7. Using materials derived from any four of the phrases described in this chapter, compose four original extended phrases. Follow the procedure for Exercise 6.

A *period* normally consists of two phrases, an antecedent and a consequent. Three- and four-phrase periods are expansions of an essentially binary structure. The *antecedent phrase* (Ant. Phr.), often compared to a question, is complete in itself. It needs, however, the fulfillment provided by the complementing or answering *consequent phrase* (Cons. Phr.). If the question and answer are to be coherent, valid, and mutually necessary, they must deal with a single subject or idea; and the answer must provide a satisfactory solution to the problem posed in the question. What happens if these criteria are not met is demonstrated in words in Table 7.1.

Table 7.1 Valid versus invalid relationships between question and answer.

Question	*Answer*	*Critique*
How many symphonies did Beethoven write?	How many symphonies did Beethoven write?	Invalid. The question is repeated, but there is no question-answer relationship.
Beethoven wrote several symphonies.	Beethoven wrote nine symphonies.	Invalid. The second statement clarifies the first, but there is no question-answer relationship.
How many symphonies did Beethoven write?	Brahms wrote four symphonies.	Invalid. The answer is not relevant to the question.
How many symphonies did Beethoven write?	Beethoven wrote nine symphonies.	Valid. There is a question-answer relationship.
How many symphonies did Beethoven write? Which of them are in the minor mode?	Beethoven wrote nine symphonies, of which only two, nos. 5 and 9, are in the minor mode.	Valid. The double question and single answer are comparable to a three-phrase musical period with double antecedent and single consequent.

A similar mutual dependency unites the phrases that form a period. Coherence and consistency are provided by the shared materials. The first (questioning) phrase closes with a comparatively weak cadence in order to ask for and make necessary the fulfillment of the second (answering) phrase.

The three standard types of two-phrase periods (both modulatory and nonmodulatory) are *parallel, sequential,* and *contrasting.* These, and the less frequently encountered three- and four-phrase periods will be examined, as well as those phrase combinations that resemble periods superficially but which must be analyzed otherwise.

TWO-PHRASE PERIODS

Parallel Construction

In a period with *parallel construction,* the beginning part of the consequent phrase is a repetition of the antecedent, but the latter part (including the necessarily stronger cadence) is different. The departure from repetition may occur at any point after the repetition has been clearly established—near the beginning, in the middle, or just before the close.

Just as it is uncommon for phrases to be less than four measures long, so periods are rarely less than eight. In slow tempo, however, one may find a four-measure period consisting of two two-measure phrases. In Example 7.1a, a *nonmodulating period,* the parallelism extends to about the middle of the consequent phrase. The first phrase ends with a weaker cadence than the second. Since there is no melodic repose at the end of m. 2, one may regard this as a covered cadence.[1] As an alternative, the example could be analyzed as a four-measure phrase (2 + 2) with a single cadence at the end.

The sixteen-measure nonmodulating period shown in Example 7.1b is less controversial. Parallel construction in the consequent phrase persists for six of the eight measures (more than half its duration), and includes such variants as octave transposition and the addition of a preliminary anacrusis. The normal weak-strong balance is found in the cadences (H.C.–P.A.C.).

Example 7.1   Period with parallel construction.

(a) MS, K. 283, ii, mm. 1–4.

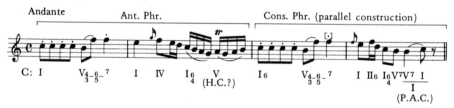

(b) BS, 14/1, ii, mm. 1–16.

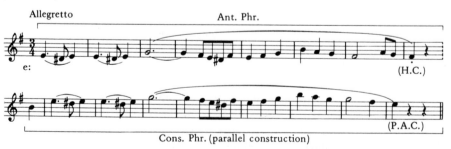

[1] A cadence is considered "covered" when the rhythmic momentum of the melody or the accompaniment does not stop, but rather continues on past the cadential point.

Parallel construction in the consequent phrase may include decorative embellishment of the materials derived from the antecedent phrase. In Example 7.2, the corresponding measures have been juxtaposed to facilitate comparison.

Example 7.2   Period (parallel construction) with melodic embellishments in the consequent phrase. MS, K. 284, ii, mm. 1–16.

Antecedent, first half

Consequent, first half

Antecedent, second half

Consequent, second half

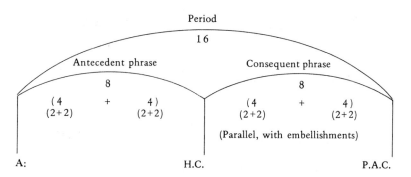

For further illustration of this principle, see the varied restatements with extended consequent in mm. 31–46 and 70–92 later in the same movement.

In the *modulating period* of Example 7.3, the consequent phrase begins in the tonic minor instead of the expected major mode. Except for the modal change, the melody in the first half of the consequent is the same as the melody in the antecedent. The consequent must therefore be regarded as parallel in construction. In the latter part of the consequent, there is a modulation to the minor dominant. The closing P.A.C. is altered by the use of a Picardy third. (Do no confuse f: I$^{\#3}$ with F:I.)

Example 7.3   Modulating period with parallel construction. MS, K. 332, ii, mm. 1–8.

In Example 7.4, a modulating period, parallel construction in the consequent phrase is disguised by the marked change in the accompaniment and the change in dynamics from piano to forte. Both phrases end with a perfect authentic cadence. The first cadence is weakened by virtue of the modulation to the dominant; the second is strengthened by the return to the tonic and by a postcadential extension (not shown in the illustration).

Example 7.4   Modulating period with disguised parallel construction. MS, K. 576, iii, mm. 1–16.

Sequential Construction

A period with sequential construction has a consequent phrase which begins with material of the same substance and content as the antecedent, but which is stated at a different degree level. (This does not include octave transposition, which is considered varied parallelism.) The consequent phrase in this instance may be either in a different key or in the same key. The difference between true modulation and temporary "tonicization" should be observed carefully.

Examples 7.5 and 7.6 are nonmodulating periods although they may appear to involve modulation to the key of the supertonic. However, the chromatically altered chords can be explained as V of II in the tonic key (D major). The E minor chord is not e:I but the II portion of a large D: I–II–V–I progression. It is worth noting there are no cadences in E minor.

Example 7.5   Nonmodulating period with sequential construction. BS, 10/3, iii, mm. 1–16.

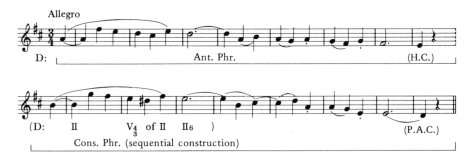

Example 7.6   Nonmodulating period with sequential construction. MS, K. 576, i, mm. 1–8.

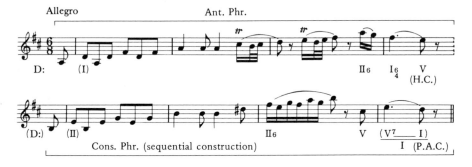

In contrast, the consequent phrase in Example 7.7 definitely modulates to a foreign key. Observe further that the sequential statement is not a step higher, but a third higher than the statement in the antecedent phrase.

Example 7.7   Modulating period with sequential construction. BS, 28, ii, mm. 1–8.

Contrasting Construction

In a period with contrasting construction, the shape of the melody line in the consequent phrase is different from that of the melody in the antecedent phrase, although one or more elements used in the antecedent usually appear in the consequent. Should the phrases lack the necessary unifying elements, they probably would not constitute period form. Such phrases would be better analyzed as a phrase group or a chain of phrases, or perhaps, as no single structural unit at all.

In Example 7.8, a nonmodulating period, there is a suggestion of sequential construction in the consequent phrase. Primarily contrasting in structure, there is in fact a blend of both sequential and contrasting types. Another element of contrast (not shown here) is provided by the accompaniment figure, which changes in the second phrase.

Example 7.8   Nonmodulating period with contrasting construction. BS, 22, iii, mm. 1–8.

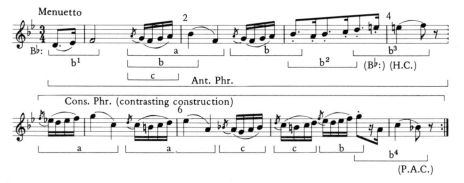

In the analysis of Example 7.8, *b* and *c* are shown as fragments of motive *a*. Closely related to *b* are *b¹* (an unembellished version of *b* that perhaps is the basic figure from which all the others derive), *b²* (which combines the rhythm of *b¹* with the shape of *b*), *b³* (in which *b¹* is embellished by an ascending appoggiatura), and *b⁴* (which is *b³* with octave displacement of the first note and a descending appoggiatura).

Considerably greater contrast may be observed in Example 7.9. The accompaniment figure changes in the consequent phrase (see complete score), as in Example 7.8. The motivic elements that relate the phrases are overshadowed by the new ideas in the consequent phrase. The first cadence, at the end of the antecedent, is an I.A.C. rather than the more common H.C. The unifying elements are shown by brackets and dotted lines.

Example 7.9   Nonmodulating period with contrasting construction. MS, K. 309, ii, mm. 33–40.

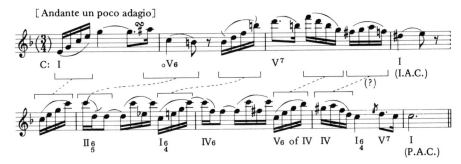

In the period that is the opening of Brahms's *Intermezzo in A minor* (Example 7.10), the intervals in the line of the consequent phrase are different from those in the antecedent, but the phrases are held together by the continuing development of the rhythmic motive first heard in m. 1. Brahms has subtly provided this motive with several alternative melodic shapes (see brackets), and ingeniously extended the second phrase to create an asymmetrical 4 + 5 structure.

Example 7.10   Nonmodulating period with contrasting construction. BW, 116/2, mm. 1–9.

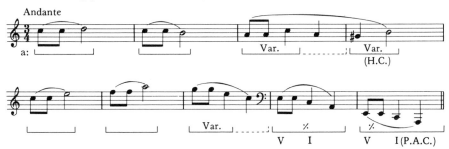

Where there is no common material, the question and answer relationship of antecedent and consequent phrases may be lacking or at best questionable. In the following example, the cadence relationships suggest those found in a typical period, but the absence of motivic relationships in both the melody and the accompaniment suggests that there may be insufficient evidence to call this group of phrases a period.

Example 7.11   Questionable period. MS, K. 281, ii, m. 1–15.

In the following example, a modulating period, there is a suggestion of parallelism in the consequent because of the repetition of the opening three notes. There is also a suggestion of sequential relationship in m. 6. In mm. 5–6, figures are used in contrary motion, a type of alteration frequently found in contrasting construction. Thus there is a mixture of all three types of construction. Additional unity is provided by a continuing Alberti bass accompaniment figure.

Example 7.12   Mixture of parallel, sequential, and contrasting construction. MS, K. 284, iii, m. 1–8.

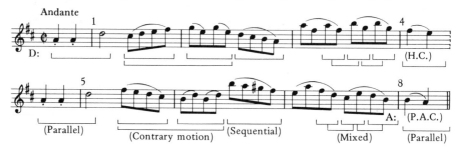

THREE-PHRASE PERIODS

The three-phrase period is an extension of the basic two-phrase period. There are two types: a double antecedent followed by a single consequent phrase, and a single antecedent followed by a double consequent phrase. Usually, the second of the paired phrases is either an exact or a slightly varied repetition of the first phrase in the pair. There must also be a greater relationship between the paired phrases than between either of them and the single, opposite phrase.

Three-phrase Period with Double Antecedent

In the following example, the antecedents are paired. The second antecedent is a sequence of the first instead of an exact repetition. The consequent is contrasting in construction; however, note the motivic similarities. Since the consequent ends on I₆ the period should be considered dissolved at that point; the materials that follow serve as a transition to the next theme. This example should be compared with the original statement in mm. 1–16, where there is a double consequent.

Example 7.13   MS, K. 283, i, mm. 72–83.

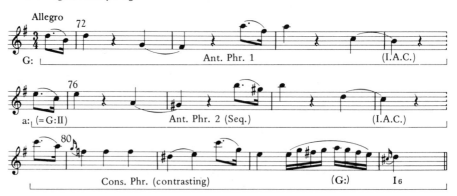

If, because of the weak cadences, this example is only viewed as part of a larger chain phrase, the structure would then be completed in m. 89 (six measures later) where there is an unmistakable cadence in G major. However, the latter measures, largely transitional in nature, have little thematic relationship to what has gone before, which suggests that the first analysis is the better of the two.

Three-phrase Period with Double Consequent

In the two examples which follow, the second consequent is a somewhat varied repetition of the first consequent phrase; both consequents display contrasting construction in terms of the antecedent. There is a different balance of cadences in the two illustrations, and one of the examples includes a postcadential extension at the close of the second consequent.

In Example 7.14 the accompaniment figure used in the antecedent continues in both consequent phrases, providing the needed cohesion. The extension which follows the cadence in m. 12 serves the entire period, not just the last phrase. It is of particular importance to observe that the extension should not be regarded as a fourth phrase. (For the complete movement of which this is only a part, see Example 21.7.)

Example 7.14   BS, 13, iii, mm. 1–17.

The three-phrase period in Example 7.15 is most interesting and rather complex. The antecedent phrase (mm. 65–68) is a variation of mm. 1–4. The second phrase (first consequent) is related to mm. 5–8; the melodic material is first stated in the bass, then is transferred to the soprano register. The third phrase (second consequent) employs the melodic material in the right hand throughout, and shows parallelism with mm. 13–16, rather than with mm. 9–12, as one might expect. The second halves of the two consequents, unlike the first halves, do not match thematically. The final cadence, which closes the entire period, as well as the consequent group and the third phrase, is stronger than the cadence at the end of the first consequent.[2]

Example 7.15   MS, K. 309, ii, mm. 65–76.

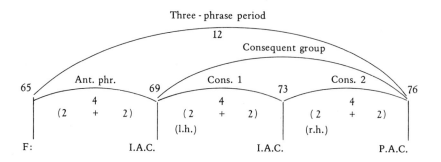

[2] Compare the repeated four-phrase period which uses the same materials in mm. 1–32.

FOUR-PHRASE PERIODS

There are several types of four-phrase periods; four of these will be considered here. In a *period with repeated antecedent and repeated consequent* the second and fourth phrases are exact repetitions of the first and third, thus: / Ant. / ∴ / Cons. / ∴ / or || : Ant. :|| : Cons. :||. The second and fourth phrases of a *period with double antecedent and double consequent* are varied repetitions of the first and third, thus: / Ant. 1 / Ant. 2 / Cons. 1 / Cons. 2 /. In a *repeated period* the second period is an exact or embellished repetition of the first period. The cadences of corresponding phrases are of the same type, thus the pattern may be either / Ant. 1 / Cons. 1 / Ant. 2 / Cons. 2 / or || : Ant. / Cons. : ||. A *double period* is somewhat like the repeated period, however the cadence of the second consequent is stronger (perhaps a different type) than the cadence of the first consequent. The cadence relationships are weak-medium-weak-strong, and the overall pattern is: / Ant. 1 / Cons. 1 / Ant. 2 / Cons. 2 /.

Period with Repeated Antecedent and Repeated Consequent

The form of the major mode middle section of the funeral march, BS, 26, iii, resembles that of the small two-part song form discussed in Chapter 11. At the same time, the rhythmic and thematic balance, and the question-answer relationship of the two parts clearly indicate the presence of period form as well.

Example 7.16   BS, 26, iii, middle section (*maggiore*).

Period with repeated antecedent and repeated consequent

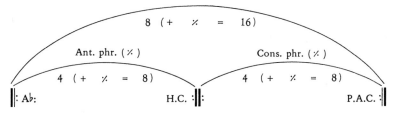

Period with Double Antecedent and Double Consequent

In Example 7.17, the second antecedent and second consequent phrases are varied repetitions of the first antecedent and consequent, respectively. In both repetitions the variation is achieved by octave transposition. As might be expected, the cadence at the end of the fourth phrase is somewhat stronger than that at the close of the third phrase since it must serve not only the phrase but also the consequent group and the entire period. Contrasting construction in the consequent group helps to make clear the binary structure of the period as a whole.

Example 7.17   BS, 28, i, mm. 1–39.

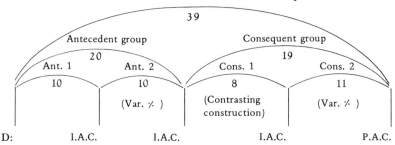

Period with double antecedent and double consequent

Repeated Period

In a repeated period, the period as a whole is repeated, rather than each phrase separately. The repetition may be exact, in which case the period may be written out twice or enclosed by the conventional repeat signs; or it may be slightly varied.

Typical variation procedures include embellishment of the melody by nonharmonic tones; chord substitution (for example, II instead of IV, $_0V^7$ instead of V or V_6, and so forth); and change in the accompaniment texture or motive.

The two antecedents customarily have matching cadences. The consequents generally have matching cadences too, but sometimes the final cadence is strengthened.

In example 7.18, the second of the paired periods is a varied repetition of the first. Melodic, harmonic, and cadential elements are substantially the same in both periods. Variation in the second period is achieved through the introduction of suspensions in the melody line and occasional octave lowering of the bass line.

Example 7.18   Repeated period. BS, 27/2, ii, mm. 1–16.

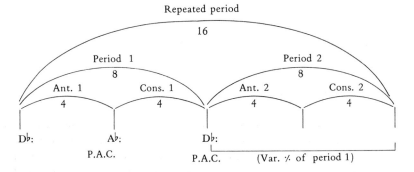

An illustration of the repeated period in which the music is enclosed by the conventional signs instead of written out twice may be found in BS, 22, iii, mm. 1–8 (see Example 7.8).

Double Period

In the double period, the cadence that closes the second consequent must be different and stronger than the cadence that closes the first consequent. The sense of completion at the end of the first period of the pair is usually weakened in order to permit the second period to close with greater finality. The double period at times resembles the single period with its weak middle and strong final cadence. Occasionally it is possible, even desirable, to analyze a passage both as a single period and, on a different level, as a double period. In such a case, all the critical factors should be carefully evaluated, particularly those at the quarter and three-quarter points. If there are "quarter cadences" then the analysis would lean in the direction of the double period. But if there are only half and closing cadences, the music is better regarded as a single period.

Example 7.19   Double period. BS, 26, i, mm. 1–16.

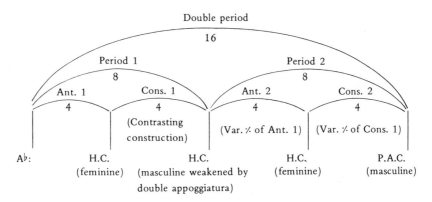

NONPERIODS

One must caution against analyzing all phrase combinations as periods. Some apparent periods are better analyzed as repeated phrases, phrase groups, chain of phrases, phrases with extensions or dissolutions, and the like.[3] A number of such types are cited below, in order to illustrate the nature of the problem, the questions to be asked, and the means of arriving at a satisfactory solution.

MS, K. 283, ii, mm. 5–8. In Example 7.1a, mm. 1–4 of this movement were analyzed as a four-measure period. We therefore expect mm. 5–8 to be a period, particularly in view of the cadence in m. 6. Examination of the cadences in mm. 6 and 8 shows them to be an I.A.C. and a H.C., respectively, both in G major. Since the second of the two cadences is weaker than the first, it cannot provide the needed sense of resolution or "answer." These four measures should be analyzed as a phrase group or chain of phrases and not as a period.

MS, K. 309, ii, mm. 33–44. This section of the movement constitutes the second or *B* theme. At first, it would appear to be a three-phrase period, grouped 4 + 4 + 4. It must be observed, however, that the three phrases have cadences as follows: C: I.A.C., C: P.A.C., and F: H.C., respectively. The last cadence is the weakest of the three, and is in the key of the next section which begins in m. 45. The first two phrases com-

[3] See the discussion of phrase group, chain phrase, and chain of phrases in Chapter 9.

pose a two-phrase period. The third is a separate phrase, outside the period, which functions as a modulatory bridge.[4]

Example 7.20, an apparent four-phrase period, must be analyzed in different terms. The opening period (mm. 1–10) is an asymmetrically balanced antecedent-consequent group (4 + 6) which modulates from the tonic key (Bb major) to the dominant (F major). The weak cadence in m. 10 is followed by an exact repetition of the antecedent phrase but only the first four measures of the consequent. At this point, the second phrase dissolves into a transition and ends rather inconclusively on a H.C. in F major. The expectation of a repeated or a double period is thwarted. The section therefore should be regarded as a *dissolved* repeated or double period.

Example 7.20   MS, K. 533/494, ii, mm. 1–22.

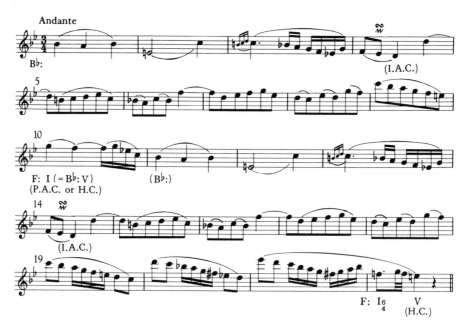

In Example 7.21 the form is not that of a period, although there are clearly two subdivisions of the 12 measures (4 + 8). The material of mm. 5–12 is too contrasting to provide any sense of "answer" to what has occurred in mm. 1–4. Furthermore, the cadence in m. 12 is clearly a half cadence in C, insufficiently strong to close a period, not an authentic cadence in G. (See m. 57 where the same chord is unambiguously C:V because of the continuation in C.)

What is the form, then? Is it a phrase group or a chain of phrases? If one questions the presence of a genuine cadence in m. 4, then the entire passage might be analyzed as a single chain phrase of two members.

---

[4] See Example 7.9; the passage as a whole should be compared with the extended period shown in Example 7.14.

Example 7.21   MS, K. 545, i, mm. 1–12.

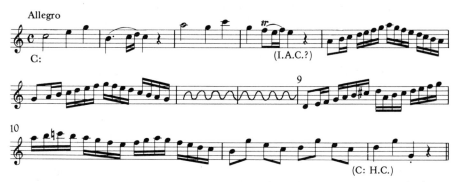

In the small binary and ternary forms such as those found in menuetto and scherzo movements (see Chapters 11–13), the materials following the first double bar sometimes form two phrases. There are theorists who view this combination as a period, but they fail to see any difference between the a^1-a^2 relationship and the b-a^3 relationship in the form which may be diagramed as $|| : a^1$-$a^2 :|| : b$-$a^3 :||$.[5] The question-answer relationship that characterizes a^1-a^2 must be distinguished from the quite different departure-return relationship of b-a^3.

It should be observed that the second part (the b-a group) consists not of a period but of two distinct sections, namely the last two of an *aba* (ternary) form which has been mixed or blended, with elements of *ab* (binary) form.

A long list of examples could be cited. Typical instances are BS, 2/1, iii (both the Menuetto and the Trio), and BS, 2/2, iii (Scherzo and Trio, of which the latter is illustrated in Example 7.22). See also the questionable period illustrated in Example 7.11 and the text which precedes it.

Example 7.22   BS, 2/2, iii (Trio section).

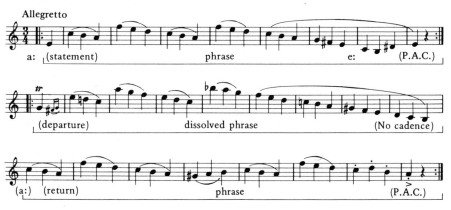

To summarize the subject of nonperiods: MS, K, 283, ii, mm 5–8 described a phrase group or chain of phrases, where the cadence relationships were incompatible with

[5] Some theorists call this very familiar musical design *rounded binary* (see the discussion of this form in Chapter 11). See also Grosvenor Cooper and Leonard B. Meyer, *The Rhythmic Structure of Music* (Chicago: Univ. of Chicago Press, 1960), pp. 83–87; and the author's opposing views in *The Journal of Music Theory*, April, 1961, p. 132.

period form; in MS, K, 309, ii, mm 33–44, a third phrase was not regarded as part of the period because of the P.A.C. at the end of the second phrase and the weak cadence closing the third phrase; Example 7.20 was described as a dissolved period; in Example 7.21 the great contrast between the phrases (or phrase members) and the too great sense of inconclusiveness at the closing cadence made it impossible to evaluate this section as a period—the form is possibly that of a phrase group, a chain of phrases, or a single chain phrase; and Example 7.22 dealt with the *b-a* relationship, referred to as a borderline case.

It is important to examine some of the following illustrations in order to develop the capacity to distinguish periods in the context of still larger forms. At least five or six should be diagramed in detail. Cadence formulas, types of antecedent-consequent relationships, thematic or accompaniment motives relevant to the form, and exceptional features should be accompanied by diagrams and, if possible, performed.

SUGGESTED EXERCISES

1. Analyze several of the following. Use the diagram technique illustrated in the text. Supplementary remarks should be added as needed.

MS, K. 457, ii, mm. 1–7	MS, K. 330, iii, mm. 33–46
MS, K. 533/494, iii, mm. 1–12	MS, K. 332, i, mm. 1–22
MS, K. 280, i, mm. 27–34	BS, 10/3, ii, mm. 1–11
MS, K. 332, iii, mm. 1–14	BS, 26, ii; mm. 1–8, 1–16, 21–30
MS, K. 283, i, mm. 1–16	MS, K. 279, ii, mm. 1–10
MS, K. 545, i, mm. 1–12	MS, K. 280, i, mm. 1–13 (first beat)
BW, 76/2, mm. 1–11	MS, K. 282, iii, mm. 1–8
BW, 116/2, mm. 1–9	MS, K. 545, ii, mm. 33–48
MS, K. 309, ii; mm. 45–52, 1–16, 17–32, 1–32	MS, K. 533/494, i, mm. 42–57
	MS, K. 333, i, mm. 23–38
MS, K. 330, ii, mm. 1–8	MS, K. 309, i, mm. 33–54
MS, K. 282, ii (Menuetto II); mm. 1–16, 25–40	BS, 26, i, mm. 1–16
	BS, 13, ii, mm. 1–16
MS, K. 333, ii, mm. 1–8	BS, 28, iii, mm. 1–32
MS, K. 547a, iii; mm. 1–8, 1–16	MS, K. 283, i, mm. 23–43
BS, 10/3, iii, mm. 1–16	MS, K. 311, iii, mm. 1–16
BS, 28, ii, mm. 1–8	MS, K. 310, iii, mm. 1–20
MS, K. 576, i, mm. 1–16	MS, K. 330, iii, mm. 1–16
MS, K. 333, ii, mm. 14–21	MS, K. 332, i, mm. 41–56

2. Using the first phrase of any of the above examples, write continuations of your own so as to achieve the following:

a two-phrase period, parallel construction, no modulation

a two-phrase period, sequential construction, no modulation

a two-phrase period, contrasting construction, no change in the basic accompaniment figure, no modulation

a two-phrase period, contrasting construction in which melodic motives provide thematic continuity; change in the accompaniment figure; no modulation a second version of any or all of the above, in which there is now a modulation in the consequent phrase

a three-phrase period with double antecedent. The second antecedent should employ one or more variation techniques.

a three-phrase period with double consequent. The antecedent should be altered so that it modulates to a related key; both consequents should cadence in the tonic key. In the first consequent, place the melody in the bass or a low register; in the second consequent, the melody should be above the accompaniment in a register similar to that used in the antecedent.

a repeated period. In the consequent phrase(s), modulate to a closely related key.

a double period

a period with double antecedent and double consequent, with the second member of each pair a variation of the first

3. Draw detailed diagrams of several possible period forms other than those provided in the text.

4. Using mm. 1–4 of Example 7.7 as a beginning, write four new continuations. Modulate to (a) F major, (b) C minor, and (c) C major, respectively; write a fourth version that remains in D minor instead of modulating to A minor. Keep the character of the original in all four versions.

Extensions of the Period

A number of the periods examined in Chapter 7 include one or more extensions. For example, the ninth measure of Example 7.10 is a repetition at the octave of m. 8. The added measure creates an asymmetrical balance of phrases (4 + 5) and helps strengthen the cadence that closes both the second phrase and the period.

Three- and four-phrase periods are extensions of the basic two-phrase type. The binary structure *ab* or *a¹a²* that characterizes the question-answer relationship is the foundation of all period forms. Thus double antecedents and double consequents should always be considered extensions of the single antecedent or single consequent. The paired group may be indicated in diagramed analysis by an arch (see Example 8.2).

The principal types of extension in phrases and periods are illustrated in Examples 8.1 and 8.2. The cadences indicated are characteristic, but other types are equally effective.

Example 8.1   Extensions of the phrase.

(a) Preliminary extension.

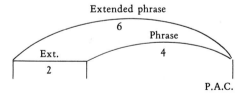

(b) Extension in course.

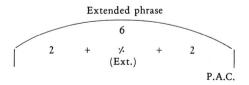

(c) Precadential extension.

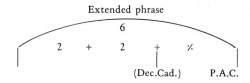

(d) Postcadential extension.

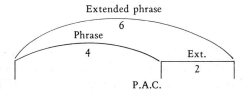

(e) Phrase repetition.

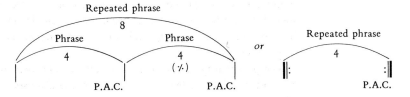

Example 8.2   Extensions of the period.

(a) Preliminary extension.

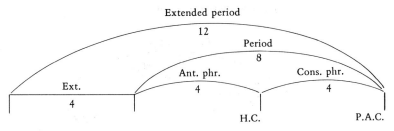

(b) Extension in course through phrase repetition
      (1) of antecedent phrase.

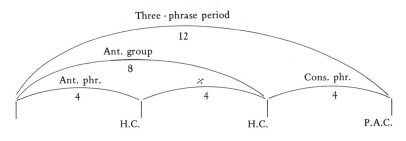

(2) of consequent phrase.

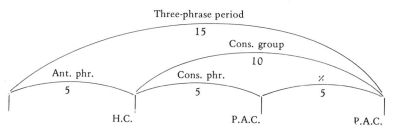

(3) of both phrases.

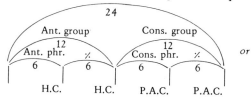

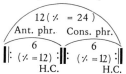

(c) Precadential extension.

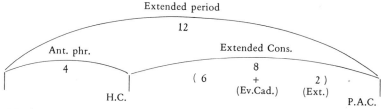

(d) Postcadential extension.

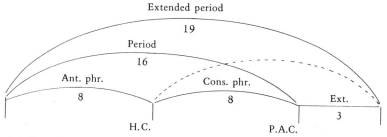

(e) Period repetition.

(1) Repeated period.

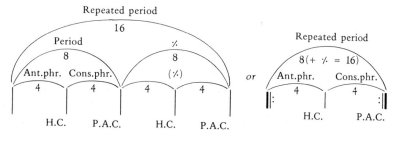

(2) Double period.

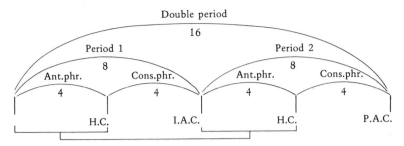

PRELIMINARY EXTENSION

A preliminary extension establishes the mood and character of the section that follows. If it is very short it may be considered part of the main body of the phrase or the period (see Example 5.9). However, if it is relatively long, or if for melodic, harmonic, or rhythmic reasons it is clearly separated or disconnected from the following material, it is better considered a prior event and not part of the main body of the phrase or period (see Example 6.11).

EXTENSION IN COURSE

Extension in the course of a period may occur within a single phrase or it may involve repetition of whole phrases. Antecedent or consequent phrases may be repeated with or without variation. These procedures have been discussed in Chapters 6 and 7 and need not be considered here. (See Examples 6.2 and 6.3 and the discussion of three- and four-phrase periods on pages 63 through 67.)

PRECADENTIAL EXTENSION

Precadential extension may prolong a period as well as a phrase. The most common means for securing such extension are one or more of the following: (a) the deceptive cadence, (b) the evaded cadence, and (c) melodic and/or harmonic backtracking.

Illustrations of precadential extension may be observed in Example 8.5, mm. 82–83 and 84–85. The first of these extensions follows an evaded cadence and melodic cesura; the second, which involves two measures of backtracking and is but a slightly varied repetition of the first, closes on a perfect authentic cadence.

POSTCADENTIAL EXTENSION

A postcadential extension that follows a consequent phrase may extend the whole period as well as the last phrase. In BS, 13, iii, mm. 1–17, the postcadential extension of five measures is too long to be an extension of the third phrase alone (see Examples 7.14 and 21.7). Compare these with the one measure extension shown in Example 7.10 which is an integral part of the phrase and is contained within the body of the period. The first of these two illustrations would be diagramed as in Example 8.2d, whereas the second would be diagramed as in Example 8.2c.

Postcadential extension sometimes serves as a codetta. There may be new treatment of material previously stated (see Example 4.3), or new materials (see Example 8.3 which follows).

Example 8.3   MS, K. 311, ii, mm. 1–12.

It may seem as if this example might be analyzed as a three-phrase period with double antecedent and single consequent, since the first two phrases are obviously similar and the last one is contrasting. The fault in such an interpretation lies in over-looking the balance of cadences in the first eight measures which could perfectly well stand alone as a period. Nor is it possible to consider this as an antecedent and double consequent, for the second phrase obviously is related thematically to mm. 1–4 and not to mm. 9–12.

Perhaps the chief evidence that mm. 9–12 is an extension and not a third phrase is that the harmonies are largely a repetition of the cadential formula, and the continued emphasis and repetition of the melody note G suggest not an "answer" to mm. 5–8 but a reaffirmation of the melodic goal already reached in m. 8.

A borderline case may be observed in Example 8.4. Here, mm. 41–44 may be analyzed as an extension, since they could be removed without damaging the balance of phrases in the period. However, mm. 37–40 could be removed instead, in which case mm. 41–44 could serve as an effective consequent phrase.

Example 8.4   BS, 2/2, iii, mm. 33–44.

It is not always necessary to have a single interpretation for every musical event; the point of view which permits a variety of evaluations on different levels is more likely to be aware of the many subtleties of art than the one which insists on categorical pigeonholes and rigid classification systems.

CONFIRMING EXTENSIONS VS. DISSOLUTIONS

The postcadential extension of a period may serve to *confirm* the previously achieved cadence, usually by repetition of the cadential chord(s) and/or melody note(s). In Example 8.5, observe the skill with which Mozart has gradually introduced into the precadential extension the bustling sixteenth note motion that pervades the accompaniment in the postcadential extension (see full score).

Example 8.5   Confirming extension. MS, K. 332, i, mm. 71–93.

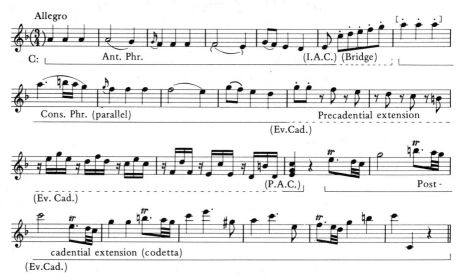

An extension may also turn into a *dissolution* if, in its course, the sense of stability achieved by the cadence is weakened or destroyed by modulation or chord alteration. In the classic era, prolongation of the cadential triad (I) and its alteration to dominant seventh structure—heard as V^7 of the immediately following key and section—is often found at the end of a middle or contrasting section at the point of return to the chief materials (*A* section or principal theme) of the movement.

Example 8.6   Dissolving extension. MS, K. 332, ii, mm. 9–21.

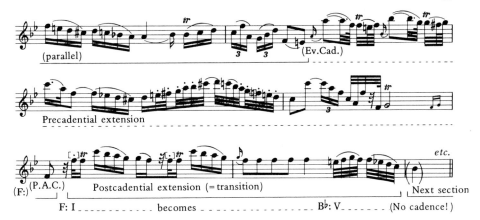

SUGGESTED EXERCISES

1. Discuss and make diagramatic analyses of the following passages.

    MS, K. 311, iii, mm. 1–16, 1–24, 249–56, 249–64, 249–69
    MS, K. 310, iii, mm. 1–20, 1–28
    MS, K. 309, ii, mm. 1–32
    Examples 8.3 and 8.6

2. Compare mm. 1–16 and 70–92 of MS, K. 284, ii.

3. Is BS, 2/3, ii, mm. 1–11 an extended period? Explain.

4. Discuss and make diagramatic analyses of the following passages.

    BS, 10/1, iii, mm. 1–16
    BS, 14/1, ii, mm. 33–51, 33–62
    BS, 22, iii, mm. 17–24, 17–30

5. Compare mm. 1–16, 45–60, and 45–67 of BS, 26, ii.

6. Using the eight-measure period that opens MS, K. 311, ii without change, devise an original postcadential extension. Utilize one or more elements derived from the given period.

7. Using the sixteen-measure period that opens MS, K. 311, iii without change, compose two different postcadential extensions. One of these should be a confirming extension, the other a dissolution ending on the dominant of B minor. Utilize elements derived from the given period in one, new material in the other.

8. Compare the extended periods in MS, K. 311, ii, mm. 1ff, 39ff, and 75ff. Discuss in some detail the functional differences among the extensions closing each of the three periods.

9. Recompose the postcadential extension in BS, 13, ii, mm. 66–73, retaining the dominant pedal point and using melodic material derived from the previous period. Write two solutions, one using materials derived from the opening measures, the other using materials derived from the closing measures. Both should illustrate the confirmation principle and have the character of a codetta.

10. Using mm. 1–16 of BS, 13, ii without change, add a two-measure extension at the beginning in order to prepare the mood and character of the following measures.

Phrases that clearly form a unit of some kind but cannot be regarded as a period fall into two kinds of phrase groups: the *chain phrase,* which is a *single,* long, developmental phrase, with two or more discrete members and one cadence; and the *chain of phrases,* which is a combination of *several* phrases, each of which has its own cadence. The binary, question-answer type relationship that characterizes the period is not present. These two loosely articulated forms provide considerable contrast to the direct, simple, declarative, tightly knit phrases and periods observed in Chapters 5–8.

Both the chain phrase and the chain of phrases should be examined for their unifying features and their contrasting elements. Sometimes the unifying elements may seem a bit elusive, or the matter of similarity and contrast may appear to be more a matter of degree than kind.

THE CHAIN PHRASE

This form is similar to a verbal sentence extended by numerous clauses and phrases. It is found with particular frequency in developmental sections and first-theme complexes of movements in sonata form. It is also commonplace in preclassical music, especially that of the baroque era.

Examples may be found in many of the preludes of BWTC. The *Prelude no. 3 in C♯ major* (BWTC, vol. 1) is a large, single chain phrase. There is only one cadence, at the end. Most of the eight-measure phrase members are set off very clearly by the regular exchange of materials between left and right hands. The work is unified by an astonishingly economical use of materials.

Opening theme statements of first movements in classical sonata form are frequently chain phrases. Example 2.1 (the opening measures of Beethoven's *Symphony no. 5 in C minor*) is a case in point. This complex phrase consists of two thematically related members (5 + 16). The cadence in m. 21 establishes the end of the chain phrase.

The sixteen measures illustrated below compose the main body of the principal theme of the indicated movement and display an *abba* construction. There are no internal cadences (except possibly the shade of a covered cadence at m. 13), and even the H.C. at the end is rhythmically weak.

Example 9.1   Brahms, *Sonata no. 3 in D minor for Violin and Piano,* 108, iv, mm. 1–16.

THE CHAIN OF PHRASES

The group of related phrases designated as a chain of phrases appears in many of the same kinds of works, movements, and sections that exhibit the chain phrase. The component members of a phrase group may have similar thematic ideas but differing treatment; both theme and texture may help to provide unity; or, if neither theme nor texture are similar, the needed continuity will be provided by other elements, such as motives, dynamics, tessitura, tone color.

In Example 9.2 it is immediately apparent that the chain of phrases includes some strong cadences but ends with a weak cadence. One may regard phrase 3 with its P.A.C. as the end of the main body of this phrase group. Phrase 4 serves largely as a dissolution or transition, rather than a fulfilling culmination. The dotted lines indicate the additional, or secondary, point of view that the opening three phrases form a period with double consequent. However, despite the dissolution in the fourth phrase, the overall form is heard as a kind of *abba* structure (actually $a^1b^1b^2a^2$) with the last phrase a modified return rather than an extension. (Compare Examples 9.1 and 9.2.)

Example 9.2   BS, 10/3, i, mm. 1–22.

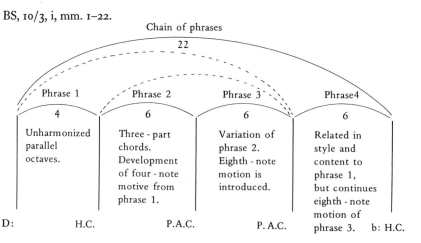

Observe that in both Examples 9.1 and 9.2, the *b* portions of the structure are thematically related to the *a* portions. The contrast is more in treatment than in substance.

The melody in Example 9.3 appears over a very consistent accompaniment texture. The three phrases exhibit considerable economy and parallelism. The rocking sixteenth note motive in the accompaniment, the modulatory scheme Ab–f–c which outlines bIV in the home key of C minor, the tonal instability resulting from the several modulations, and the cadential relationships (P.A.C.–P.A.C.–H.C.) are of considerable interest. The last cadence is the weakest of the three, but it is strengthened somewhat by a postcadential group of fourteen measures (extension-transition) that is largely an expansion of c:V.

It should also be observed that the phrase prior to the H.C. is extended by one measure. Thus it ends on the first beat of the fifth measure, also the beginning of the next four-measure group (creating an elision), rather than on the weaker fourth measure. The extra rhythmic weight provides additional strength to the weak cadence.

Example 9.3   BS, 7, ii, mm. 25–37.

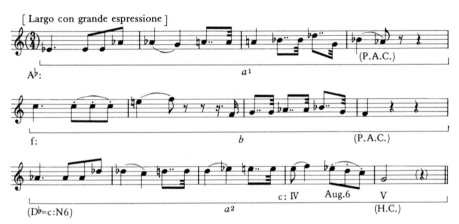

Examples 9.1 and 9.2 have in common a suggestion of the rounded form[1] *aba*. The *abba* form, an extension of the simpler *aba* pattern (see Example 9.3), also shows binary tendencies because its second half serves as a mirror of the first half. Example 9.4 exhibits not only ternary design, but also considerable thematic contrast among the constituent members. There are suggestions of cadence in mm. 4 and 12, and the example may thus be regarded as a borderline case, that is, either a chain phrase or a chain of phrases. A strong H.C. on the dominant of the key of the following section appears in mm. 21–22. As in Examples 9.2 and 9.3, the final phrase dissolves the previous established tonality, and is in effect a modulating transition to the next section of the movement.

---

[1] This term describes a form whose last section is more or less an exact repetition of the first section. The return is comparable to the completion of a circle or cycle, hence the word "rounded."

Example 9.4   BS, 14/1, i, mm. 1–22.

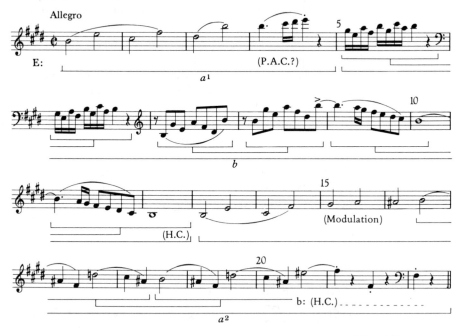

The preceding examples have illustrated thematic statements. The following examples will show how similar procedures are used in typical development sections, such as those in movements in sonata form.

The large middle section of BS, 2/1, i (mm. 49–100) is composed of three parts (mm. 49–55, 56–81, and 81–100). The *first* part is a chain phrase of two sequentially related members which closes on a half cadence. The *closing* part of this section (mm. 81–100) is also a chain phrase but one of several members, some of which are rather contrasting but all of which are unified by the common harmonic emphasis on f:V. The *middle* portion (see Example 9.5) is a rather asymmetrical chain of phrases which consists of two distinct but closely related chain phrases. There are several repetitions and modulating sequences which move ultimately to f:V. A half cadence closes each chain phrase.

Example 9.5 BS, 2/1, i, mm. 56–81.

Brahms's *Rhapsody in E♭ major* (BW, 119/4), his last composition for solo piano, is a particularly interesting example of phrase group construction. The opening sixty measures are divided symmetrically into three groups (20 + 20 + 20). Each twenty measures is further subdivided into four groups (5 + 5 + 5 + 5). Elements such as the repeated quarter notes help to unify the sixty measures. The middle twenty clearly form a contrasting group, the third group is a modified return, and the whole is thus another illustration of the *aba* pattern.

Each group of twenty can be seen as a chain of phrases if each five-measure unit is regarded as ending with a cadence, or as a single chain phrase if only the final cadence of each group is regarded as sufficiently strong to be labeled as such. Observe below the alternative analyses of mm. 1–20.

Example 9.6   BW, 119/4, mm. 1–20.

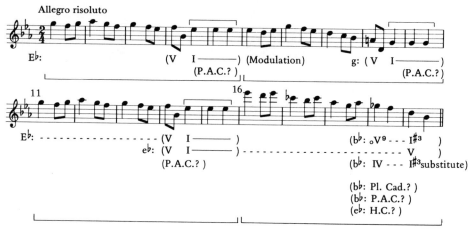

For further illustration of the chain phrase see Examples 23.1, mm. 1–20 (Haydn); 23.2, mm. 11–28 and mm. 51–74 (Mozart); and 23.5, mm. 33–52 (Stravinsky).

SUGGESTED EXERCISES

1. Diagram, adding supporting commentary and discussion where needed, the following:

> MS, K. 331, ii (Menuetto), mm. 1–18, 19–30, 31–48. Compare these.
> MS, K. 332, i, mm. 1–22
> MS, K. 475 (*Fantasy in C Minor*), mm. 1–25
> MS, K. 330, ii, mm. 9–20, 29–36. Compare these.
> MS, K. 330, iii, mm. 21–32
> MS, K. 283, iii, mm. 41–73
> MS, K. 279, i, mm. 1–16
> MS, K. 280, i, mm. 27–43
> BWTC, Vol. 1, *Prelude no. 17 in A♭ major*, mm. 1–18
> BS, 13, i, mm. 137–94 (the middle section without key signature)
> BS, 10/2, i, mm. 67–117 (the middle section, from the double bar to the change of key signature)
> BW, 118/5, mm. 1–16. Do the cadences occur on the first or the fifth beat of the measure? Are these sixteen measures a phrase group or a double period? State the case for each point of view. Compare mm. 48–57.
> BW, 79/2, mm. 1–8. In what keys are the two cadences?

2. Compose short exercises to the given specifications. Diagram each.

> Using the first phrase of any of the examples in this chapter, compose a chain phrase of about twelve measures, altering the cadence of the original phrase if necessary.
>
> Using the first phrase of any of the examples in this chapter, compose a chain of

phrases of sixteen to twenty measures, altering the cadence of the original phrase if necessary. Use one or more modulating sequences. End on the dominant of a third-related key.

Compose a twenty-measure chain of phrases following the general plan of Example 9.6. Use different materials, cadence plans, and modulations, but adhere to the five-measure grouping and the rhythmic character of the original.

Recompose the music illustrated in Example 9.5. Assume that the same motives are employed and that the length of the whole section is the same, but that it begins in the key of F♯ minor, proceeds to B minor, then to C♯ major (the latter changing enharmonically to D♭), and closes on C (f:V) as Beethoven does.

Polyphonic Devices 10

Polyphony is a musical texture in which two or more relatively independent melodic lines are brought into simultaneous association. The preferred consonances and the allowable dissonances vary according to the style and the period. Lines achieve independence largely through the favoring of contrary (rather than parallel) motion, contrasting (rather than duplicating) rhythms, and different (rather than similar) phrase structure.

Polyphonic works may or may not employ the device of imitation (compare, for instance, *Prelude no. 6 in D minor* and *Prelude no. 7 in Eb major,* BWTC, Volume 1). The ways in which imitation may be used are numerous; they have led to an array of complex structures which would otherwise be unattainable.

In this chapter the concept of imitation will be defined, the chief techniques or modes of usage will be demonstrated, and the meanings of terms associated with its practice will be clarified.

IMITATION

Imitation is a type of repetition. Specifically, it is immediate or close repetition in a different voice on the same or a different scale degree. Imitation should not be confused with sequence, which is immediate repetition at a different scale degree in the *same* voice.

Example 10.1   Imitation and sequence compared.

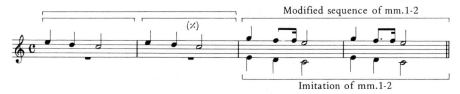

For an illustration of imitation see Example 5.2 where the melodic phrase in the bass line

appears in the alto line a few beats later.

The degree of subtlety with which the principle of imitation may be employed is illustrated in Example 10.2. Both lines grow out of a single motive, the filled-in third (C#–D#–E). In the upper voice this motive is repeated in modified sequences. In the lower voice the figure is turned upside-down (inverted) and decorated by a series of anticipations, then repeated sequentially. The lower voice is thus a somewhat disguised imitation of the upper voice.

Example 10.2   BWTC, Vol. 1, *Fugue no. 14,* mm. 4–7.

(a) Imitation.

(b) Analysis of motive development.

Basic motive   Reduced rhythmic   Decorated by neighboring tone
                      values

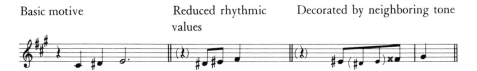

Inverted and decorated by double   Inverted and decorated by anticipations
neighboring tone

The relationship between a musical statement and its imitation in another voice is measured in terms of vertical *interval* and horizontal *distance*. Thus, in Example 5.2, the imitation begins at the upper twelfth (or fifth) at a distance of a half-measure. In Example 5.16, the imitation is at the octave below after two measures. In Example 10.2a, the imitation in contrary motion begins at the unison and, allowing for the anticipation, after three beats.

Imitation may be exact or, as observed in Example 5.2, varied in a number of ways. In varied or free imitation the *general outline* of a motive or melodic shape (rather than the exact shape), or the rhythmic element of a melodic idea only may be maintained. Changes in the original intervals may be introduced. See, for instance, Example 2.1 where the opening motive consists of three repeated tones followed by a descending leap of a major third. In the following measures, the imitation at times involves the interval progression of a minor second, a minor third, or a perfect fourth. At the end of the quoted passage, the three repeated tones are reduced to two, and two stepwise progressions replace the single leap of a third. Despite the pitch changes, the basic rhythmic figure is clearly heard in each of the repetitions and imitations.

CANON

Canon is strict imitation that continues for a considerable length of time. The procedure may be employed for a structural section or throughout a whole movement or work. The term is discusssed more fully in Chapter 17. It is sufficient here to note an interesting example of a two-voice canon at the octave after one beat in MS, K. 576, i, mm. 28–33; at mm. 63–67 it appears after one measure; and at mm. 70–74 after half a measure.

INVERSION

Inversion is a type of mirror technique in which an ascending line becomes a descending line and vice versa (see Example 10.2). In inversion, it is customary for the numerical value of the intervals to remain unchanged, but the interval quality (major, minor, etc.) is adjusted to accommodate the scale and mode. Thus, in C major the progression C–D–E–A–G (M2–M2–P4–M2) when inverted becomes G F E B C (M2–m2–P4–m2). If the original interval qualities were retained, the resultant pitches (G–F–Eb–Bb–C) would not be in C major.

A melodic line may occur in simultaneous inversion. An illustration of this procedure may be found in Example 15.3 ("Theme"). Here the intervals of the leaps are slightly changed in the inversions; the intervals themselves are inverted. Example 10.3 illustrates a figure in contrary motion, doubled in thirds.

Example 10.3   Figure in contrary motion. BWTC, Vol. 1, *Fugue no. 6*, closing measures.

STRETTO

Stretto is a type of imitation, as imitation is a type of repetition. The term denotes a quasi-canonic overlapping of two or more statements of a relatively compact thematic idea. It is most commonly used in connection with the fugue where the subject or theme may be introduced in a second voice before it has been completed in the first (see Examples 19.3 and 19.4). A stretto is described in the same terms as a canon, that is, the interval and distance between the opening notes.

DIMINUTION

Diminution is the proportional reduction of rhythmic values. In duple meter, for example, the rhythmic values are halved; thus:

in diminution is:

COMPRESSION

Compression, a similar procedure applied to pitches, is relatively rare and seldom used with rigor or consistency. The intervals are reduced in value. Thus, the diatonic progression:

becomes chromatic:

when it is compressed. The procedure is employed by Debussy in his *Prélude à L'après-midi d'un faune.* Here, the melodic line of the opening two measures, played by the unaccompanied flute, is contained within the interval of a tritone. Later variants are confined to the smaller intervals of the perfect fourth and the diminished fourth.[1]

AUGMENTATION

Augmentation is the reverse of diminution. Here the rhythmic values are increased; usually they are doubled. If the meter is triple or compound triple, the values might be tripled rather than doubled in order to avoid the sense of metrical conflict that would result. See Example 19.6 for an illustration of inversion, stretto, diminution, compression, and augmentation.

EXPANSION

Expansion is the opposite of compression. It is a rather neglected procedure and examples are not easily found. One instance may be observed in MS, K. 547a, i, where the stepwise motive D–Eb–F–G (at mm. 94–95) is inverted and slightly expanded in the following measure (C–A–G–F♯) and more fully expanded in the sequences of mm. 106–12 where the scale line becomes a broken chord (E–A–C–Db, and so forth).

---

[1] See Exercise 1c at the end of this chapter. Measures 2–3 display contrary motion of a rhythmically altered two-note figure. In m. 4, in the bass, there is chromatic compression in contrary motion against the diatonic three-note figure in the top voice. Compare m. 9 with m. 4.

RETROGRADE

Retrograde (sometimes called *cancrizans,* after the Latin word for crab) is, like inversion, a type of mirror device. In inversion, the figurative mirror is held horizontally —that is, vertical images are affected as ascending lines become descending, and vice versa. In retrograde, the imaginary mirror is held vertically, so that left-to-right becomes right-to-left.

Example 10.4   Inversion and retrograde compared.

Original figure	Inversion	Retrograde	Inversion and retrograde combined
(a) WXYZ	ＭXＡZ	ZYXW	ZＡXＭ
(b) X	OOOO	X	OOOO
(c) OOOO	X	OOOO	X

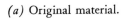

Double Counterpoint (also called invertible counterpoint) is a procedure in which two or more simultaneous melodic lines exchange positions, the upper becoming lower and vice versa. If three or four voices are involved, the terms *triple* or *quadruple counterpoint,* respectively, are sometimes used. The similar exchange of melody and chordal accompaniment in a homophonic texture is frequently encountered; however, since that music is not contrapuntal the term *double counterpoint* would obviously be inappropriate.

The most commonly used double counterpoint is that at the interval of an octave. There is no change in harmony except for the difference in chord inversion. Double counterpoint at the twelfth or the tenth is rarer. The difficulty involved in making this device work harmonically at other intervals almost precludes such usage.

Example 10.5   Double counterpoint.

(a) Original material.   *(b)* Double counterpoint of *(a)*
at the octave.

(c) Double counterpoint   *(d)* Double counterpoint of *(a)*
of *(a)* at the twelfth.[2]   at the tenth.

[2] See also Example 6.8.

Fragmentation is an important means of developing thematic ideas both in homophonic and polyphonic styles. (See Examples 2.8 and 19.10.) It is mentioned here because it is found frequently in polyphonic music and because it is often associated with the other techniques described. In brief, if one were to define *xxyy* as a single motive, then *xx, yy, xy, x,* and *y* would be derived fragments.

SUGGESTED EXERCISES

1. Identify the devices employed in each of the following illustrations:

    (a) BWTC, Vol. 2, *Prelude no. 22,* mm. 1–7.

    (b) Schumann, *Studies for Pedal Piano,* 56/6, mm. 1–10.

(c) Brahms, *Variations on a Theme by Joseph Haydn*, Variation 4, mm. 1–5, 9–16
(octave doubling omitted).

(d) BWTC, Vol. 1, *Fugue no. 22,* mm. 67–75 (in open score).

(e) Bach, *The Art of Fugue,* Contrapunctus, 7, mm. 1–8 (in open score).

(f) Kohs, Variation on a phrase from *L'Homme Armé.*[3]

[3] The example was written expressly for this text. See also Kohs's extended keyboard variations on the same theme (Mercury Music Corp., New York, 1947). The melody, a fifteenth-century French folk song, appeared frequently as one voice in fifteenth- and sixteenth-century polyphonic masses.

2. List, in order of appearance, every instance of inversion, stretto, and augmentation of the subject in BWTC, Volume 1, *Fugue no. 8*. Indicate the measure and beat, and identify the voice (soprano, alto, bass) of each. Note any irregularities such as incomplete statements, chromatic alterations, modal changes, and so forth.

3. Write short examples (four to five measures) of the following, identifying each.

> two-voice canon at the octave
> two-voice canon at the fifth above
> imitation involving motive inversion
> stretto in two voices, with the second entry in diminution
> double counterpoint at the twelfth

Small Song Forms: Binary Form 11

Except for the comparatively rare one-part form,[1] the shortest and least complex of the instrumental forms of the baroque and classical eras are binary (*ab*) and ternary (*aba*) song forms. These forms have their origin in folk songs and dances, from which their directness and simple structure are derived.

Most of the movements in the instrumental suites of the baroque era, either polyphonic or homophonic in texture, are stylized dances in binary form (see for example the minuets, gavottes, and gigues, of Bach, Rameau, and Froberger). The prelude, overture, or similarly titled first movement, usually a more elaborate form, is the chief exception.

The classic era tended to favor three-part design (see the minuet or trio sections of the stylized dance movements in Mozart, Haydn, or Beethoven sonatas, string quartets, and symphonies).

A song form is usually somewhat larger and more complex than a period. Each of the two or three parts may be composed of one or more phrases, periods, or phrase groups. The contrasting part (*b*) is not a great departure from the principal part (*a*). It is quite common for thematic elements of *a* to reappear in *b*. The chief contrast between the parts is in tonality, or, if there is no genuine modulation, in harmonic emphasis or direction and in the treatment of the thematic materials. The parts need not be of equal length, but they generally balance each other. A second or third part is sometimes considerably lengthened by developmental procedures.

Some of the binary forms which will be examined in this chapter are complete movements; others are structural sections within a movement. In either case, each of the two parts is repeated quite formally and exactly, thus: ||: *a* :||: *b* :||. The first part may remain in the tonic key; more frequently it modulates from the tonic to a closely related key. In major mode the modulation is usually to the dominant; in minor, to the dominant or the relative major.[2] Part two continues from the point where part one leaves off, and closes with a cadence in the tonic key. Part two, thus, is roughly a tonal mirror of part one.

---

[1] See, for example, BWTC, Volume I, *Prelude no. 3 in C♯ major* (a chain phrase), and Chopin's *Preludes nos. 1, 2, 4,* and *20.*

[2] Among the first thirty of the Scarlatti sonatas in the Kirkpatrick edition (all of which are in two-part form) eighteen are in major keys and modulate from I–V in part one. Of the twelve in minor keys, eight modulate to the dominant and four modulate to the relative minor.

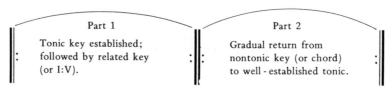

Parallel materials are often used in part two, particularly in the closing measures. Parallelism between the opening measures is less common, except perhaps in the gigue where thematic materials that open *a* may appear in inversion at the beginning of *b*.

Each of the two parts ends with a strong cadence, usually a P.A.C., although the first part may end in a H.C. if no modulation has occurred. As a rule there is no transition or continuing momentum between *a* and *b*. If there are first and second endings at the end of either part, the cadence of the first ending is generally weakened by continuing motion that serves as a bridge or connecting link in the return to the beginning of the part.

A cadence within either of the parts is usually a comparatively weak one. Closing cadences frequently are strengthened by extensions, pre- or postcadential, or both.

In Example 11.1, thematic parallelism relates the two parts which are of unequal length. Part one ends on a cadence that is more Db:V that Ab:I. Part two ends firmly on Db:I. There are no cadences within the parts, each of which is thus simply a phrase. A short bridge or transition leading to the repetition of the scherzo follows the measures shown here.

Example 11.1   BS, 26, ii (Trio).

The whole movement cited in Example 11.2 is a large three-part form, *ABA,* in which each of the parts is itself a small part form. The first large part (*A*), cited here, is a small binary form, *ab,* with both sections repeated.

Part *a* (mm. 1–8) modulates from the tonic key (F) to the dominant key (C) where it closes on a P.A.C. Part *b* (mm. 9–20) returns by way of several transient modulations to the original key. Both parts employ the rhythmic motive ♪♪♪ | ♩. and it may be noted that the closing cadences have corresponding material.

Each part consists of two phrases. Part one is a period. Part two is best regarded as a chain of phrases.

Example 11.2   MS, K. 330, ii, mm. 1–20.

The whole movement of Example 11.3 is in rondo form (*ABACA*), which will be studied in detail in Chapters 21–22. The *C* section cited here (mm. 32–39) is a small binary form with the usual formal repetitions, balanced phrases (4 + 4), modulatory scheme, and so forth.

Example 11.3   MS, K. 570, ii, mm. 32–39.

The two parts of Example 11.4 are six and twelve measures long, respectively—proportionately the same as those observed in Example 11.1. Part *a* modulates to the key of the dominant. Part *b* returns to the tonic after excursions to the relative minor and the supertonic keys. Part *a* is a chain phrase (perhaps a chain of phrases, if one admits the possibility of a cadence in m. 2). Part *b* clearly is a chain of phrases (4 + 4 + 4). The continuing half-measure accompaniment motive in the bass (four eighth notes in a consistent zigzag pattern) is a significant unifying factor.

Example 11.4 Bach, *Suite no. 3 in D major for orchestra,* ii (Air).

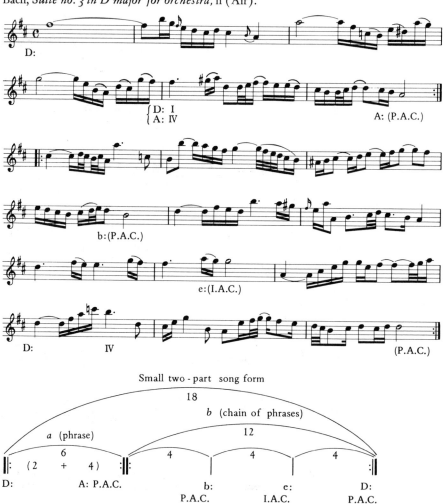

Each of the two parts of Example 11.5 is thirty-two measures long. Part *a* proceeds from the tonic (G) to the dominant key (D); part *b* begins in D and returns to G. Although *b* is in no sense a repetition of *a*, it does employ the same thematic elements. The exchange of sixteenth note and eighth note motion in nearly all but the closing measures of part *b* is particularly striking (compare Examples 11.5a and 11.5b).

Example 11.5   Opening and closing measures of both parts. Bach, *Partita no. 5 in G major for Clavier,* Corrente.

(a) Opening and closing measures of part *a.*

(b) Opening and closing measures of part *b.*

The second part of the binary form in Example 11.6 is an ingenious development of elements derived from part one. If part one were described as a^1b^1, part two would be $a^2a^3b^2b^3$.

Example 11.6   Mozart, *Symphony in C major,* K. 96, iii (Trio).

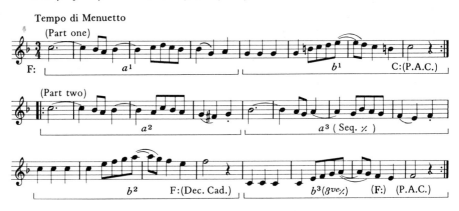

In Example 11.7 the two parts are twelve and sixteen measures long, respectively. Part one is a chain phrase of well-defined four-measure groups $(4 + 4 + 4)$ which may be labeled *abc.* (Observe that since *a* and *c* use related material there is a suggestion of ternary design within part one.) Part two consists of two chain phrases $(8 + 8)$, and, with reference to the material of part one, may be described as *aabc.* The series of close imitations is of particular interest in the developmental *aa* group.

Example 11.7   Mozart, *Symphony in D major*, K. 133, iii (Menuetto).

(*a*) Part one (*abc*).

(*b*) Part two (*aabc*).

SUGGESTED EXERCISES

1. List the chief similarities and differences among the binary forms illustrated in this chapter. Consider such factors as motives, key scheme, cadence types, phrase and section balance, and thematic parallelism.
2. Analyze in some detail one of the Scarlatti keyboard sonatas.
3. Analyze the Allemande, Corrente, Air, Sarabande, Gavotte, and Gigue of the *Partita no. 6 in E minor for Clavier* by Bach.

4. Using the formal structure and proportions of one or two of the compositions described above as the frame of reference, compose one or more original works in small two-part song form. Each example should be accompanied by a diagram showing essential details.

5. Analyze the following portion of Prokofiev's *Classical Symphony*.[3] Using the same harmonic scheme, compose an original work of similar proportions.

[3] Copyright 1926 by Edition Russe de Musique. Copyright assigned to Boosey and Hawkes, Inc., for all countries. Reprinted by permission.

Small Song Forms: Ternary Form 12

Many of the characteristic properties of the small three-part song form (a^1ba^2) are variable. Thus, for example, it may be a complete movement, or it may be a section of a larger form. There may be formal repetitiois of a^1 and ba^2 respectively (high probability), or there may be no formal repetitions. The three parts may be of equal length (low probability), or a^1 may equal the length of ba^2 combined; or the balance may be asymmetrical. The a parts may correspond in every detail (low probability), or a^2 may differ from a^1 in one or more particulars. Part a^1 generally modulates, whereas a^2 remains in the tonic key. Part b may contain new materials, perhaps in combination with elements from a, or it may be based solely on elements derived from a. Part b may be in a closely related key (occasionally it may be in a remote key), or it may involve a shift of harmonic emphasis—away from the tonic—without a change of key. Part b may close on a half cadence, or it may dissolve, either in the course of a postcadential extension that has turned into a retransition, or without any cadence whatsoever. Part a^2 may be followed by a codetta, or there may be no codetta.

The a sections characteristically end in strong, usually authentic, cadences. But even this rule has its exceptions; see, for example, the trio portion of BS, 2/3, iii, in which the final cadence is replaced by a dissolving retransition to the scherzo. These variables, together with others such as tempo, mode, and so forth, may be combined in many ways. A few of them are suggested in the following examples.

The first twelve measures of MS, K. 570, ii, make up the A^1 section of a large rondo ($A^1BA^2CA^3$ + coda). The A^1 section is a small three-part song form (a^1ba^2).

Each of the three parts is four measures long. Parts a^1 and a^2 are identical in every respect. Part a^1 is repeated, and ba^2 is repeated as a unit.[1]

Each a part is a period with parallel construction. Part b is a single four-measure phrase with a half cadence at its close. There is no modulation in b, but there is a greater emphasis on the dominant than is found in either a section. There is some relationship between the melodic lines of b and a^1, but the overall impression in b is of thematic contrast. In b the lack of modulation (which provides tonal *unity*) balances nicely with the presence of new materials (which provide thematic *contrast*).

---

[1] The repetition of a^1 and of ba^2 provides a mixture of binary in what would otherwise be an unambiguous ternary form. In the diagrams which follow, this binary element is indicated by dotted lines. See also the pertinent discussion of nonperiods in Chapter 7.

Example 12.1   MS, K. 570, ii, mm. 1–12.

The measures of Example 12.2 comprise the *D* section of a modified rondo form ($A^1BA^2CA^3DA^4BA^5$). As in Example 12.1, the small three-part song form cited is but a portion of a larger structure.

In part *b* there is development of material derived from a^1. In a^2 the thematic material is transferred from the upper to the lower register. The balance of symmetrical but unequal sections (8 + 6 + 8) and the key scheme (modulation to the relative major and return to the tonic) are of additional interest.

Example 12.2   MS, K. 533/494, iii, mm. 95–116.

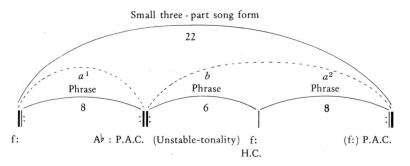

Unlike Examples 12.1 and 12.2, the specimen of small ternary form in Example 12.3 is without the customary formal repetitions. Thus there is no suggestion of binary form. Furthermore, there is a very distinctive retransition between the main body of *b* and a^2.

The key scheme is striking and bold, involving enharmonic changes and distant third-related keys: ab (= g♯) to C♭ (= B) to D (leading tone of ab: V). At the beginning of part *b*, C♭ (major) changes both enharmonically and modally to b (minor). The dominant area (ab: V) is emphasized in the retransition to heighten the expectation of the return to the tonic key.

As in Example 12.1, the *a* sections, though parallel in material, have different tonal objectives. The consequent phrase in a^2 is slightly extended to provide the additional cadential strength that is needed after the excursion to tonally remote areas.

Example 12.3   BS, 26, iii, mm. 1–30.

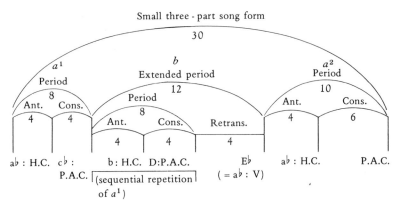

Small three - part song form

Example 12.4   MS, K. 576, ii, mm. 1–16, 17–43, 44–59.

This movement from Mozart's last piano sonata is a large *ABA* design in which each part is itself a small *aba*. The form of the movement as a whole is thus:

A^1	B	A^2	Coda
a^1 b a^2	c^1 d c^2	a^1 b a^2	
(mm. 1–16)	(mm. 17–43)	(mm. 44–59)	(mm. 59–67)

It is instructive to compare the three small ternary forms in order to see their similarities and differences on several levels. It is also useful to compare them with Examples 12.1, 12.2, and 12.3.

SUGGESTED EXERCISES

1. Analyze the following works, all examples of small three-part song form. Use diagrams, and supplement them with commentary as needed:

   BW, 118/1; 118/3, mm. 1–40; 119/1
   MS, K. 331, i (Theme); ii (both Menuetto and Trio); and iii, mm. 1–24
   BS, 14/2, ii, mm. 1–20
   MS, K. 570, iii. Compare mm. 1–22, 23–42, and 45–56, each of which is a small three-part song form.
   MS, K. 284, iii, mm. 1–17
   BS, 7, iii (Allegro). Discuss in detail the relationship between the *a* and *b* sections, and between the two *a* sections. Does the coda begin at m. 70 or m. 86? Indicate the evidence to support your hypothesis.
   BS, 22, iii (Menuetto). Analyze and discuss as suggested above.

2. Examine the Menuetto and the Trio sections of the second or third movements, as the case may be, in Beethoven's symphonies nos. 1, 2, 3, 5, 7, 8, and in all six of the string quartets which make up opus 18. Make a comparative study of these movements, considering such matters as section balance, key structure, relationship of *b* and a^2 to a^1, motive development, presence or absence of retransition, coda, and so forth. Are there any practices found in the quartets which are not found in the symphonies, or vice versa? How do these movements compare to the Beethoven piano sonatas you have examined?

3. Given the a^1 section of any of the works listed in the above exercises, compose a new *b* section and rework a^3 so it has different proportions and structural details.

4. Using any of the illustrations or diagrams in this chapter as models, compose several short compositions. Key and tempo may be different.

Sometimes musical forms are clear and unambiguous. Frequently, however, composers enjoy stretching formal concepts, mixing, compressing, or distorting them in any number of ways in order to achieve heightened expressivity. Considerable esthetic satisfaction may be derived by the listener who is prepared to observe the ingenuity and the subtlety with which a composer may bend or adapt elemental formal concepts according to the purposes and the power of his expressive will.

Although small binary and ternary forms are rather distinct, they have certain common properties, for example, the tonal scheme (tonic key to related area to tonic), and the frequent formal repetition of sections (in binary form: *a* repeated, *b* repeated; in ternary form, a^1 repeated, ba^2 repeated). If the similarities are emphasized and the differences suppressed, it may be difficult to decide whether the form is binary or ternary. The best example of this middle ground is *incipient ternary* form (some theorists prefer the term *rounded binary*). The designation *incipient ternary* connotes a form that is *almost* three-part, a form moving in the direction of, or on the way to becoming, ternary design. The word "rounded" in the term *rounded binary* suggests that the binary structure is closed or rounded off in the manner of a circle by virtue of the return of opening materials in the closing portion of part two.

The form $||{:}a^1a^2{:}||{:}ba^3{:}||$ in which the four components are of comparable or equal length is regarded by some theorists as more binary than ternary. This view is generally associated with the questionable corollary view that ba^3 is comparable in form to a^1a^2. (See the discussion of this matter in Chapter 7.) Although it may appear to be a minor distinction, it is important to devote some attention to the reasons that support these opposing views, in order to prepare for even more problematical situations that will arise in the larger forms considered in later chapters.

The case for the term binary or rounded binary form as an appropriate designation rests largely on the following evidence: (a) the balanced proportions, (b) the scheme of formal repetitions, and (c) the strength of the closing cadences.

Those who suggest that ternary or incipient ternary form is the better term point to the presence of (a) return following departure or episode, which may or may not involve compression or telescoping of a^1 and/or a^2 in the latter portion of part two (a^3); (b) the tripartite tonal or key scheme (tonic to related area to tonic); (c) the lack of unity in ba^3 with respect to the materials and/or the procedures used; and, particularly critical, (d) the bridge or retransition between b and a^3, which provides not only separation and modulation but also a sense of aroused *expectations* for the return of *a.*

Five examples of this fusion of binary and ternary principles will be considered, followed by illustrations of extension and dissolution.

INCIPIENT TERNARY (ROUNDED BINARY) FORM

The opening eight measures in Example 13.1 make up part one, which is repeated. Part two is also eight measures long. There is no bridge or preparation for the return of *a,* and, because the same thematic materials are used throughout the trio, there is very little sense of departure and return.

Example 13.1   BS, 22, iii (Trio).

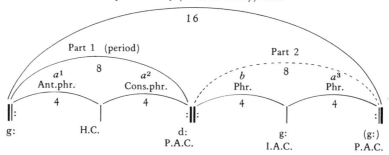

Because of the great similarity of material in all parts, the form in Example 13.2 is rather indistinct. Each phrase appears to be a variation of the other phrases, and instead of being formally repeated, part two is written out twice. In the second statement of part two, the melody is exactly the same as in the first statement, but the harmonization differs considerably. Thus, $ab(a)$ is expanded to $\|{:}a^1a^2{:}\| |b^1a^3b^2a^4| \|$. Both part one and part two are heard as four balancing phrases $(4 + 4 + 4 + 4)$. If only the melodic element is considered, the music is heard as *abab-baba,* a mirror procedure which further emphasizes the binary aspect of the form.

Example 13.2   BS, 28, iii (Trio).

(a) Part one (a^1a^2).

(b) Part two $(b^1a^3b^2a^4)$.

The passage illustrated in Example 13.3 is a small island of major in a sea of minor. (A minor is the prevailing key of this movement.) In its proportions and in its pattern of formal repetitions it resembles the two Beethoven examples cited above. However, since the contrast is more striking between the outer a sections, a^3 seems more like a continuation of b and less like a return. The formal repetitions of the two parts contribute further evidence of binary structure.

An impression of ternary design, however, is created by the tonic pedal point which is used in a^1, a^2, and a^3, along with a distinctive accompaniment texture not found in b. The fact that the quasi-return of a employs the materials of mm. 5–8 rather than mm. 1–4 is of particular interest. As a result, there is no exact correspondence with either a^1 or a^2. Mozart must be given credit for giving the impression or suggestion of a return to the beginning without actually having done so.

Example 13.3   MS, K. 310, iii, mm. 143–74.

(a) Part one (a^1a^2).

(b) Part two (*ba*³).

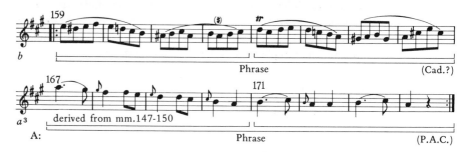

Examples 13.4 and 13.5 illustrate incipient ternary form as found in many of Bach's solo, chamber, and orchestral works. In the two movements cited, each of the three divisions closes with a well-defined cadence.

In the Menuet of Bach's *Partita no. 4 in D major for Clavier,* part one closes on on a H.C. in the original key. Note that part two modulates to the relative minor, closes midway on a P.A.C., and then continues in a quasi-return to the materials, but not the key, of the opening *a*. The tonic key is not firmly secured until the D: P.A.C. in the closing measures. The absence of tonal parallelism in the second half of part two weakens the sense of ternary form considerably, though the proportions (8 + 12 + 8) contribute materially to a sense of ternary symmetry.

Example 13.4   Bach, *Partita no. 4 in D major for Clavier,* Menuet.

(a) Part one. Period? (*a*¹)

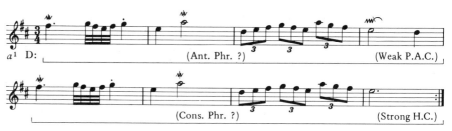

(b) Part two. Two phrase groups (*ba*²).

Many of the factors that created ambiguity in Example 13.4 also appear in Example 13.5. The use of full orchestra only in the *a* sections (timpani are absent and there is but limited use of trumpets in *b*) suggests that the composer had ternary design in mind. The motive used in a^1a^2 is inverted in *b* and restored to its original position in a^3, a further indication of three-part structure.

The motive, however, is inverted at the beginning of *b* and near the end of a^3. Thus a^3, in this respect, is a mirror of *b*. Binary design is furthered not only by the provision in part two of the mirror element not found in part one, but also by the absence of any preparation for the return of *a*.

Example 13.5   Bach, *Suite no. 3 in D major for Orchestra,* Gavotte.

(a) Part one. Period (a^1a^2).

(b) Part two. Two phrase groups (ba^3).

EXTENSION AND DISSOLUTION

A song form may be shortened by dissolution (see Example 13.6) or lengthened by extension (see Examples 13.7, 13.8, and 13.9).

Dissolution in the last part of a ternary song form may cause it to be shorter than the corresponding first part. In Example 13.6, the Trio (*B* in the ternary form A^1BA^2) dissolves into a retransition[1] that leads to A^2. (Compare this with Example 12.3.)

Example 13.6   BS, 14/1, ii, Trio.

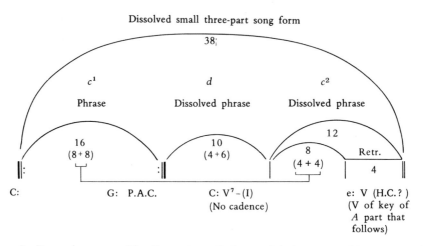

In Example 13.7, unlike Example 13.6, the modulating retransition occurs after a closing cadence, extending rather than shortening the form. The materials are derived from, and thus anticipate the return of, the scherzo proper (A^2 in the A^1BA^2 design).

Example 13.7   BS, 26, ii, Trio.

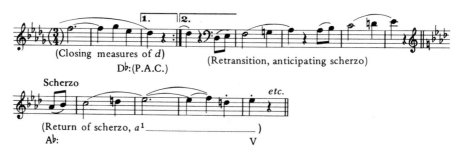

---

[1] A *transition* is a secondary section or passage which leads from one main section to another. A *retransition* is a type of transition in which the music proceeds to a *restatement*, as for example between *B* and A^2 in the form A^1BA^2. A *bridge* is a brief connecting link better viewed as part of a section rather than as a section in itself.

In the larger context, a transition, retransition, or bridge is usually heard as a *terminal* portion of the *previous* main section (as in Example 21.7 mm. 107–20) unless it is separated from the preceding section by a cadence (as in the same example, mm. 18–24), in which case it may be heard as an *initial* part of the *following* main section.

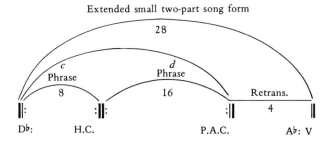

Extended small two-part song form

Marie's lullaby aria in Act I of Berg's opera *Wozzeck* is a small binary form (a^1b^1) (a^2b^2) plus codetta. The *a* sections are in 6/8 meter, *b* sections are in 3/4. The instrumental codetta, which also serves dramatically as a dissolution, continues the mood and meter of *b* while employing the motive that opens *a*.

Example 13.8   Berg, *Wozzeck*,[2] Act I, mm. 372–416. (Vocal line, text omitted.)

[2] Wozzeck by Alban Berg, © copyright 1926, Universal Edition. Used by permission of the Publisher, Theodore Presser Company, sole representative, U.S.A., Canada and Mexico.

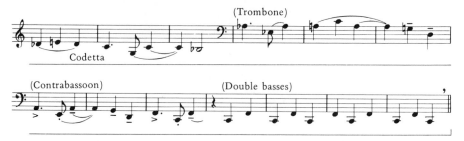

Das verlassene Mägdlein ("The Forsaken Maiden"), by Hugo Wolf with a text by Mörike, is an example of closed form, with *a* sections that surround a middle group of twice the size and of two parts. The whole work may be viewed as a^1bca^2 (or *a–bc–a*) in which the two sections *bc* take the place of *b* (one section).

In addition to this expansion of the ternary concept, there are a short introduction, interludes between the sections, and a coda. These use material derived from (a) the immediately following section (see the introduction and the first two interludes), (b) the immediately preceding section (see the third interlude), or (c) the basic motive of the entire song ♩♫ (see the coda). It is instructive to see the manner in which these formal decorations seem to point inward, toward the center. This very original idea and the almost unrelieved use of the rhythmic motive indicated above contribute greatly to the musical expression of the poem, both as symbols of concentrated and unrelieved misery and as technical means for generating and maintaining a musical mood.

Example 13.9   Hugo Wolf, *Das verlassene Mägdlein* ("The Forsaken Maiden") reduced score.

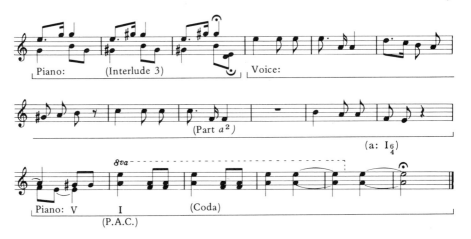

SUGGESTED EXERCISES

1. Analyze both the scherzo proper and the trio section of BS, 2/2, iii, each of which is a small song form. Diagram each. Discuss any evidence of rounded binary or incipient ternary form, extension, and so forth.

2. Analyze similarly BS, 14/2, ii, mm. 1–20; and iii (scherzo), mm. 1–22.

3. Make diagrams of Examples 13.2, 13.3, 13.4, 13.5, and 13.9. Use the techniques employed in Examples 13.1, 13.6, and 13.7.

4. Make a comparative analysis of the dance movements in Bach's *Suite no. 3 in D major for Orchestra,* emphasizing the manner in which the composer has combined binary and ternary elements.

5. Compose original music to fit the specifications of any two of the diagrams in this chapter. The substance of the music should not be related to any of the quoted sources.

John Dewey Library
Johnson State College
Johnson, Vermont 05656

Large (Compound) Song Forms: Song and Trio 14

Small song forms may be combined in a larger *ABA* grouping called compound song form. The most common types are listed below.

Example 14.1   Typical compound song forms.

(a) Both *A* and *B* are small three-part song forms.

$$\| \quad a^1 \quad :\|: \quad b \quad a^2 \quad :\|: \quad c^1 \quad :\|: \quad d \quad c^2 \quad :\| \quad a^1 \quad b \quad a^2 \quad \|$$

(with section brackets labeled A^1, B, A^2)

(b) *A* is three-part, *B* is two-part.

$$\| \quad a^1 \quad :\|: \quad b \quad a^2 \quad :\|: \quad c \quad :\|: \quad d \quad :\| \quad a^1 \quad b \quad a^2 \quad \|$$

(with section brackets labeled A^1, B, A^2)

(c) Both *A* and *B* are two-part.

$$\| \quad a \quad :\|: \quad b \quad :\|: \quad c \quad :\|: \quad d \quad :\| \quad a \quad b \quad \|$$

(with section brackets labeled A^1, B, A^2)

The form described in Example 14.1a is that of the standard minuet (or scherzo) and trio of solo, chamber, and symphonic works in the classic and romantic eras. As a rule, the *A* sections are identical except for the lack of formal repetition in A^2. In fact, the music usually is not written out for A^2; the indication "da capo" (from the beginning), or the abbreviation D.C., sometimes with the additional qualification "senza repetizione" (without repeating) appears at the end of *B* (the trio). The form described in Example 14.1b is an alternate form of that shown in 14.1a; the only difference is that *B* has fewer parts. Baroque dance movements such as the Minuet I–Minuet II–Minuet I or Gavotte I–II–I generally display the form shown in Example 14.1c. Any of the three types may be embellished by a coda.

A minuet is a stately, dignified dance in triple meter. A scherzo is its faster and livelier counterpart. The so-called trio *(B)*, actually a second minuet or scherzo, derives its name from the late baroque practice of writing the second of a pair of dances for only three instruments (for example, in an orchestral suite, for two oboes and a bassoon) in contrast to the fully orchestrated first dance. The trio is usually lighter in texture and less complex than the surrounding dances. The key may be the same, or it may be the parallel major if the minuet (or scherzo) is in minor. If a closely related key or, more rarely, a remote key is used, there may be a modulating retransition between B and A^2.

If any of these forms is found in a slow movement, the character is likely to be that of a stylized song rather than a dance. Part A^2 is then written out rather than indicated by the da capo sign, and frequently displays assorted variation techniques. Formal repetition of the smaller parts may be present but it is neither necessary nor characteristic. In slow movements, key contrast in B is characteristic rather than exceptional, as it would be in dance movements. The meter may be duple or triple. However, duple or compound duple generally is used in slow movements that are adjacent to minuets, in the interest of variety and contrast. In slow movements, a retransition between B and A^2 is characteristic (as it is between b and a^2 in the small three-part song form a^1ba^2) in contrast to the faster dance movements where it is relatively rare.

In Example 14.2, the minuet is in F minor, the trio in the parallel F major. Both are small three-part song forms.

Example 14.2   BS, 2/1, iii.

(a) Minuet.

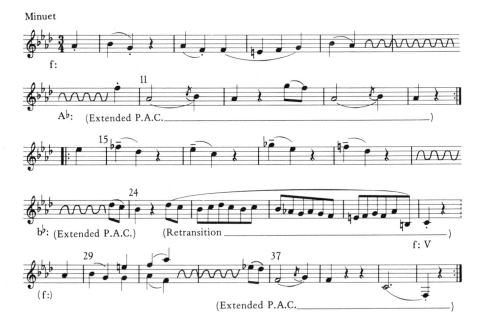

(b) Trio.

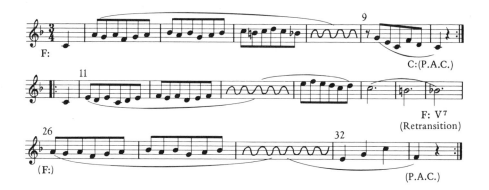

(c) Minuet da capo.

A¹: Minuet—Small three-part song form

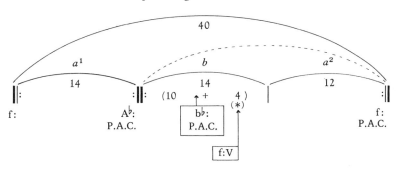

B: Trio—Small three-part song form

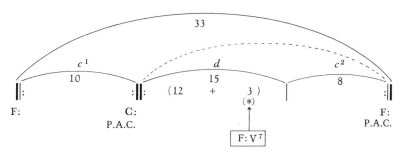

A²: Minuet da capo—*A¹* without repetition of the subdivisions

In Example 14.3, the trio is in the unorthodox subdominant key, necessitating the retransition to *A²* (repetition of the scherzo proper). In the course of this, the harmony shifts from subdominant to dominant of the principal key as preparation, and there is anticipation of the thematic material to follow, further heightening the expectations. The scherzo is ternary, the trio binary in form.

Example. 14.3   BS, 26, ii.

A^1: Scherzo—Small three-part song form

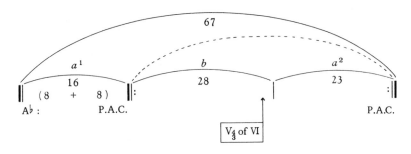

B: Trio—Small two-part song form

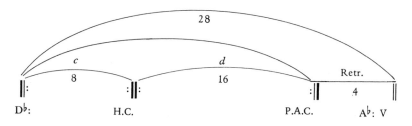

A^2: Scherzo da capo—A^1 without repetition of the subdivisions

The menuetto and trio of Example 14.4 are thematically related rather than contrasting. Such contrast as may be found is provided largely by the modal alteration (minor to major) and the manner in which the material is used. The basic motive of the trio derives not from the beginning of the menuetto, but from its cadences. Mozart has transformed a closing idea into an opening, initial statement in the c section and develops it in a series of canonic sequences in d. In the analysis, the above-mentioned chief motive is labeled (x).

Example 14.4   Mozart, *String Quintet in G Minor,* K. 516, ii (reduced score).

Menuetto (A^1. Small three-part song form.)
a^1 (period)

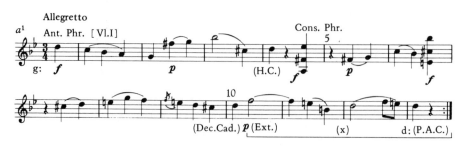

b (chain phrase) and *a*² (extended period)

Trio (*B*. Small three-part song form.)

*c*¹ (extended phrase)

d (phrase) and *c*² (extended phrase)

Menuetto da capo (senza repetizione) (A^2).

The elements of the slow movement of MS, K. 576, ii are in remarkable balance, and display an unusual degree of exact symmetry. The overall form is:

A^1 $\qquad\qquad$ B $\qquad\qquad$ A^2 $\qquad\qquad$ *Coda*
a^1 b a^2 $\quad$ c^1 d c^2 $\quad$ a^1 b a^2

There are no formal repetitions within A or B. A^2 is written out. The coda is based on elements derived from the beginning of B. Although the middle part (B) is quite contrasting in key and texture, its central portion (d) utilizes material that is markedly similar to the b portion of A^1.

Example 13.9 illustrated a small song form which had an *ABCA* design, an expansion of the statement-departure-return inherent in the simpler *ABA* form. In MS, K. 570, iii, a similarly organized movement diagramed below, each large division, with the exception of the last, is a small three-part song form; thus:

A^1 $\qquad\qquad$ B $\qquad\qquad$ C $\qquad\quad$ A^2 $\quad$ *Coda*
a b a $\quad$ c^1 d c^2 $\quad$ e^1 f e^2 $\quad$ a $\quad$ (using materials from B and C)

In A^1 the two a parts are identical, hence no distinction is made in the diagram. But in B and C the outer parts have different key schemes. Part B is in the original rather than a contrasting key; C, in addition to providing key contrast, is preceded by a transition and followed by a retransition. This evidence seems to suggest the possibility of an alternate grouping, *AB-C-A* + coda, rather than the more likely and expected *A-BC-A* + coda design.

The diagram shows how the movement as a whole is related to the compound song form type. It is an example of one of the ways in which forms may be stretched "out of shape." The need to define formal categories in flexible rather than in rigid terms should now be more understandable. Description should not be confused with pre- (or pro-) scription.

The tripartite scherzo and trio form in Beethoven's *Symphony no. 4 in B♭ major,* 60, iii, is expanded to *ABABA* by the repetition of the trio and the two repetitions of the scherzo proper. The overall scheme is as follows:

A^1	B^1	A^2	B^2	A^2
Scherzo	Trio I	Scherzo	Trio II	Scherzo
(90 mm.)	(85 mm.)	(90 mm.)	(85 mm.)	(41 mm.)
‖ :a^1: ‖ ‖ :b a^2 : ‖	c^1 d c^2	a^1 b a^2	Exact	a^2 (only)
	(without	(without	repeti-	(a^1 and b are
	repetitions)	repetitions)	tion of	suppressed)
			Trio I	

Another example of a scherzo with repeated trio may be found in Beethoven's *Symphony no. 7 in A major,* iii. In Brahms's *Symphony no. 2 in D major,* iii, there are two different trios which are very subtly related to each other and to the outer A sections, with a resulting $A^1BA^2CA^3$ form (similar to the *rondo* discussed in a later chapter). The fact that A^3 begins in the "wrong" key (the subtonic) following a dissolving retransition, and slips into the "correct" tonic key only in the course of the statement is of particular interest.

SUGGESTED EXERCISES

1. Diagram each of the following movements.

> MS, K. 331, ii
> MS, K. 330, ii
> MS, K. 282, ii
> BS, 28, ii
> BS, 10/2, ii
> BS, 27/1, ii
> BS, 14/1, iii
> A movement from a string quartet by Haydn, Mozart, or Beethoven

2. Compose a compound song form using one of the illustrations as a model for form. Details such as key and length may be altered, but the chief structural elements should be retained.

3. Explain or define in general terms the form of the final (fourth) movement of Bach's *Brandenburg Concerto no. 1 in F major*. Describe the form of each of the principal subdivisions.

4. Of the several movements of Bach's *Suite no. 1 in C major for Orchestra,* some may be small song forms. Identify any which are compound song forms and diagram them showing the most important structural details.

Variation *procedure*, in varying degrees, is apparent in nearly all music. Variation *form* is a product of the consistent and continuous use of variation throughout an entire work or movement. If the variation principle is used only intermittently, or if it is limited to certain sections of a work or movement, some other principle must be responsible for the larger structure. This chapter first will consider movements in which variation is evident in one or more sections, but not throughout; then movements in which variation is the paramount structural principle will be examined.

VARIATION PROCEDURE

Occasional, short-term variation, as distinguished from consistent, continuous variation, may appear in various forms: phrase, period, section of a part form, and so forth. A few typical examples, beginning with small structural units and proceeding to larger ones, will be considered here.

Variation In A Repeated Phrase

The consequent phrase of the period in Example 15.1 is not only parallel in construction, but it is also a variation of the antecedent phrase. Variation is accomplished by means of nonharmonic embellishments and short notes which replace rests or the latter part of long notes.

Example 15.1   MS, K. 545, ii, mm. 1–4, 9–12.

The nonadjacent phrases in Example 15.2 do not play similar roles in the structure, but they are related in a subtle and very unusual way. The pitch lines show melodic parallelism, but the rhythmic values are dissimilar. A quasi-pedal point on the dominant is an additional feature of the second version.

Example 15.2   MS, K. 333, iii, mm. 56–60, 76–80.

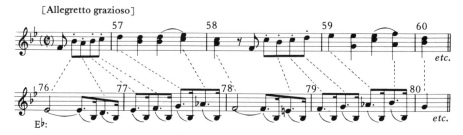

The next illustration demonstrates a type of theme and variations, with the following structure. Mm. 79–82: Theme (four-measure phrase; closes on Ab:H.C.). Mm. 83–86: Variation 1[1] (both voices inverted; the upper is syncopated). Mm. 87–90: Variation 2 (voices in original positions; syncopation transferred to the lower voice which is doubled in thirds). Mm. 91–94: Variation 3 (inversion and syncopation return to the upper voice; third doubling remains in the lower voice). Mm. 95–98: (*not* a variation, but an episode extending and strengthening the cadence, and establishing mm. 79–98 as a phrase group). Mm. 99–102: Variation 4 (the theme in the upper voice is accompanied by a descending scale in eighth notes in the lower voice). Mm. 103–06: Variation 5 (upper and lower voices exchange material [double counterpoint], then dissolve into the retransition at c:V. Variations 4–5 comprise a dissolved phrase group). (See Example 21.7, mm. 79–106.)

Example 15.3   BS, 13, iii, mm. 79–106. Opening two measures of the theme and each variation.

---

[1] Variations are not numbered in the printed score.

Variation in a Repeated or Double Period

In Example 15.4, the sixteen measures (8 + 8) at the return of the original key signature correspond to mm. 1–8 which were repeated *exactly* and formally. The initial statement at m. 39, however, is followed by a *varied* repetition. The form in both cases is a repeated period. The opening of each period is shown below to illustrate the variation technique employed. The accompaniment is not varied and therefore omitted from the illustration.

Example 15.4   BS, 28, ii, mm. 39–40 and 47–48 compared.

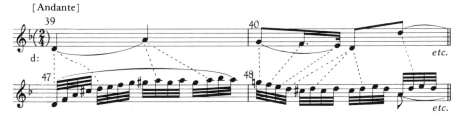

The principal theme in Example 15.5 is a repeated period in which the second statement is varied by means of quasi-canonic imitation.

Example 15.5   MS, K. 576, i, mm. 1–2 and 9–10 compared.

A fine specimen of invention and craftsmanship, the repeated period in Example 15.6 is also a good example of Mozart's ability to reconcile baroque polyphony (the "learned" style) with rococo homophony (the "gallant" style), most notably achieved in the finale of his *Symphony no. 41 in C major.*

Each period has an antecedent phrase which closes on a half cadence, and a sequentially related consequent phrase which closes on a perfect authentic cadence. The thematic idea in the upper voice in period 1 is transferred to the lower voice in period 2 and altered at phrase endings in order to accommodate the desired cadences. Canonic imitation is a notable feature in period 2. To facilitate comparison, the two periods are placed in paired staves.

Example 15.6   Variation in a repeated period. MS, K. 533/494, i, mm. 41–57.

(a)   (Ant. Phr. 1)

(b) (Ant. Phr. 2)

(H.C.)

(c) (Cons. Phr. 1)

(P.A.C.)

(d) (Cons. Phr. 2) (Suggestion of canonic imitation in contrary motion)

(P.A.C.)

Measures 1–16 of MS, K. 309, ii, constitute a double period (8 + 8, in which each eight-measure period consists of two phrases, 4 + 4). Measures 17–32 constitute a varied repetition of this double period. In the second double period the general outline of the melody is preserved. However, a considerable number of embellishments such as grace notes, neighboring and passing tones, and chromatic inflections have been added.

Variation in a Repeated Larger Structural Division

The overall form of BS, 10/1, ii is *ABABA*. The final *A* is short, and also functions as a coda. Each of the previous *A* sections has a double statement of the theme. Every statement of the unvaried melody is provided with a different accompaniment based on the same underlying harmonies. The general character of the variations is indicated in Example 15.7.

Example 15.7   Variations in the statements of the *A* theme. BS, 10/1, ii.

Measures 53–60 of MS, K. 309, ii, make up the B^2 section of a movement whose form is $A^1B^1A^2B^2A^3$. In B^2, which is a variation of B^1 (mm. 33–44), the accompaniment is largely the same as in B^1. But the melody in B^2 is a highly elaborate, quasi-coloratura version of B^1.[2] The closing measures of both B^1 and B^2 serve as retransition, with parallel materials; in contrast to the main body of B^2, the variation procedure (neighboring tone embellishment) here is in the lower voice while the upper voice is largely unchanged.

Example 15.8   MS, K. 309, ii, mm. 33ff and 53ff compared.

[2] Compare Example 15.8 with 15.7 in which it is the accompaniment, not the melody, that is varied.

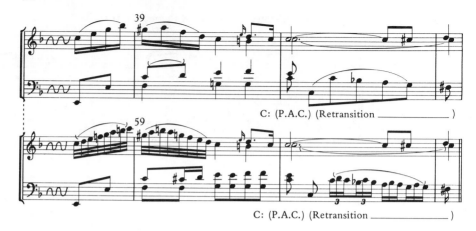

C: (P.A.C.) (Retransition _____)

C: (P.A.C.) (Retransition _____)

VARIATION FORM

In the following illustrations, variation is used consistently and is the chief structural principle. Observe that in homophonic variations, as a rule, there is a *harmonic* constant in the several variations, melody, accompaniment figure, texture, mode, tempo, and so forth being subject to change. In contrast, there usually is a *melodic* constant in polyphonic variations, the other factors, including harmony, being subject to alteration. This should not be construed as a formula or rule, but as a description of general practice.

The harmonic constant in homophonic variations is sometimes slightly modified. For example, substitute chords may be used, especially in the course of the phrase and less commonly at phrase endings. Thus, V–of–V may be used instead of II, II instead of IV, $_0$V^7 instead of V, or vice versa. However, the more important details of harmonic structure—beginnings, endings, cadence types—and phrase lengths and proportions are preserved in all the variations.

Strict variations are sometimes numbered, sometimes not; in any case, clear cadences appear at regular, periodic intervals corresponding to those in the theme.

Sectional (or *noncontinuous*) *variations* are usually separated by a brief pause, and numbered; *continuous variations* follow each other without interruption (they may dovetail by means of elision) and are not numbered.

Free (in contrast to "strict") *variations* do not preserve the phrase structure and the harmonic design of the theme. In such variations, the form is unique and unpredictable. A movement in variation form may combine these two types of procedure, as observed in Example 15.11.

Character variations may be distinguished from *ornamental variations*. In ornamental variations, the changes are largely decorative; as a result, there is little change of mood or expressive substance. In character variation, the variations are markedly different in style, mood, and substance. Examples of character variation may be observed in Variation 11 of Example 15.10, and in Example 15.12.

Example 15.9 which follows is *not* labeled variation form as such. Example 15.10 *is* so identified and the variations are numbered. In both, there is a short final extension or coda designed to avoid an abrupt conclusion.

In Example 15.9, the theme is followed by three variations and a coda. Each of the four sections, excluding the coda, is a small song form (incipient ternary or rounded binary). Part one (a^1a^2) is an eight-measure period, with parallel construction, which modulates to the dominant key. Part two consists of a first phrase (b) that is decidedly contrasting in material and tonally unstable, a second phrase (a^3) in the original key, and a third phrase that serves as codetta.[3] Between Variations 2 and 3 there is a four-measure bridge or interlude on the dominant, an exceptional feature in this otherwise "strict" variation form. The material of the brief coda is derived from the theme.

In Variation 1 the melody, which was originally in the upper voice, appears in the tenor against a syncopated accompaniment figure in the soprano register. The theme returns to the upper voice in Variation 2, borrowing the syncopation feature used in the accompaniment in Variation 1. In Variation 3 the melody is buried in a succession of sixteenth notes played by the right hand against prevailing slurred quarters in the left.

The opening measures of the theme and each of the three variations which appear in Example 15.9 demonstrate the variation techniques used.

Example 15.9   BS, 14/2, ii. Opening measures of the Theme and Variations 1, 2, and 3.

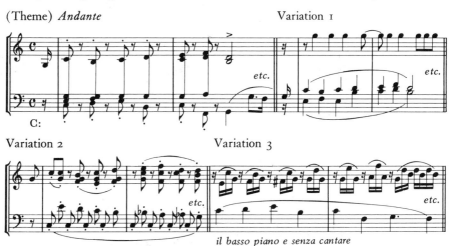

In Example 5.10 the theme is a small song form, $\|$ $:a^1a^2:$ $\|$ $:ba^3:$ $\|$. Each of the twelve numbered variations has the same form as the theme, and each explores one or more characteristic devices or motives. Part one of the theme is an eight-measure period. In part two, b is a four-measure phrase extended to five by the interpolation of a complete measure rest, and a^3 compresses the materials of a^1a^2 into a single four-measure phrase.

---

[3] For the distinction between coda and codetta, see the explanations on pages 265 and 267. For an illustration, see Example 23.3.

Example 15.10   MS, K. 284, iii. A description of the variations and the opening measures of each.

(a) Theme.[4]

(b) Variation 1. Eighth note triplets fill in the leaps and decorate the chief melody notes. A light chordal accompaniment replaces the Alberti bass figure of the theme.

(c) Variation 2. Two-part texture is predominant. There is a sense of dialogue between lower and upper voices, and rhythm contrast between triplets and sixteenth notes.

(d) Variation 3. The harmony underlying the theme is retained. Running sixteenth notes provide a new melody line, eighth notes doubled in octaves provide a new bass line.

[4] By a remarkable coincidence, the themes of Examples 15.9 and 15.10 are quite similar. Compare:

(e) Variation 4. The melody is simplified. The accompaniment is a figure composed of a broken chord and repeated neighboring tones in running sixteenth notes.

(f) Variation 5. There is a new melody, based on the rhythmic motive  and a new bass figure, largely in parallel thirds.

(g) Variation 6. Still another new melody in quarter notes (note the crossing of hands) is accompanied by a tremolo-like sixteenth note figure in the middle register.

(h) Variation 7. A plaintive melody in the minor mode is accompanied by repeated chords in eighth notes.

(i) Variation 8. The major mode returns. New motives are introduced and developed in dialogue style. The harmony is simplified (for example, I is followed at once by V without the intervening VI and II).

(j) Variation 9. The texture is largely two-voice, and there are suggestions of canonic imitation at the fifth below, the octave above, and in contrary motion. The use of such polyphonic devices in an essentially homophonic work provides useful textural contrast.

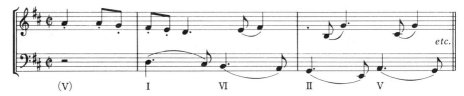

(k) Variation 10. A tremolo figure in sixteenth notes appears as accompaniment to a melody which is based on a simplified version of the original harmony. In part *b* there is exchange of materials between left and right hands and extensive chromaticism.

(l) Variation 11. Here the formal repetitions of *a¹a²* and *ba³* are abandoned in favor of varied repetition. The result is *a¹, a², a¹* varied, *a²* varied, *b, a³, b* varied, *a³* varied. The tempo changes to adagio cantabile. A melody in the style of a vocal aria appears in the upper voice.[5] Some florid scale passages in mm. 11, 13, 26, 30, and 32 suggest the *fioriture* of a coloratura soprano. The accompaniment is an Alberti bass figure in sixteenth notes.

[5] The melody given here corresponds to that in the first printed edition rather than the autograph. See the edition of MS edited by Nathan Broder, published by Theodore Presser, Bryn Mawr, Pa., 1956.

(m) Variation 12. There is a return to fast tempo (allegro), and for the first time triple meter is used. A new melody touches on some of the notes in the original line. As in Variation 11, the *exact* repetitions of parts one and two are replaced by *varied* repetitions. The closing phrase is extended several measures in the manner of a codetta, in order to strengthen the final cadence of the movement.

Allegro

(V) I V$_5^6$

The fourth movement of Beethoven's *Symphony no. 3 in E♭ major* is a large design that may be called a unique form; it illustrates rather nicely the principle of free variation. Not all the variations are free; however, the strict and the free variations tend to form larger sections within the movement as a whole. Thus the "free" alternation between strict and free variation is itself an element that contributes to the movement's unique shape.[6]

Example 15.11   Free variation. Beethoven, *Symphony no. 3 in E♭ major,* iv. Summary of overall design:

(a)

(b)

1. Introduction
2. *(a)* *(a:* Var. 1) *(a:* Var. 2) *(a + b:* Var. 3) (Bridge)
3. (First fugal development of *a*) (Development of *b*) (*a* in march style)
4. (Short development of *b + a*) (Second fugal development of *a*) (Bridge)
5. *(b:* Var. 4) *(b,* without repeated sections, *adagio:* Var. 5) (Bridge)
6. Coda *(presto)*

The variations in Example 15.12 are strict or formal, but because of the great contrasts of mood and expressive effect between the variations, they tend to be character variations rather than ornamental ones. The opening measures of the theme and each of the variations are cited to show the character contrasts.

[6] In the diagram, strict variations are numbered, free variations are not numbered.

Example 15.12   Character variation. Beethoven, *String Quartet in A major,* 18/5, iii. Opening measures of the Theme and Variations.

(a)   Theme: Andante cantabile

(b)   Variation 1.

(c)   Variation 2.

(d)   Variation 3.

(e) Variation 4.

(f) Variation 5.

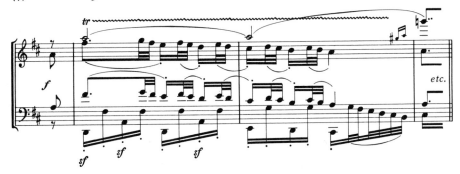

Even greater contrasts may be found in Elgar's *Enigma Variations* for orchestra, and in Richard Strauss's tone poem *Don Quixote,* which is close to being a concerto for cello and orchestra. In the Elgar and Strauss works the variations are free in their inner phrase structure, but are sectional and numbered. The *Symphonic Variations* for piano and orchestra by César Franck are free rather than strict, continuous rather than sectional, unnumbered, and character rather than ornamental; in addition, the work is a one-movement concerto for piano and orchestra.

Transitions, Bridges, and Extensions

Transitions or bridges between variations may be used in order to effect needed modulations (see Example 15.11), to provide contrast, or to provide larger section grouping (see Example 21.7, mm. 95–98).

Extension at the beginning or at the end of a series of variations may expand this form, as any other form. Observe that the finale of Beethoven's *Symphony no. 3 in Eb major* cited in Example 15.11 begins with an introduction and closes with a coda; the former serves to establish the dominant of the prevailing key (Eb major), while the latter emphasizes the tonic, and serves additionally as a sort of coda for the entire symphony. The sonata movement cited in Example 15.9, a theme with three variations, has a coda but no introduction. In the final variation of the movement illustrated in Example 15.10, there is an extension of the last phrase in the manner of a codetta, rather than a separate and distinguishable coda.

In Brahms's *Variations on a Theme of Haydn,* the variations are all strict except for the last one, which merely paraphrases elements of the theme and is a variation form known as ground bass (see Example 16.4). The finale, a series of continuous variations based on a five-measure theme, is followed by a coda which relates rather closely to the initial theme and helps round off the overall form of the work. The same composer's variations based on a Handel theme consist of strict variations followed by a fugue that also serves as a coda to the composition as a whole.

SUGGESTED EXERCISES

1. What evidence of variation can be found in BS, 22, i, mm. 93–104?

2. Discuss the relationship between mm. 73–82 and 83–90 in MS, K. 533/494, ii. Compare these measures with mm. 1–22. What is the relationship between mm. 1–22 and 73–90? Describe the variation techniques.

3. Compare the thematic ideas of the contrasting formal divisions of Brahms's *Symphony no. 2 in D major,* iii. Explain the relationship of the material at mm. 33, 107, 176, 194, and 219 to that in the opening measures of the movement.

4. When the main theme of BS, 22, ii reappears after the middle section, it is varied. Describe the means used. Is there precedent for this type of elaboration earlier in the movement?

5. Compare the several statements of the main theme in BS, 22, iv. In which statements is there evidence of variation? What techniques are used?

6. BS, 27/1, ii is a scherzo and trio. Compare A^2 with A^1.

7. Compare mm. 9–16 with mm. 1–8 in BS, 27/2, ii. See also mm. 25–36. Is the latter group similar to mm. 1–8, 9–16, or both? In what respect(s) is it different from both?

8. Is there any evidence of variation in the opening section (mm. 1–39) of BS, 28, i?

9. Analyze MS, K. 547, iii in detail. Indicate the form of the theme and identify the techniques used in each of the variations.

10. Analyze BS, 26, i in detail. Use the procedure indicated for Exercise 9.

11. Write a short essay comparing the variation techniques used in the following movements of Beethoven string quartets: 18/5, iii; 74, iv; 127, ii; 131, iv; 132, iii; 135, iii.

12. Write an essay discussing the variation techniques used in one or more of the following works:

> D'Indy, *Istar Variations* (for orchestra)
> Bach, *Goldberg Variations* (for harpsichord)
> Beethoven, *Diabelli Variations* (for piano)
> Franck, *Symphonic Variations* (for piano and orchestra)
> Richard Strauss, *Don Quixote* (symphonic poem)
> Hindemith, *Symphonic Metamorphosis on Themes by Carl Maria von Weber*
> Vaughan Williams, *Variations on a Theme by Thomas Tallis* (for string orchestra)
> Beethoven, *Symphony no. 3 in E♭ major,* iv; and *Symphony no. 9 in D minor,* iv
> Elgar, *Enigma Variations* (for orchestra)
> Brahms, *Variations on a Theme by Joseph Haydn* (for orchestra; also for two pianos)

Polyphonic Variations:
Ostinato, Ground Bass, Passacaglia, Chaconne   16

Polyphonic variations differ from homophonic variations primarily in texture. Although the two types are distinct, they should not be regarded as absolutely mutually exclusive. Example 15.10, Variation 9, shows the use of imitation in the course of variations that are primarily homophonic in orientation. In Example 16.6, Variations 1 and 2, homophonic texture appears in a variation form that is largely polyphonic in character. In the final movement of the *Symphony no. 3 in E♭ major,* Beethoven displays considerable ingenuity and originality in his juxtaposition of the two types of variation in alternation. Bartók, in the second movement of the *Concerto no. 3 for Piano and Orchestra,* uses the technique of *chorale variation* (a type of polyphonic variation) in the *A* parts of a three-part form, enclosing a rather impressionistic and comparatively homophonic *B* part that is *not* in variation form.

This chapter is concerned with the terms *ostinato, ground bass* (*basso ostinato* in Italian, and sometimes referred to simply as *ground*), *passacaglia,* and *chaconne.* All are variation forms in which there is multiple and continuous repetition of a thematic idea, usually melodic (in the chaconne it may be harmonic), and in a single voice—generally the bass—although migration to another voice and return can occasionally be observed as an exception to the "rule." The chief interest in these types of variation lies not in the thematic repetitions but in the continually changing material in the associated voices and in the continually changing harmonies which result. The several kinds of variation technique that may be applied to a (usually) *single* statement of a pre-existent melody—so-called *cantus firmus* treatment—will be discussed in Chapter 20.

OSTINATO

The term *ostinato* frequently is used in a generic sense to refer to all the indicated forms except the more harmonically oriented chaconne. In a more limited sense, it refers to the continuous repetition of a short melodic idea, generally a *motive,* in one voice. The idea may also be a *phrase* in length. If the ostinato appears in the lowest voice the more specific term *basso ostinato* is preferable.

In Example 16.1 there is a one-measure, three-note ostinato in the middle register. The figure appears throughout the *A* sections of the movement which is in *ABA* form. The quotation includes the retransition to and the opening measures of the third part. The ostinato figure illustrated in Example 16.2 also is one measure long. There are four notes descending stepwise in the bass register. In Example 16.3 the four-note ostinato creates a sense of cross meter against the 3/2 time signature. In addition, there is a three-beat ostinato in the soprano line. The overlapping ostinati create a very tightly knit structure.

Example 16.1 Ostinato in the middle register. Bizet, "Carillon" from *L'arlésienne Suite no. 1.* (Excerpt, reduced score.)

Example 16.2 Ostinato in the bass register. Brahms, *Symphony no. 1 in C minor,* iv, second theme. (Excerpt, reduced score).

Example 16.3   Overlapping ostinati. Stravinsky, *Symphony of Psalms*,[1] iii (excerpt, reduced score, strings and brass omitted).

GROUND BASS

The term *ground bass, basso ostinato,* or simply, *ground,* is best used if the melodic idea is a *phrase* in length rather than a motive; very rarely is it longer. The line is more a harmonic bass than a tune, but there are occasional instances of truly melodic character; see, for example, the five-measure theme used in Example 16.4.

A ground bass theme usually is first stated alone, a characteristic that is shared with the passacaglia. The following example is exceptional in that the accompanying voices

[1] *Symphony in Psalms* by Igor Stravinsky, Copyright 1931 by Edition Russe de Musique; Renewed 1958. Copyright and Renewal assigned to Boosey and Hawkes, Inc. Revised Edition Copyright 1948 by Boosey and Hawkes, Inc. Reprinted by permission.

enter before the end of the first statement. Two of the upper voices begin as imitations of the bass (see brackets). There is continuous elision of phrases, since the B♭ at the beginning of each phrase is also heard as the conclusion of the previous phrase. (An alternate analysis which views every fifth measure as a half cadence is tenable. It is also possible to see the ties and suspensions as obliterating the cadences completely.)

Example 16.4   Ground bass. Brahms, *Variations on a Theme by Joseph Haydn,* finale (opening measures).[2]

[2] The illustration is taken from the two-piano version (op. 56b) rather than the simultaneously published orchestral version (op. 56a).

Chromatic ground basses of the baroque era frequently involve descending motion by half-steps from the tonic to the dominant, followed by a cadential leap back to the tonic. This use of chromatic harmony for the central portion and diatonic harmony for the cadential portion of a phrase clearly presages the nineteenth-century practice of chromaticism in such composers as Wagner and Franck.

Perhaps the best known chromatic ground basses are those by Purcell (in the "Lament" aria of the opera *Dido and Aeneas*), and by Bach (in the "Crucifixus" of the *Mass in B minor*) which show striking similarity both in construction and in expressive effect.

Example 16.5   Chromatic ground basses.

(a)   Purcell, "Dido's Lament" from *Dido and Aeneas*.

(b)   Bach, "Crucifixus" from the *Mass in B minor*.

PASSACAGLIA AND CHACONNE

The terms *passacaglia* and *chaconne* appear to have been used interchangeably by composers of the baroque era. Today, the Passacaglia from the *Passacaglia and Fugue in C minor* for organ, and the Chaconne from the *Partita in D minor for Unaccompanied Violin*, both by Bach, are generally regarded as models. Using these works as reference points, Willi Apel states[3] that a passacaglia is "based on a clearly distinguishable ostinato[4] that normally appears in the bass but that may occasionally be transferred to an upper voice."[5] In a chaconne, on the other hand, the "theme" is only "a scheme of harmonies . . . usually treated so that the first and last chords are fixed whereas the intervening ones can be replaced by substitutes."

The two types are similar in tempo, which is generally slow; in meter, which is generally triple; and in mode, usually minor. Composers, particularly in the nineteenth and twentieth centuries, have sometimes departed from one or more of these secondary characteristics. A useful though little recognized distinction should also be made between the bass line quality of the basso ostinato (or ground) and the more tuneful and melodic nature of the passacaglia theme.

In the *Passacaglia in C minor,* the theme first appears unaccompanied in the pedals; except as noted below, it remains in the pedals throughout. Following the initial statement there are twenty variations, each with different accompanying materials or procedures. These are based on a relatively small number of motives, providing a remarkable sense of unity and consistency. The changes in texture and motive usage generally occur at the cadences in order to strengthen and reinforce the sense of phrase structure inherent in the bass line. (See Example 16.4, in which the cadences that would otherwise appear every five measures have been deliberately suppressed or markedly weakened.)

Example 16.6   Bach, *Passacaglia in C minor.* The theme and the beginning of each variation.

The theme

★ (First half is the subject of the fugue which follows.)

[3] See *Harvard Dictionary of Music,* edited by Willi Apel, 3rd ed., (Cambridge: Harvard Univ. Press, 1970).

[4] The term is used here in its generic sense.

[5] See Example 16.6; only in Variations 11–13 is the theme in an upper voice rather than in the bass. In the curious *Variations for Violin and Continuo* by Heinrich Biber, cited in the *Historical Anthology of Music* (Cambridge: Harvard Univ. Press, 1950), there are attempts to treat the sixteen-measure theme canonically; in one variation, short segments are repeated antiphonally in an exchange between upper and lower voices.

Variation 1   Variation 2

Homophonic texture. Sequential use of ♪ | ♩. ♫ ♩.

Same style and motive. Different harmonization.

Variation 3   Variation 4

Flowing eighths based on ♪♫♫ | ♩ or ♫♫ | ♩. Imitative style.

Imitative style using ♫ | ♪ in stepwise motion.

Variation 5   Variation 6

Same motive and style with the addition of leaps. Bass participates in the imitation.

New motive ♫♫♩ introduced. Imitation in upper voices only. *Ascending* stepwise motion prevails.

Variation 7   Variation 8

Same materials. *Descend-ing* stepwise motion pre-vails.

Same materials. Ascend-ing, descending *and con-trary* motion used.

Variation 9   Variation 10

Same rhythmic motive, but with new melodic contour using ascending leap. Bass participates in the imitation.

Continued use of motive, but now in the soprano line only. No imitation. Harmonic support in homophonic style.

Variation 11   Variation 12

Theme is transferred to soprano line. Soprano line of Var. 10 is employed as the lower voice. Two-part texture. Pedals silent.

Theme continues in the soprano line. Motive  reintroduced. New motive in the bass line (cascading échappées) subsequently imitated in the other voices.

Variation 13   Variation 14

Theme is in middle register, occasionally ornamented. Pedals silent. Further development of sixteenth note motive.

Theme reverts to the bass, as lowest note of arpeggiated harmonies.

Variation 15   Variation 16

Similar to Var. 14. Notes of the theme appear alternately in high and low register.

Theme returns to pedals, sustained notes. New variant of with tied notes creates effect of crescendo in each measure.

Variation 17   Variation 18

New sixteenth note motive (triplets). Alternately descending and ascending motion.

Slight change in the rhythm of the theme. New variant of motive.

Variation 19   Variation 20

New variant of   Continuation of the style
♪ ♪♪♪ ♩ in four-voice   of Var. 19. Texture thick-
texture.   ens to five voices.

In retrospect the variations may be viewed as grouped 5 + 5 + 5 + 5 on the basis of common characteristics.

Var. 1   2   3   4   5
(Homophonic style,   (Continuous   (Motivic unity)
motivic unity)   eighths)

(Variations 1–5 use several motives composed of eighths and sixteenths. There is gradually increasing momentum.)

Var. 6   7   8   9   10

(Variations 6–10 are based on a single motive of four sixteenth notes of which the last is accented. The mounting intensity is continued.)

Var. 11   12   13   14   15

(The theme is in an upper voice)   (Arpeggiated chords based
                                            on the four sixteenth note
                                            motive. Absence of sus-
                                            tained theme in any voice)

(Variations 11–15 have irregular features. There is a gradual reduction in intensity. The theme does not appear in the pedal part)

Var. 16   17   18   19   20
(Same motive as   (New triplet mo-   (Same motive as   (Same motive as
Vars. 6–10)   tive)   Vars. 4–5)   in Vars. 6–10,
                                                            slightly varied)

(Variations 16–20 constitute a quasi-reprise because of the reintroduction of motives and procedures used in the earlier variations. There is mounting intensity to the close.)

The Chaconne from Bach's *Partita in D minor for Unaccompanied Violin* consists of a four-measure theme in homophonic style followed by sixty-two variations. Perhaps because of the limitations of the instrument, there is not much polyphonic texture (this is true even of the fugal movements in the three sonatas for unaccompanied violin). Frequently there is but a single line, occasionally there are arpeggiated chords; only now and then can a sense of real polyphony be discerned. The movement exhibits stately character, slow tempo, triple meter, minor mode, and the emphasis on the second beat typical of the sarabande. There is no clearly repeated bass melody, as there is in the Passacaglia. The chord structure is not identical in each of the variations, some of which may be grouped by their common use of a single variant of the original harmonies. The "theme," if it may be called one, is simple enough to be varied and remain recognizable. If the basic harmonic set is defined as I–II(or IV)–V–I, there can be little dispute as to the so-called "liberties" Bach has permitted himself.

A comparison of the harmonic structure of the "theme" (mm. 1–5) with that of two of the variations (Var. 12, mm. 49–53; and Var. 48, mm. 193–97) will reveal the method used throughout.

Theme:	I		$II_{(\frac{4}{2})}$	$V_{(\frac{6}{5})}$	I	VI	II_6	I_6	$_0V_6$		I
									4		
Var. 12:	I	V_6 of VII	VII	V_6 of VI	VI	II_6		V			I
		5		5		5					
Var. 48:	I		$II_{(7)}$	I_6	IV	V_6 of V	I_6		V		I
							4				

Both the chord structure and the bass line are subject to alteration. As a rule, the bass line moves in a descending stepwise pattern from D to A, with or without embellishments, in either a diatonic or chromatic progression; it then leaps from A to D. The following bass lines are derived from the variations indicated, and display representative procedures.

Example 16.7 Bach, *Partita in D minor for Unaccompanied Violin*, Chaconne.

(a) Bass line of the theme (mm. 1–5).[6]

(b) Bass line of Variation 4 (mm. 17–21).

[6] The theme begins on the second beat of measure 1 and ends on the first beat of measure 5. The phrase, therefore, is exactly four measures long.

(c)   Bass line of Variation 12[7] (mm. 49–53).

(d)   Bass line of Variation 48[8] (mm. 193–97).

As illustration of the manner in which the variations may be grouped the following are cited: (a) Theme and Variations 1–2–3 using the same bass line (see Example 16.7a); (b) Variations 4–5 using a chromatically embellished variation of the original line (see Example 16.7b); (c) Variations 12–19 using a zigzag line, emphasizing the interval of an ascending fourth or its inversion, the descending fifth (see Example 16.7c). Observe also that in Example 16.7d the bass line moves upward from tonic to dominant, instead of downward.

The movement has an overall tripartite form (A^1BA^2) largely caused by the change to major mode in the middle section. A^1 comprises the theme and the first thirty-two variations. There are nineteen variations in B. A^2 consists of eleven variations of which the last two are an extended reprise of the opening statement of the theme.

Repetitions of an ostinato, ground bass, or passacaglia theme characteristically appear on the same scale degrees. As a result, the opportunities for modulation are considerably limited and tonal monotony may result. One solution to this problem is the transposition of the repeated figure to other scale degrees, usually with modification of some of the intervals to fit the harmony and the resulting alteration of the exact melodic shape. Another is transposition to other keys in which case less drastic alteration is required. In either case, small changes are usually called for in order to secure the necessary joints or connections.

This technique may be observed in the slow movements of *Sonata no. 2 in A major* and *Sonata no. 3 in E major for Clavier and Violin* by Bach; both are in the relative minor of the main key of the work. In the first, the repeated figure is only a half measure long, and more properly called an ostinato; in the second, it is a four-measure figure which makes up an entire phrase and therefore designated a ground bass. Example 16.8 illustrates selected measures from each movement.

[7] This variation may also be viewed as built on the harmonic circle of fifths, as the root progression is I–IV–♭VII–III–VI–II–V–I.

[8] See the harmonic analysis of this variation on page 154.

Example 16.8 Transposing ostinato and modulating ground bass.

(a) Bach, *Sonata no. 2 in A major for Clavier* and *Violin,* iii (in F♯ minor). Transposing ostinato (selected measures).

(b) Bach, *Sonata no. 3 in E major for Clavier and Violin,* iii, (in C♯ minor). Modulating ground bass (selected measures).

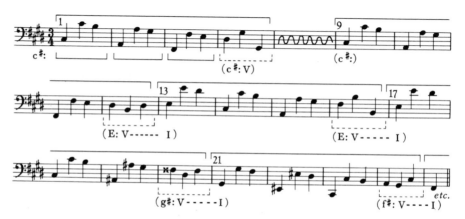

It is evident in these examples that by continuously redefining the constant, it is possible to make the rigid ostinato formula slightly flexible. In Example 16.8a, the apparently constant octave leap between the first two notes is altered (in mm. 19–20) to the leap of a sixth or a third. The second beat of the figure first appears to be a triad outline, but as early as m. 2 the figure becomes a seventh chord outline, with the same general shape. In Example 16.8b the four-measure ground bass is a complex of one-measure motives treated sequentially; only gradually is it apparent that the fourth measure is a variable unit that is assigned whatever material is needed to accomplish the desired modulation and cadence. In every fourth measure the V chord which is needed to establish the key is the factor determining the melodic shape; in this sense each fourth measure *is* a constant.

SUGGESTED EXERCISES

1. Write a short paper discussing the terms ostinato, basso ostinato, ground bass, passacaglia, and chaconne. You may wish to consult other texts and reference works; if you do, be sure to credit your sources properly. Use musical illustrations as needed.

2. Analyze the final movement of Brahms's *Variations on a Theme of Haydn*. Discuss the procedures used in each of the five-measure variations. Describe the means used to weaken or thwart the recurring V–I cadences. Is there evidence of larger grouping, such as that observed in the Bach *Passacaglia in C minor?* Support your statements with evidence.

3. Discuss the variation technique used by Brahms in the last movement of his *Symphony no. 4 in E minor*. Trace the eight-note ostinato figure (E–F♯–G–A–A♯–B–B–E) through each of the variations.

4. Examine one of the standard anthologies containing baroque music. Make up a list of several compositions that employ the techniques discussed above. Describe each example briefly. Credit your sources.

5. Stravinsky is well known for the frequency with which he uses ostinato devices. Examine several scores (for example, *Le Sacre du Printemps, Capriccio for Piano and Orchestra, Histoire du Soldat, Symphony of Psalms*) and make a list of selected passages where such devices appear. Indicate title, edition, page, measure numbers. Describe the usage in each instance.

6. Utilizing the three-note figure of Example 16.1, the four-note figure of Example 16.2 or 16.3, or the chromatic ground bass of Example 16.5a, compose a work of about one page in length. Provide a brief analysis and description of your work.

7. Compose a short work in which you employ a transposing ostinato or modulating ground bass of your own choice. If you choose the latter alternative, plan the modulatory scheme so that you proceed from the tonic to closely related keys and return to the tonic at the close. Use a postcadential extension or codetta as necessary.

Canon is defined as a rule or law; in music, it denotes strict imitation, in either a section or a complete movement. If the appearance is quite brief, the term *canonic imitation* is more appropriate.

Canons are classified as either finite or infinite. Finite canons are performed once and have a specific and predetermined close. Infinite canons are performed, or capable of being performed, several times and do not have a prescribed end; the performance stops only at an arbitrarily chosen point.

An *infinite* (or *perpetual*) *canon* is sometimes called a *round*. This is because of the circular pattern that results from the continual repetition of the melody in the participating voices which enter one after the other in the following manner:

```
(Voice 1):   a b c d a b c d a b c d
(Voice 2):     a b c d a b c d a b c
(Voice 3):       a b c d a b c d a b
(Voice 4):         a b c d a b c d a
```

Familiar examples of this type are *Row, row, row your boat, Three blind mice,* and *Frère Jacques.*

A *finite canon* has a definite ending point; in two voices it may be symbolically represented as follows:

```
(Voice 1):   a b c d e f g h ... z
(Voice 2):     a b c d e f g h ... z
```

The second voice (or *comes*) imitates the first (or *dux*) quite strictly to the very end. When the leading voice has run its course (to z), it may either drop out; sustain the last factor as a held or tied note to the end; or proceed with free material, to maintain the full sonority and texture to the end.

Canons can also be classified according to the number of voices participating in the imitation. The round previously described is an example of four-part canon; the example of a finite canon which followed is a two-part canon. If one or more of the scored voices is not involved with the imitation (see Example 17.4), the term *accompanied canon* is appropriate.

If two canons sound simultaneously, the result is a *double canon.*

(Voice 1): a b c d e . . . j k
(Voice 2): p q r s t . . . y z
(Voice 3):   a b c d e . . . j
(Voice 4):   p q r s t . . . y

Because such technical demands make the achievement of genuinely musical results difficult, procedures of this complexity are seldom attempted. There are a number of examples of double canons in *Orgelbüchlein* (a collection of chorale preludes for the liturgical year) by Bach.

A canon is also properly described in terms of the (vertical) interval and the (horizontal) distance between the opening notes. Thus, one may refer to a canon at the octave after one measure, a canon at the fifth after two beats, and so forth. The canonic interval can be reckoned either above or below the leading voice. It is possible, although rare, to have the imitating voice appear in inversion, augmentation, diminution, retrogression, or any of several possible combinations.[1] The following examples show just a few of the many ways a musical idea may be imitated canonically.

Example 17.1   Canonic imitation.

(a) Canon at the octave below, after one measure.

(b) Canon at the fifth above, after two beats.

(c) Canon at the third below, after one beat.

(d) Canon at the tritone above, after three beats.

[1] See the discussion of these terms in Chapter 16. Illustrations of many of these rare procedures may be found in the canons that form part of Bach's *Musical Offering*.

(e) Canon in inversion, at the fifth, after one measure.

(f) Canon at the octave below, in retrograde and augmentation.

(g) Three-voice canon at the fourth below after one measure, and at the octave after three measures.

The numerical value of the intervals is not altered in canonic imitation. The interval *quality* may be changed as necessary to maintain the desired key. In Example 17.1g, the second voice has F♮ in m. 4, not F♯, in order to preserve the key of A minor. If this prescription is not followed, the voices will be in different keys (see Example 17.2). Where the style is consistently chromatic, all twelve degrees of the scale are used, and tonality is obscure, this problem tends to disappear (see Example 17.1d).

Example 17.2 Correct vs. incorrect canonic imitation in diatonic style.

(a) Correct *(b)* Incorrect

If a modulating melody is used in canon there are additional problems for the composer, since the lines modulate at different points; the solution does not lie in the erroneous method illustrated in Example 17.2b. To avoid contradictory tonalities as well as a sudden modulatory shift, a modulating canon must be composed in such a way that a neutral area, an area of tonal ambiguity, occurs for several beats or measures while the modulation is taking place. The composer should provide the pivotal common-chord area with tones that belong to both old and new keys. See the modulation to the dominant and return to the tonic in Example 17.1g, the six modulations in the illustration of Exercise 1 at the end of this chapter, and Example 17.3 which follows.

Example 17.3 Tonal ambiguity in a modulating canon. Bach, *Sonata no. 2 in A major for Clavier and Violin*, iii (in F♯ minor), opening measures. (The left-hand part for the clavier is omitted.)

It should be remembered that canon is a technique or procedure, not a form. A given form may employ canonic means, or a canon may be invested in a particular form; it is not important here to decide which comes first in the composer's planning. It is important to distinguish form from procedure. See, for example, (a) MS, K.

576, i, in which canonic imitation is used in connection with thematic statements and developments in the larger context of sonata form; (b) Franck, *Sonata in A major for Violin and Piano,* iv, in which the *a* sections of the opening *ababa* group are based on a canonically treated principal theme; and (c) Haydn, *String Quartet in D minor,* 76/2, Menuetto (not including the Trio), which is a canon between the upper and lower strings.

In Bach's *Goldberg Variations* for harpsichord, the harmonic structure of a highly ornamented melody in the style of a vocal aria is the basis of thirty variations. (The work closes with a reprise of the aria.) Every third variation is a canon, except for no. 30, which is a quodlibet (a work in which two or more pre-existent melodies appear simultaneously in counterpoint).[2] Each canon is at a progressively larger interval. Thus the first canon is at the unison, the second canon is at the interval of a second, and so forth up to the interval of a ninth. The enormous expressivity which is obtained despite the severe limitations imposed by the formal, harmonic, and canonic demands is one of the wonders of the musical world. It is also eloquent testimony to the notion that formidable technique and intellect are no barrier to expressive utterance.

The nine canons should be examined in full; only the opening measures of each are indicated here.

Example 17.4   Canonic variation. Bach, *Goldberg Variations.* Opening measures of the theme (Aria) and the canonic variations.[3]

(a) Theme (Aria), (3/4).

(b) Variation 3, canon at the unison after one measure, (12/8).

---

[2] A popular example of quodlibet is the combination of Dvořák's *Humoresque* with *Way Down Upon the Swanee River.*

[3] The harmonic structure of the opening measures of the aria and of each variation is I, V_6, $_0V_6$ of V, V, or a slight modification of that plan. Thus, it is evident the variations are based upon the harmony (not the melody) of the "theme."

(c) Variation 6, canon at the second after one measure, (3/8).

(I - - - - - - - - - - - - - - - - V) [V$_5^6$]

(d) Variation 9, canon at the third (below) after one measure, (C).

(I - - - - - - - - - - - - V) [Actually, substitute for V]

(e) Variation 12, canon at the fourth (below) after one measure, (3/4). (Canon in inversion.)

(I - - - - - - - - - - - - - - - - - - V)

(f) Variation 15, canon at the fifth after one measure, (2/4). (Canon in inversion.)

g: (I - - - - - - - - - - - - - - - - - V)

(g) Variation 18, canon at the sixth after a half measure, (₵).

G: (I - - - - - - - - - - - - - - - V)

(h) Variation 21, canon at the seventh after a half measure, (C).

g: (I - - - - - - - - - - - -V⁽⁷⁾)

(i) Variation 24, canon at the octave (below) after two measures, (9/8).

G: (I - - - - - - - - - - - V)

(j) Variation 27, canon at the ninth after one measure, (6/8).[4]

(I - - - - - - - - - - - - - -V) [V⁶₅]

See further, Robert Erickson's discussion and illustration of Bach's *Musical Offering* and *The Art of Fugue,* Hindemith's *Ludus Tonalis,* and Webern's *Symphony,* op. 21;[5] and the article on canon in the *Harvard Dictionary of Music* which includes discussion of types, historical background, noteworthy examples and significant didactic works.

---

[4] This is the only one of the nine canons lacking a "free" third voice in the bass.

[5] *The Structure of Music,* 2nd ed. (New York: The Noonday Press, 1959), pp. 142–57.

SUGGESTED EXERCISES

1. Analyze the following canon, noting such features as interval and distance, overall form, key structure, modulatory procedures, cadences, the character of the accompaniment, and so forth.

2. Identify and describe the procedures in each canon included in any anthology.

3. Write a paper describing in some detail the several canons in Bach's *Musical Offering*.[6] Provide short illustrations of the procedures used.

4. Write several two-part canons of moderate length (15–20 measures in compound meter), using the procedure and nomenclature suggested in Example 17.1. The specifications you choose should include various intervals, distances, keys, and modes. Some of the imitations should be above, others below the leading voice. *Procedure:* First write the opening measure(s) in both voices. Then add short segments to each, checking frequently to ensure harmonic propriety and rhythmic balance. Be sure the second voice continues the canon up to and including the last note in the final cadence. Work backward from the last notes for at least one or two measures.

5. Write a three-voice composition of moderate length in which the two upper voices are in canon and the bass voice is "free." Modulate to the relative major or minor, then to the dominant, and finally back to the tonic. The last phrase should be a more or less exact restatement of the opening phrase. Plan the pivot areas in the modulations carefully, and mark them as in Example 17.3. Procedure as in Exercise 4.

6. Using the opening four measures of Variation 18 of Example 17.4g as a beginning, continue the canon and accompanying voice for another twelve measures, using the same style and motives. Use the following harmonic plan as a guide:

$$(\text{mm. } 5\text{–}8){:} \quad (\text{G}){:} \text{ III } / \text{ G:IV}_6 / \text{ e: II}^7 \quad \text{V}^9 / \frac{\text{V}}{\text{I}} \text{–I } /$$

$$(= \text{e:VI}_6 \qquad\qquad (\text{e:I} = \text{G:VI})$$

$$(\text{mm. } 9\text{–}12){:} \quad (\text{G}){:} \text{ V}^6 \text{ of V } / \text{ V } / \text{ V of V } / \text{ V}_6 \text{ (V}^7) /$$

$$(\text{mm. } 13\text{–}16){:} \quad (\text{G}){:} \text{ I} / \text{ II}_6 / \text{ V——}^7 / \text{ I } /$$

---

[6] Realization of the enigma canons may be found in the Hans T. David edition (G. Schirmer, New York, 1944) and in the Lea Pocket Score edition (New York).

The Invention 18

The procedure known as *invention* is often associated with the familiar two-voice keyboard compositions of that name by Bach and the similarly constructed three-voice sinfonias which are generally referred to today as the three-voice inventions. The same style is also used occasionally in partita and sonata movements, in several of the preludes of *The Well-Tempered Clavier,* and occasionally in association with chorale variation.

The invention can be identified by its distinguishing characteristics. There is consistent and fairly continuous use of one motive or a small number of short motives; these are treated imitatively and equally in each of the several voices. Counter-motives are regularly used as counterpoints to the chief motive(s), resulting in considerable double counterpoint.[1] There are either few or no episodes.[2] There usually are several (three or four) sections, each closing on a well-defined cadence. The sections do not use contrasting material since the motives persist throughout, but they do employ different developmental procedures and/or contrasting keys.

The motives may have a generalized shape, rather than a particular one. That is, the intervals may change while the linear direction or character and the rhythm remain unchanged. It is in this particular respect that the invention may differ greatly from the sometimes similar fugue. (See Table 19.1.)

The opening statement is usually imitated immediately at the octave (see Examples 18.1 and 18.3, and *Two-voice Inventions nos. 1–4, 6–9, 11, 13*). The initial tonic statement may be answered at the dominant level (as in Examples 18.4 and 18.5, and *Two-voice Inventions nos, 5, 10, 14, 15*), or there may be immediate development without a formal "answer" in the second voice, but this is rare (see Example 18.2 and *Two-Voice Invention no. 12*).

The following excerpts illustrate some of the typical procedures employed in the invention. Examples 18.1, 18.2, and 18.3 are in two voices; 18.4 and 18.5 are in three voices.

TWO-VOICE INVENTION

at the octave; consistent use of two motives, one in sixteenths, the other in eighth
In the *Two-Voice Invention no. 4 in D minor* by Bach, there is characteristic imitation

[1] See Example 10.5 and the text that precedes it.
[2] An episode in an invention is a structural division in which the complete motive(s) is (are) absent.

notes; varied interval contours within the basic motive shapes; sequence and inversion;[3] and sectional form. There is a nice balance between unity and variety in the first section which modulates from D minor to the relative key, F major.

Example 18.1   Bach, *Two-voice Invention no. 4 in D minor,* opening section.

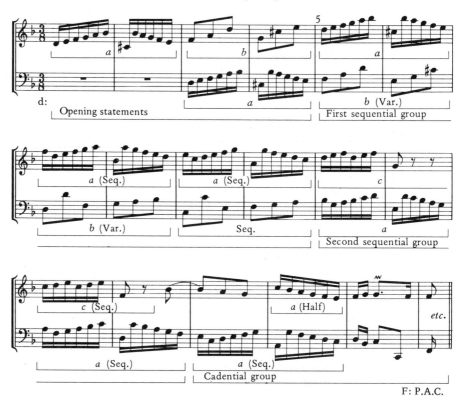

In Example 18.2 there is no formal "answer" to the opening statement. In m. 2 the sequential pattern begun in the upper voice in m. 1 continues over a tonic pedal point. A modulatory development in mm. 3–5 leads to the relative minor key (D minor). The underlying stepwise line F–Eb–D–C–Bb–A–B♮–C–C♯–D in the upper voice (mm. 1–4), and the circle of fifths D–G–C–F–Bb–E–A–D in the root progression (mm. 4–6), both of which are designed to assist the modulation to D minor, are of particular interest. Motive fragments are indicated by superscripts: thus y^1 is a fragment of *y*.

Motives *x* and *y* have generalized rather than particular shapes. In the measures cited below, the first half of *x* appears variously as the following succession of intervals: 4–3–2–2–3 (mm. 1, 3, 4, 6), 3–4–2–2–4 (m. 1), 3–3–2–2–3 (mm. 2, 3, 4, 5, 6), and 2–2–2–2–3 (m. 2). The second half of *x* is more consistent (usually 3–3–3–2–2) changing only in m. 2 to 3–2–3–2–2.

---

[3] Inverted *a* motive first appears in the second section, mm. 22–23.

Example 18.2   BWTC, Vol. 1, *Prelude no. 11 in F major,* mm. 1–6.

The following excerpt is from Kohs's *Invention no. 7 in E* (using the scale E–F–Gb–A♯–B–C–Db–E, a modified Phrygian mode). Note that only a few motives are used (*a, b, c, d*) but that they are varied in a number of ways. For instance, in mm. 3–6 the half-step motive in the right hand (Gb–F) takes on four rhythmic guises. And the rhythm first found in the right hand in m. 5, where it is associated with *two pitches,* is applied later to *repeated tones* (mm. 11ff). Additional formal interest is provided by canonic imitation for seven measures, beginning with the lower voice in m. 8 (see brackets).

Example 18.3   Kohs, *Invention no. 7 in E*[4] (excerpt).

[4] *Ten Inventions for Two Voices* by Ellis B. Kohs, © Copyright 1954 by Ellis B. Kohs; reprinted by permission of American Composers Alliance, 170 W. 74th St., New York, N. Y., 10023.

Expansion of *abcd* (in canon)

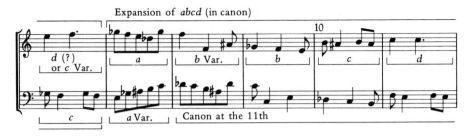

Expansion of *a d*

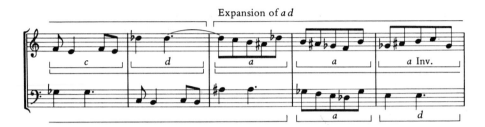

Expansion of *b d*

Ostinato

THREE-VOICE INVENTION

Perhaps the most remarkable of Bach's three-voice inventions (or sinfonias) is the one in F minor. Three melodies, each two measures long, are used in triple counterpoint, the principle of double counterpoint extended to three voices. Only two of the voices are heard in the first phrase. The third voice, the soprano, first heard in m. 3, imitates the alto, while the alto imitates the bass which continues with a third motive. There are occasional episodic developments, usually modulatory in character, each based on elements derived from the given motives. Much of the expressivity of this invention is an outcome of the chromatic harmonies that derive from the *b* motive, which is very much like the chromatic ground basses illustrated in Example 16.5.

Example 18.4   Bach, *Three-voice Invention no. 9 in F minor,* opening measures.

* Analysis of episode showing derivation from a¹.

Example 18.5 displays short connecting bridges; a developmental episode based on motive fragments; the use of rather complex motives which include sequentially developed fragments; and several motive variants. Unlike Example 18.4, in which one voice had a delayed entrance, all three voices participate in the opening statement.

Example 18.5   BWTC, Vol. 1, *Prelude no. 19 in A major,* mm. 1–12 (in open score).

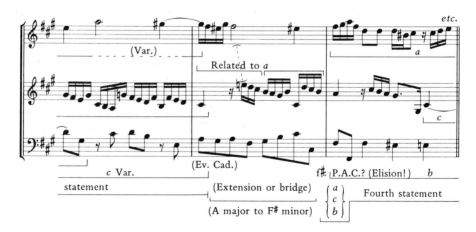

SUGGESTED EXERCISES

1. Copy and analyze thoroughly one of the two-voice and one of the three-voice inventions by Bach. Identify and label the motives. Analyze the harmonic and the key structures. Locate the chief cadences. Indicate the overall form.

2. Write in musical notation the chief motive(s) used in the following *Preludes*, BWTC, Volume 1:

no. 3	*no. 18*
no. 11	*no. 19*
no. 14	*no. 20*
no. 15	*no. 23*

3. Compare the procedures of motive development in the invention-style *Preludes* listed in Exercise 2 with the procedures used in the following *Preludes* (same volume):

no. 1	*no. 6*
no. 2	*no. 10*
no. 5	*no. 22*

4. Analyze the first movement of Bach's *Sonata no. 2 in A major for Clavier and Violin*. Identify all motives and motive fragments. The chief motives of the first half of the movement are:

   and:

   A third motive:

which first appears in m. 8, is used with great frequency in the second half. Draw a diagram showing the key areas, cadences, and the large structural divisions.

5. Compose a two-voice invention based on the half-measure motive used in *Prelude no. 10,* BWTC, Volume 1, mm. 1ff. Modulate from E minor to G major to B minor; then return to E minor in the closing part.

6. Write a three-voice invention using as one of the motives the two-measure sixteenth note line that opens BWTC, Volume 1, *Prelude no. 5* (m. 1 to the F♯ on the first beat of m. 3). Use *Prelude no. 19* of the same volume as a model for procedure and overall form. Make a diagram of *Prelude no. 19* to serve as a guide.

Fugue

The term *fugue,* like invention, denotes a compositional style or procedure rather than a specific form. Fugal style evolved in the second half of the seventeenth and the first half of the eighteenth centuries from such vocal antecedents as the motet, chanson, and madrigal, and such instrumental forms as the ricercare, canzona, and fantasia; it came to full flower in the works of J. S. Bach. Composers of the classic and romantic eras used it sparingly, except for incorporating short fugal sections into larger, generally homophonic forms. Fugue has been used in the twentieth century by such composers as Stravinsky, Hindemith, and Bartók not only as a procedure for short sections, but also for complete movements, and with modern harmonic vocabulary, syntax, and tonal orientation. The fugue, with its sensitive balance of contrapuntal and harmonic organization, marks the high point in polyphony of the late baroque era, much as sonata form is the most notable achievement in homophony of the classic era.

Despite its many unmistakable characteristics, fugue is not easily defined or described. Any formula inevitably is an oversimplification. No two fugues have the same formal outline; the "typical fugue" does not exist except as a musical abstraction. Despite its elusive character, an attempt will be made to describe its principal, most commonly appearing features. But it is important to keep in mind that any one trait may be altered or disguised in one or more ways, or may not be present at all.

A fugue is a polyphonic work—vocal, instrumental, or both—in a specific number of voices or parts, usually three or four, possibly five, rarely more or fewer.[1] It is characteristically monothematic[2] and imitative, with an open form.[3] The theme, or *subject* as it is generally called, enters in one voice after another, the first entry being without any accompanying material whatever.[4] There is gradual thickening of texture as the voices enter in turn, with entrances alternating at tonic and dominant levels. Following

---

[1] The ricercare in Bach's *Musical Offering* is, in fact, a six-voice fugue. His only two-voice fugue is the one in E minor, BWTC, Volume I. The fugues in his sonatas for unaccompanied violin simulate several voices, but the exact number is often problematical.

[2] Double and triple fugues, which have two and three subjects, respectively, are extensions of the fugal concept.

[3] In "open form" there is continuous expansion and growth rather than the sectional return at the end found in "closed forms" such as the ternary *aba* and the *abaca* rondo.

[4] The term *accompanied fugue* is appropriate if "free" accompanimental material, not related to the fugue proper, appears in one or more associated voices.

the initial set of entries, subject statements appear in more or less regular alternation with episodes, an episode being a section in which the *complete* subject does *not* appear, and in which there is development of previously stated and/or new material.[5] Up to the point where the first episode appears, a fugue is almost indistinguishable from a canon. The freedom of the episodes not only makes fugue different from canon; it also provides the greater challenge to the composer's imagination and sense of fantasy.

These episodes frequently are modulatory, except when they appear near the end of the fugue. At that point, after one or more modulations, they may help to restore the tonic key and a sense of tonal stability. Episodes also help to provide some relief from the frequently repeated subjects. The alternations of subject and episode that characterize the main body of most fugues may be likened to the repeated cycles of harmonic tension and resolution, and of dissonance and consonance.

For interest, variety, and dramatic intensity the subject may be introduced in inversion or stretto in the latter part of a fugue. Less frequently, it is introduced in augmentation, diminution, or rarely, in retrograde motion. Combinations of these, for example, augmentation *and* stretto, may be used.

Manfred Bukofzer observed that "the one formal feature that all fugues had in common was continuous expansion, realized in a chain of fugal exposition."[6] One may add to this very cautious statement the observation that the most highly regulated or formalized portion of a fugue is the opening section. It is known as the *exposition*, and during its course each voice in turn has one statement of the subject.[7] The less predictable events which follow the exposition constitute the *development*. The development section may be divided into a number of subsections according to such factors as tonality, consistency of procedures used, and cadences.

EXPOSITION

A fugue normally opens with only one voice sounding, without harmonic or contrapuntal accompaniment.[8] The opening thematic idea, the *subject,* may be as short as a motive (see BWTC, Volume 1, *Fugues nos. 9, 17, 19*), but more frequently it is the length of a melodic phrase (see BWTC, Volume 1, *Fugue no. 2,* two measures long; *Fugue no. 15,* four measures and one beat in length; *Fugue no. 24,* three measures long). The subject usually is striking and concise, terminating with a melodic cadence (see BWTC, Volume 1, *Fugues nos. 6, 8, 10, 12, 13, 14, 20, 23, 24*). This melodic cadence, however, may be weakened by continuing motion or dissolution (see BWTC, Volume 1, *Fugues nos. 1, 5, 9, 11, 18, 22*). The subject may be followed at once by a short connecting link or bridge (BWTC, Volume 1, *Fugue no. 7*) leading to the countersubject (see the discussion of this term below). A subject may remain in the tonic key, which it usually clearly defines; or it may modulate to the dominant in its course. Other possibilities not found in classical procedure may appear in twentieth-century fugues.

[5] A notable exception is BWTC, Volume 1, *Fugue no. 1,* which has no episodes.

[6] Manfred Bukofzer, *Music in the Baroque Era* (New York: W. W. Norton, 1947) p. 362.

[7] Similar structures later in the fugue are known as counterexpositions, or numbered as second, third exposition, and so forth.

[8] Exceptions may be found in works that are quasi-fugal, in double fugues, accompanied fugues, and so forth.

The term *response* (or *answer*) denotes the reappearance of the subject at the interval of a fourth or fifth in the second voice (other intervals are used in some twentieth-century fugues). The "normal" subject-response key relationship is tonic-dominant. If a subject begins on the dominant note, it may be followed by a response that begins on the tonic note. Thus it is possible for the subject-response *key* relationship to be I–V while the relationship of scale degree *first notes* is the reverse, 5–1. (See BWTC, Volume 1, *Fugues nos. 7, 11, and 24.*)

There are two types of response, real and tonal. A *real response* is an exact transposition: both the numerical value and the quality of intervals are unchanged. In the minor mode, the response is associated with the dominant *key* (minor mode), not the dominant *chord* (major triad). If the subject is in the major mode it may be impossible to distinguish between short-term modulation to the dominant key and progression to the dominant chord (that is, between C:I–G:I and C:I–V). Examples of real response may be found in BWTC, Volume 1, *Fugues nos. 1, 5, 6, 15.*

In a *tonal response* there are a small number of interval changes designed to (a) assure gradual modulation, (b) redirect a modulation, or (c) prevent an undesired modulation. The change of interval is never more than one degree, for example a fourth may be changed to a fifth, or a second to a third. Most frequently, the change is made so that the important tonic and dominant notes in the subject are matched by their opposites in the response. Thus, a tonic note in the subject is matched by a dominant note in the response; and a dominant note in the subject is matched by a tonic note in the response. For example: in BWTC, Volume 1, *Fugue no. 2 in C minor,* the C–G (1–5) relationship of the descending fourth in the subject is changed to G–C (5–1), a descending fifth, in the response. Because of the change in this one note, the subsequent interval is changed from a second to a third.

This tonal adjustment makes it possible for the response to modulate gradually from the tonic to the dominant key, instead of plunging into it directly and awkwardly without preparation. In this way, the new key is permitted to be the goal of the response, achieved by the cadence at its end. The emphasis is on dynamic *becoming* rather than on static *being.*

If the subject modulates to the dominant key, then a tonal response may be used to prevent a second modulation to the supertonic, and to secure a return to the tonic key (BWTC, Volume 1, *Fugue no. 18*).

See further the tonal responses in BWTC, Volume 1, *Fugues nos. 3, 7,* and *11,* among others. *Fugue no. 4* is exceptional in that both a real and a tonal response (second and fourth entries) are found in the exposition section; the former (mm. 4–8) is real, the latter (mm. 12–14) is tonal and also rhythmically foreshortened.

The opening voice continues while the answering voice states the response. If the material used in this continuation of the first voice recurs as a regular and constant contrapuntal companion of the subject and/or response it is designated the *countersubject.*[9] However, if this material does *not* regularly recur, it is considered a "free" counterpoint and not given an identifying label (see BWTC, Volume 1, *Fugues nos. 8* and *19*). Although usually contrasting in contour and rhythm, the countersubject may borrow one or more elements from the subject (see the analysis of Example 19.10,

[9] The material accompanying the subject may be so striking in character and so regular in its appearances that its designation as *second subject* is appropriate, especially if it first appears simultaneously with the opening statement of the subject rather than as a counterpoint to the first response. See, for example, the fugue which follows Bach's *Passacaglia in C minor.*

and Example 10.2 where the upper line is the response and the lower line is the countersubject).

Small changes in the intervals of the countersubject which are designed to make the connecting joints articulate properly or to accommodate the differences between subject and tonal response, are to be expected and do not require special terminology. See the countersubjects in BWTC, Volume 1, *Fugue no. 2* (Example 19.10), mm. 3–4, 7–8; *Fugue no. 7*, mm. 3–4, 6–7.

A *bridge* is a short link that connects structural sections; it is often found between subject and response or *vice versa* (see BWTC, Volume 1, *Fugue no. 6*, m. 5; *Fugue no. 7*, second half of m. 2). It is usually direct, not discursive or developmental in character, and thus quite different from an episode with which it is sometimes confused.

An *episode* is a developmental section between statements of subject or response. It is distinguished primarily by the fact that in its course the *complete* fugue subject does not appear. Fragments of the subject (BWTC, Volume 1, *Fugue no. 2*, mm. 5–6) or of the countersubject (*Fugue no. 12*, mm. 10–12) may be treated in imitation or sequence or both. New material may be employed (*Fugue no. 13*, mm. 7–11). It is comparable in length and structural weight to the subject itself, although it may be shorter or longer than the subject.

If there is an episode in the exposition section, it is most likely to occur between the second and third entries. This may be due to the need to (a) modulate back to the tonic key, (b) provide a centrally located section in which short relief from the subject may be secured, or (c) prepare for the next entry of the subject. (See, for instance, BWTC, Volume 1, *Fugue no. 2*, mm. 5–6; *Fugue no. 7*, second half of m. 4 through m. 5.) In *Fugue no. 12*, there is an episode between the third and fourth entries. A four-voice exposition with *no* episode may be found in *Fugue no. 18*. As already noted, *Fugue no. 1* has no episodes at all—either during or following the exposition—a most exceptional procedure.

Following the opening statements of subject (S) and response (R), the remaining voices enter and continue the pattern of S–R and I–V alternation. Thus the *order of entries* in a three-voice fugue is the pattern S–R–S, in a four-voice fugue S–R–S–R, and in a five-voice fugue S–R–S–R–S. The S entries are tonic in emphasis, the R entries are dominant. Irregular procedure appears occasionally. For example, in BWTC, Volume 1, *Fugue no. 1*, the order is S–R–R–S (I–V–V–I).

Since subject and response have a I–V relationship, they are usually coupled in voices whose ranges are a fifth apart (soprano-alto, alto-tenor, tenor-bass) or an octave and a fifth apart (soprano-bass). It follows that the second S and R appear in voices whose ranges are an octave higher or lower than the first S and R. Typical orders of entry are indicated in Example 19.1.

Example 19.1   Typical orders of entry of subject and response.

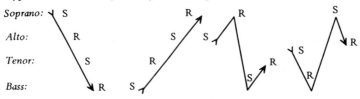

If there is a countersubject (CS) it generally appears in the voice which last carried the S or R. This procedure makes it possible for the CS to appear as the *continuation* of the S or R. It also ensures equitable distribution among the several voices. Example 19.2 illustrates typical procedure.

Example 19.2   Typical distribution of the countersubject (CS).

Soprano:	(S. . . . . .)	(CS. . . . . .)	E. . . . .)	(Free. . . . .)
Alto:	▬	(R. . . . . .)	p i. . . . .) s	(CS. . . . . .)	(Free. . . . .
Tenor:	▬	▬	o ▬ d	(S. . . . . . .)	(CS. . . . . .)
Bass:	▬	▬	e ▬	▬	(R. . . . . . .)

The exposition ends when the last of the several voices completes its opening statement. There may be a sense of cadence at that point, but frequently the cadence is weakened or destroyed by such devices as deceptive harmonic progression, sequence based on figures derived from the end of the subject statement, and suspension. The first six fugues of BWTC, Volume 1 have expositions that close in the following ways: *no. 1,* sequential continuation of a motivic figure weakens the cadence at m. 7; *no. 2,* I_6 is used instead of I at m. 9 (inversion instead of root position); *no. 3,* the cadence at m. 7 is weakened by a suspension; *no. 4,* there is a deceptive cadence *and* a suspension at m. 17; *no. 5,* there is an authentic cadence at m. 6; *no. 6,* V^7 is used at m. 8 instead of V in order to avoid a half cadence.

The exposition may be followed by a counter exposition (that is, a second set of entries) which probably would adhere to the tonic-dominant order of the first exposition. The number of voices at the beginning of a counterexposition may be reduced, and the order of entry different. The counterexposition may be regarded either as an extension of the exposition, or a part of the development section, according to (a) one's view of the proportions, (b) the extent to which there is parallelism with preceding or following materials, and (c) the relative strength of the cadences closing each section.

DEVELOPMENT

In the development which follows the exposition, the number of entries, episodes, and formal divisions, as well as the choice and order of keys may vary; the use of inversion, stretto, or other special devices is optional. Some developments are comparatively brief and compact, others are extended. As a rule, larger works have more complex forms and a correspondingly greater number of structural levels. The characteristic feature of most development sections, and the chief point of departure in their analysis, is the regular alternation of subject (or response) and episode in closely related keys (or with suggestions of removal from the tonic), with a return to the tonic key at the end.

The overall *key scheme* varies widely. It is possible for a fugue to stay entirely within the limits of the tonic and dominant keys (see Example 19.11; there are entries in mm. 11 and 25 that *suggest* the subdominant, but both should be analyzed as centered on c:IV rather than f:I). More frequently, there are one or more modulations to closely related keys such as the relative major or minor, and keys with a signature having a differential of one sharp or one flat. The subdominant area or key is largely reserved for a section near the close, to facilitate a large IV–V–I progression which will reinforce the sense of completion needed at the final cadence (see Example 19.11, m. 25).

Analysis of *Fugues nos. 7* and *11* in the major mode and *Fugues nos. 12* and *14* in the minor mode (BWTC, Volume 1) illustrates typical key schemes and groupings in the development section. It must be stressed that these are not standard types, but only examples of the *kinds* of types—a list which could be extended indefinitely.

Fugue no. 7 (E♭)	R[10]	(E♭)[11]	(Tonic)
	R	(c)	⎫ (Minor mode group)
	S	(c to g)	⎭
	S/R[12]	(E♭ to B♭)	⎫ (Return to the tonic)
	R	(E♭)	⎭
Fugue no. 11 (F)	S	(F)	⎫
	R	**(C)**	⎬ (Counterexposition)
	S	(F)	⎭
	S	(d)	⎫
	S	(d)	⎬ (Stretto) ⎫ (Two minor mode
	S	(d)	⎭ ⎬ groups, one in the
	S	(g)	⎫ ⎬ relative minor, the
	S	(g)	⎬ (Stretto) ⎬ other in g: (g: =
	S	(g)	⎭ ⎭ d:IV and also F:II)
	S	(F)	(Return to the tonic)
Fugue no. 2 (c)	S	(E♭)	(Relative major)
	R	(c to g)	(Tonic to dominant)
	S	(c)	⎫
	S	(c)	⎬ (Tonic group)
	S	(c)	⎭
Fugue no. 14 (f♯)	S[13]	(f♯)	⎱ (Tonic)
	R	(c♯)	⎰ (Dominant)
	S	(f♯)	⎫
	S[13]	(b)[14]	⎬ (Largely tonic)
	S	(f♯)	⎭

[10] An entry in the development is indicated as S unless there is good reason to call it R, for example, if the form of the *tonal* response is used, or to show a dominant relationship to an adjacent tonic statement.

[11] Capitals indicate major mode, lower case minor mode.

[12] S/R indicates statement has elements of both S and R.

[13] The subject is inverted.

[14] The key of b, in a larger sense, is an expansion of f♯: IV.

Note that only *Fugue no. 11* has a counterexposition. Of the two fugues in major keys, one has considerable tonic emphasis, the other dwells considerably in related minor key areas. Of the two in minor, only *Fugue no. 2* has a statement in the major mode, and only in *Fugue no. 14* is there a strong suggestion of the subdominant near the close.

Melodic *inversion* of the subject, in which ascending lines become descending and vice versa, is used alone in four fugues in BWTC, and in conjunction with stretto in eight. Inversion almost always appears more than once if it appears at all. It is more commonly found in paired or grouped statements than in an isolated position, such as that found in *Fugue no. 14*. See the two consecutive statements in inversion in BWTC, Volume 1, *Fugue no. 23*, mm. 18–21, and the three inverted statements in BWTC, Volume 2, *Fugue no. 4*, mm. 24–29. In Volume 2, *Fugue no. 8*, the final statement of the subject appears in the soprano line simultaneously with its inversion in the tenor. Like other devices designed to show the manifold potential of the subject, inversion tends to appear only in the latter part of the fugue. Because it does not create much dramatic tension, it might be expected to appear earlier than stretto or augmentation.

The term *stretto* refers to overlapping statements of the fugue subject in two or more voices. It is really a type of canonic imitation. The participating voices in stretto should be described, as in a canon, in terms of the interval and the distance between the first notes. Thus, one may speak of a stretto at the octave above after two beats, and so forth. Almost a third of the fugues in BWTC employ the device, some to a greater degree than others. Like inversion, it is almost always used at least twice.

It is not uncommon to find a group of stretti in double counterpoint. Instances of such stretti in two voices may be observed in abundance in BWTC, Volume 1, *Fugue no. 1;* there is a stretto at the fifth above after one beat in mm. 10–12, and at the fourth below in mm. 14–15.

A four-voice stretto in the same fugue is quoted in Example 19.3. One observes remarkable variety among the intervals and distances. The soprano entry on C is followed after one beat by the alto on G. Two beats later the tenor comes in on A, and finally we hear the bass on D, after another two beats (actually, the entrance is a half beat "too soon"). The modulation from C major to D minor should not pass unobserved. (A five-voice stretto has been quoted in Chapter 10, Exercise 1d.)

Example 19.3   Four-voice stretto. BWTC, Vol. 1, *Fugue no. 1*, mm. 16–18.

A somewhat irregular stretto, involving a rhythmically altered subject in quasi-augmentation, may be observed in Example 19.4. The subject in the middle voice is partially augmented, that is, *some* of the notes are lengthened. The last two notes are missing. In the soprano, the last note is delayed by one beat. And in the bass, the subject is dropped after one measure in favor of a free part. Dissolution or discontinuation of a stretto is not uncommon; generally, however, this occurs only if continuation of the stretto would result in undesired harmonies.

Example 19.4   Three-voice stretto, one voice in quasi-augmentation. BWTC, Vol. 1, *Fugue no. 8,* mm. 24–26.

A proportional increase in the rhythmic values of a melodic line results in *augmentation*. Note values are usually doubled: eighth notes become quarters, quarters become half notes. In triple or compound triple meter the values may be tripled so that the relationship between strong and weak pulses is not violated. Thus, an eighth note in 9/8 would become a dotted quarter.

The term *double augmentation* is appropriate if the values are quadrupled (see the bass line in Exercise 1e, Chapter 10). Partial or quasi-augmentation has already been cited (see Example 19.4).

A particularly interesting example of fugue subject augmentation appears in BWTC, Volume 1, *Fugue no. 8,* the last twenty-six measures. There are three consecutive statements, one in each of the several voices. The consistent use of augmentation in these measures, and its absence in previous portions of the fugue, is an important factor in the overall form. A rare example of augmentation in Beethoven is the final statement of the main theme of the first movement of his *String Quartet in C♯ minor,* op. 131, mm. 99ff, in the cello part.

Augmentation is sometimes associated with stretto (see *Fugue no. 8,* BWTC, Volume 1). In Chapter 10, Exercise 1e, there is an astonishing combination of augmentation, double augmentation, inversion, and stretto in a passage of only eight measures! Following the initial tenor entry in m. 1, the soprano answers in m. 2 with the subject in augmentation, inversion, and stretto; the alto joins in a measure later in diminution, inversion, and in stretto with the soprano; and in m. 5 the bass presents the subject in double augmentation, inversion, and in stretto with the soprano. In m. 6, there is an incomplete statement in the tenor, in stretto with the bass; and in mm. 7–8 a complete statement in the alto, in stretto with the bass. There are five stretti in all, each involving at least one voice in augmentation.

Diminution is the opposite of augmentation—a reduction of the rhythmic values, usually by one-half. In triple or compound triple meter, a dotted half note may become a quarter, or a dotted quarter may become an eighth note (reduction by one-third rather than by one-half) to prevent disruption of the metrical structure (see Examples 19.6a and 19.6b).

Diminution appears in musical literature even less frequently than the comparatively rare augmentation. Its use in BWTC may be seen in Volume 2, *Fugue no. 9,* mm. 26–29, where the subject appears in each of the four voices, in both diminution and stretto; and in mm. 30–32, where the original subject is in stretto with its diminution.

Example 19.5   Diminution and stretto combined. BWTC, Vol. 2, *Fugue no. 9*, mm. 26–32.

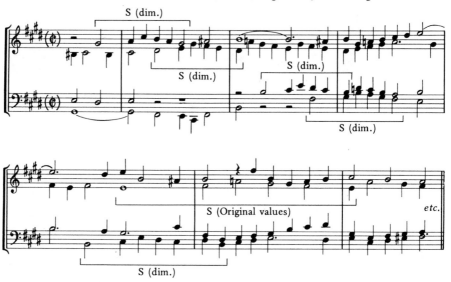

Beethoven used these special devices with increasing frequency in his later years. The fugal finale of BS, op. 110 provides several illustrations. The fugue subject, in 6/8 meter, is largely in dotted quarters, a rising sequence of ascending intervals of the fourth (see Example 19.6a). Following the interruption caused by the return of materials from the preceding movement (adagio), there is an exposition of the inverted subject in G major (quite remote from the prevailing key of A♭!). This is followed by a develop-ment which includes stretti that combine augmentation in one voice with diminution and occasional interval alteration in the others (19.6b); and double diminution in one voice with inversion in the other (19.6c).

Example 19.6   Augmentation, diminution, compression, inversion, and stretti. BS, 110, iv.

(a) The fugue subject.

(b) Stretto with augmentation, diminution, and interval compression (some fourths become thirds, some thirds become seconds).

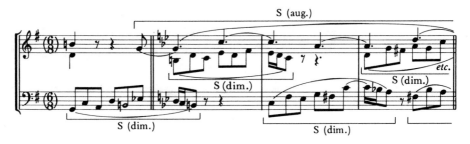

(c) Stretto with inversion in one voice and double diminution in the other.

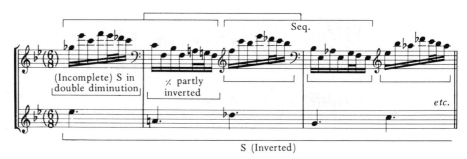

Of all the means by which a fugue subject may be varied, *retrograde* motion or retrogression is the least used. This is probably because the rhythmic proportions of the original melody cannot be immediately recognized when the time order is reversed, a problem which does not arise in the other devices. It is also the most difficult to use with good musical effect because of the awkward rhythmic proportions that frequently result. Nevertheless, it has been revived in the twentieth century by those who employ serial techniques in twelve-tone compositions. In this style, retrograde and inversion and their combination provide some of the fundamental principles for both small and large scale instrumental and vocal works including opera. (See, for example, Schoenberg's music from op. 23 on; and Berg's opera *Lulu*.)

The classic examples of retrograde motion are found in some of the canons which form a portion of Bach's *Musical Offering*. No less remarkable is Beethoven's use of the device in the fugal finale of his *"Hammerklavier"* Sonata (BS, op. 106). The very striking subject and its retrograde form are shown in Example 19.7.

Example 19.7   Retrograde motion. BS, 106, iv.

(a) Fugue subject (in B♭ major).

(b) The subject in retrograde motion (in B minor).

In addition to the more or less standard procedures already discussed, a fugue subject may be altered by means of other devices, for example: (a) change of mode, either major to minor (BWTC, Volume 1, *Fugue no. 11,* mm. 36–40) or minor to major (BWTC, Volume 1, *Fugue no. 2,* mm. 11–13); (b) small interval changes, other than those found in a tonal response (BWTC, Volume 2, *Fugue no. 11,* mm. 85–89; *Fugue no. 2,* mm. 7–8); (c) transposition within the key, for example to the supertonic level, in contrast to a statement in the supertonic key (BWTC, Volume 1, *Fugue no. 6,* mm. 8–10); (d) lengthening or shortening of the opening or closing notes, and occasionally others (BWTC, Volume 1, *Fugue no. 8,* mm. 12–14; and Examples 19.3 and 19.4); and (e) addition of embellishments such as passing or neighboring tones (BWTC, Volume 1, *Fugue no. 8,* m. 39; *Fugue no. 11,* mm. 64–68, as illustrated in Example 19.8).

Example 19.8   Ornamental variation of the subject. BWTC, Vol. 1, *Fugue no. 11.*

(a) The subject, mm. 1–4.

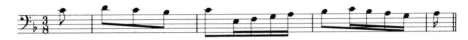

(b) The subject varied by means of embellishment, mm. 64–68.

Extension in the course of the subject, caused by interpolated sequences based on elements (motives) of the subject, is also used as an altering device (BWTC, Volume 2, *Fugue no. 11,* mm. 89–95).

PROCEDURES RELATED TO FUGUE

Double Fugue

There are two kinds of *double fugue.* In one type, the two subjects are introduced simultaneously and then recur throughout the fugue as inseparable and equal thematic companions. The fugue which follows Bach's *Passacaglia in C minor* is a well-known example of this type. Some theorists prefer to regard such paired thematic ideas as subject and countersubject, and consider the "premature" appearance of the countersubject merely an exception to the rule, rather than an indication of a different type.

A second kind of double fugue has a first subject and exposition, followed by a short development; a second subject and exposition, followed by a short development; and a third section in which the two subjects are used simultaneously. The "Confiteor" of Bach's *Mass in B minor,* which is a double fugue of this type, employs the following two subjects.

Example 19.9   Two subjects of a double fugue. The "Confiteor" of Bach's *Mass in B minor*.

(a) First subject

(b) Second subject

(c) The two subjects combined

Triple Fugue

Triple fugue is an extension of double fugue. It normally extends the second type of double fugue just described, thus there are three distinct expositions. The chief examples by Bach are the so-called "St. Anne" *Fugue in E♭ major* for organ (the closing work of the *Clavierübung*), and the final and unfinished fugue of *The Art of Fugue*. The latter is particularly interesting because the third subject consists of the four notes B♭–A–C–B♮, the letters in Bach's name (B being the German for B♭, and H the term for B♮).

Fugue no. 4 in BWTC, Volume 1, is a somewhat irregular example. Subject 2 first enters in the soprano in mm. 35–38 following the cadence in E major, in a texture of reduced voices but already in counterpoint with the first subject. Subject 3 first appears in the tenor in mm. 49–51, in the subdominant (!) key and in counterpoint with Subject 1 and a portion of Subject 2. It does not have a separate exposition, the widely separated initial entries are not in tonic-dominant alternation, and the customary reduction in the number of voices is lacking.

Accompanied Fugue

Fugal style can be adapted in many ways. Modified, it may be used in contexts where the label "fugue" would otherwise require considerable qualification. Thus, fugal procedures are found in such instrumental forms as the French overture, and in sacred choral works with instrumental accompaniment such as the cantatas and the monolithic *Mass in B minor* by Bach. The opening "Kyrie" of the latter work is an *accompanied fugue*. It is so called because (following a four-measure introduction) the opening orchestral exposition of the subject is accompanied by supportive harmonic material unrelated to the subject. In the five-voice choral exposition that follows, the orchestra not only doubles the vocal parts but also freely accompanies them. The "Confiteor" of the Mass, described in Example 19.9, is also an accompanied fugue. The *Sonatas for Clavier and Violin* by Bach, *no. 1,* ii; *no. 2,* ii and iv; *no. 3,* ii and iv; *no. 4,* ii and iv; *no. 5,* i, ii, and iv; and *no. 6,* i, are all, in varying degrees, fugal in style, but the opening subject statement in each instance is provided with a continuo-type accompaniment in the bass.

Fugato

Brief or limited fugal procedure is called *fugato.* It is an incipient fugue, incomplete rather than fully realized. A fugal exposition begins but is shortly followed by dissolution. There may be an extremely short-lived development or none at all.

Fugato may be employed at the beginning, as for example in BS, 10/2, iii; Mozart, *String Quartet in G major,* K. 387, iv; and Wagner, *Die Meistersinger,* Prelude to Act 3. More frequently, it appears in development sections in the course of a movement or an operatic act, as in Verdi's *Falstaff,* final scene; Beethoven's *Symphony no. 3 in E♭ major* (the fourth movement includes two fugal episodes or *fugati*) and *Symphony no. 7 in A major,* ii, mm. 183ff; and Mozart, *Symphony no. 41 in C major,* iv, mm. 36ff and 372ff.

Fughetta

A *fughetta* is a miniature fugue. The essentials and characteristics of a fugue are present, but the proportions and dimensions are considerably reduced. The fughetta, which is short, is also a complete movement and should not be confused with the fugato which is incomplete and merely a section of a piece. For example, see Variation 10 of Bach's *Goldberg Variations.*

Fugue versus Invention

Invention and fugue are sometimes not clearly distinguished because of the similarities between them. The following comparison may be helpful in analyzing borderline cases.

Table 19.1   Invention and fugue compared.

Invention	Fugue
Number of voices usually two or three.	Number of voices usually three or four (sometimes five, rarely two or six).
Immediate imitation of opening statement is not necessary (sequential treatment in one voice is possible).	Immediate imitation of the opening statement is the rule.
The second voice enters at the octave, fourth, or fifth.	The second voice enters at the fourth or fifth, *not* at the octave.
Continuous imitation and sequential repetition of a short motive *is* characteristic.	Continuous sequential repetition is *not* characteristic.
Episodes are neither necessary nor typical.	Following the exposition, statements are normally separated by episodes.
Interval changes in a motive are not unusual.	Interval changes in the subject are rare, except as found in the tonal response.

Two Bach fugues are presented complete and diagramed in Examples 19.10 and 19.11. The first, Example 19.10 (BWTC, Volume 1, *Fugue no. 2),* is for three voices. It is distinguished by great conciseness of form and economy of resource. The episodes are highly organized developments of previously stated motives and display a minimum of new material. None of the special devices (stretto, inversion, and so forth) is used. However, there is considerable double counterpoint, notably in the related episodes 1 and 4, 2 and 5. The final statement of the subject occurs over an explicit tonic pedal point (compare the implicit tonic pedal near the end of Example 19.11).

Fugue no. 2 in BWTC, Volume 2 (Example 19.11) is in the same key, but it is for four voices. It is irregular in that the fourth voice (the bass) does not appear at all in the exposition section, and does not appear in the development until late in the fugue. (Some of Bach's organ fugues share this peculiarity, the organ pedals entering only with the climactic final statements.) The second half of the fugue (mm. 14–28) consists of three sections which may be distinguished from each other largely by virtue of the presence or absence of stretto. Some of the stretti are associated with inversion or augmentation or both. Consecutive subject statements in the second of these sections provide marked contrast to the imitative surrounding sections.

Example 19.10   BWTC, Volume 1, *Fugue no. 2.*

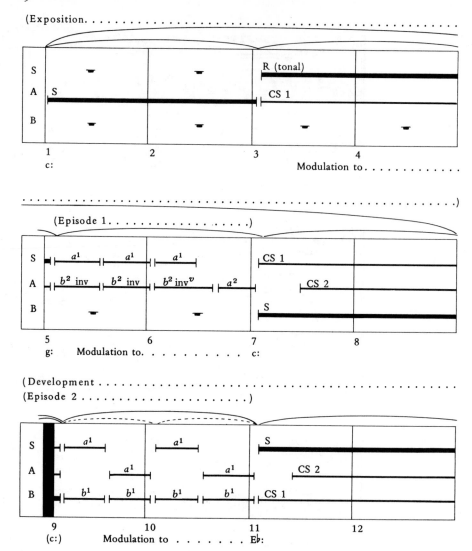

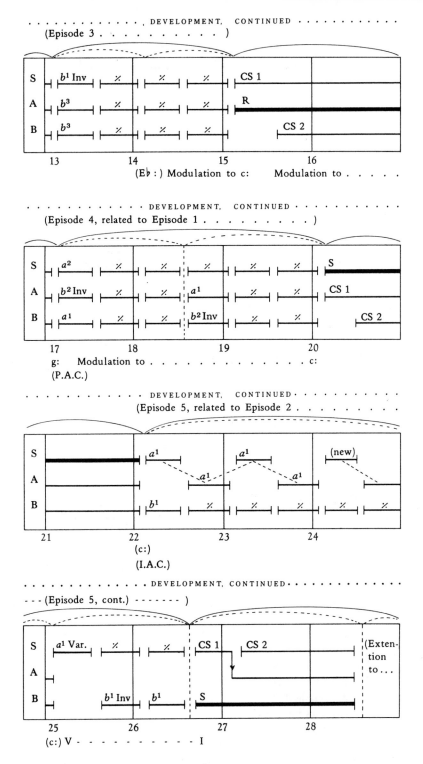

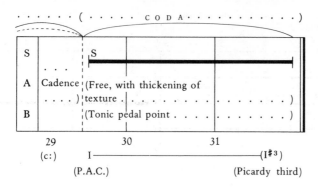

Subject (S), and motivic fragments a^1 and a^2.

Response (R), (tonal).

Countersubject 1 (CS 1), and motivic fragments b^1, b^2, and b^3 (b^3 is an augmentation of half of b^1—see the dotted brackets).

Countersubject 2 (CS 2), and motives derived from both S and CS 1.

S and R are indicated by a heavy line.

Extended rests are indicated by ➤.

Variant is indicated by Var, or a raised $v^{(v)}$.

Inv indicates inversion.

⁒ indicates motive repetition.

Imitations are indicated by dotted diagonals. (‗ ‗ ‿ ‿ ‗ ‗).

Spaces not accounted for are either free melody lines or short rests.

Example 19.11   BWTC, Volume 2, *Fugue no. 2.*

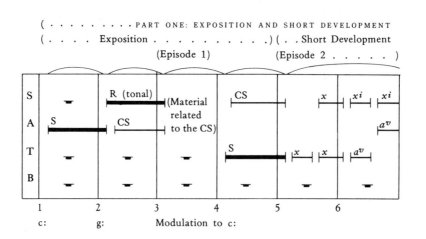

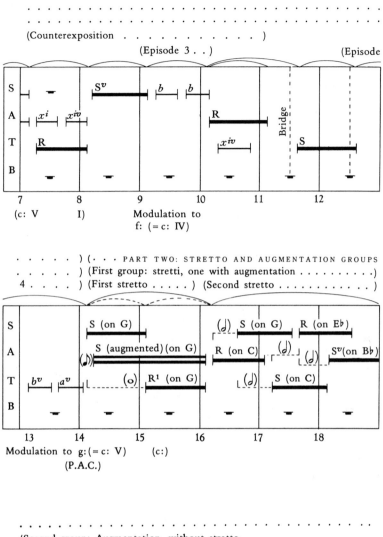

(Counterexposition . . . .)

(Episode 3 . .)   (Episode

| | 7 | 8 | 9 | 10 | 11 | 12 |

(c: V   I)   Modulation to
                          f: (= c: IV)

. . . . . .) (. . . PART TWO: STRETTO AND AUGMENTATION GROUPS
. . . . . .) (First group: stretti, one with augmentation . . . .)
4 . . . .) (First stretto . . . . .) (Second stretto . . . .)

| 13 | 14 | 15 | 16 | 17 | 18 |

Modulation to g: (= c: V)   (c:)
(P.A.C.)

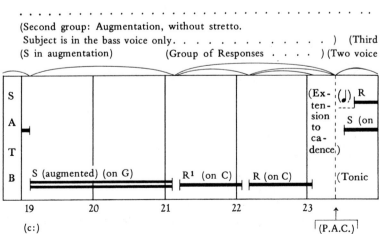

(Second group: Augmentation, without stretto.
Subject is in the bass voice only. . . . .) (Third
(S in augmentation)   (Group of Responses . . . .) (Two voice

| 19 | 20 | 21 | 22 | 23 |

(c:)   (P.A.C.)

PART TWO: STRETTO AND AUGMENTATION GROUPS, CONTINUED...)
group: Two stretti, without augmentation; (Coda) . . . .)
stretto)   (Four voice stretto . . . . .)   (Cadenza-like extension)

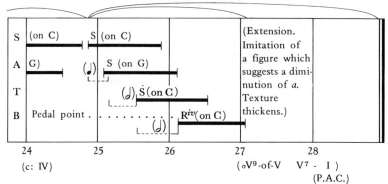

Subject (S), and motivic fragments *a* and *b*.

Response (R), (tonal).

Countersubject (CS).

Episode motive, *x*.

S and R are indicated by a heavy line.

Augmentation of S is indicated by a double heavy line.

Extended rests are indicated by ➥ .

Raised *v* $^{(v)}$ indicates variant.

Raised *i* $^{(i)}$ indicates inversion.

Raised *iv* $^{(iv)}$ indicates variant of the inversion.

Distance between stretto entries is indicated by (♪), (♩), and so forth.

Spaces not accounted for are either free melody lines or short rests.

SUGGESTED EXERCISES

1. Analyze two or more fugues in BWTC. At least one should be in minor, and one in major mode. At least one should be for three, and one for four voices. Use the diagram technique illustrated above. Discuss the regular and irregular features of each.

2. Draw diagrams showing the structural details of two hypothetical fugues. These should differ considerably, and should not conform to the structure of any of the fugues analyzed in Exercise 1.

3. Why is *Fugue no. 10*, BWTC, Volume 1, called a fugue rather than an invention? See Example 19.10.

4. Discuss Beethoven's use of fugal procedure in the first movement of his *String Quartet in C♯ minor*, op. 131.

5. Write a short essay discussing Brahms's use of fugal procedure in his *Variations and Fugue on a Theme by Handel*.

6. Write an essay on the use of fugue in Franck's *Prelude, Chorale, and Fugue* for piano.

7. Hector Berlioz, a decided romanticist, spoke out frequently against the academicians of his day. Yet one finds fugal procedure in a number of his works. Write a short essay considering such evidence as may be found in *The Damnation of Faust, Harold in Italy,* and the *Requiem Mass*.

8. Write an essay on the use of fugue by Hindemith, Bartók, and Stravinsky.

9. Write an essay on the chief prefugal forms of the Renaissance and baroque eras. Note briefly the chief similarities to and differences from the fugue.

10. Write an essay on *The Art of Fugue* by Bach.

11. Compose a four-voice fugal exposition using a subject based on the notes do–re–mi–fa–mi (scale degrees: 1–2–3–4–3) in the major mode. Compose a second version for three voices in the minor mode, using a different order of entries.

12. Compose a three-voice fugue for piano, and/or a four-voice fugue for organ, on an original subject or on the subject indicated in Exercise 11. If both fugues are tried, write one in a diatonic, the other in a chromatic style. Following approval of your exposition section, explore the possibilities of stretto, inversion, and so forth, using various intervals, distances, and scale degrees (a detailed list is best). (Composition majors with previous experience in writing fugues, may wish to try a double or even a triple fugue.) Make a schematic diagram of the projected work before continuing further, showing clearly the key and section structure and the location of any of the special devices. In general, all the subjects and responses should be sketched first, before the episodes have been worked out in too great detail. Episodes should be planned in terms of the role they are to play, both motivically and with respect to possible modulation. The development should be undertaken only following approval of the preliminary stages. The final "polishing" may involve a reconsideration of some of the musical joints—beginnings and endings of statements and episodes—possible additional use of double counterpoint, expansion of final cadence or section, and so forth.

Chorale variation, like invention and fugue, is a procedure rather than a form. It is a composition in which a chorale or hymn tune serves as the basis for one or more variations. There are many ways in which variation technique may be applied. Sometimes variation is combined with other procedures such as the motet, invention, fugue, or suite, or several types of variation may be used simultaneously.

The term *chorale variation* is broad in its application, and not associated with any specific instrumentation. One type of chorale variation, the *chorale prelude* (sometimes called *organ chorale*), is customarily performed as an organ solo.

In the baroque era, chorale variation was based on a pre-existent melody, usually a German Protestant hymn or chorale. Thus it is a kind of *cantus firmus* composition, a type that was widely used during the Middle Ages and the Renaissance in connection with polyphonic settings of Gregorian melodies.

Chorale variation developed as part of the Protestant church service as an instrumental, or sometimes instrumental and vocal, embellishment and development of the chorale that was sung by the congregation.[1] Although most of the compositions described in this chapter are for organ solo, the procedures used appear also in movements for solo voice and/or chorus with organ or orchestra in many cantatas of the period, notably in many Bach works, including his larger *St. Matthew* and *St. John Passions.*

In more recent times, both sacred and secular works have been written in this style. Traditional melodies as well as newly composed ones in the style of a chorale have been used (see, for example, Hindemith's symphony, *Mathis der Maler,* i and iii; and Bartók's *Piano Concerto no. 3,* ii).

Classification of the many varieties of chorale variation is difficult because of the many mixed types and subtypes. Apel identifies eight types of organ chorale.[2]

1. Cantus firmus chorale: the chorale in long notes is treated as a cantus firmus, usually in the bass.

---

[1] Probably all music students are familiar with Bach's harmonizations of the traditional chorales, but some may not realize that Bach did not compose any of the melodies, except for a few whose authenticity is in doubt.

[2] *Harvard Dictionary of Music,* edited by Willi Apel, 3rd ed. (Cambridge: Harvard Univ. Press, 1970) article on organ chorale.

2. Chorale motet: each phrase of the chorale is treated in imitation, in a series of expositions.
3. Chorale fugue: the first phrase of the chorale is treated fugally throughout, the whole chorale appearing in an additional voice.
4. Figured chorale: continuous chorale in the soprano; motivic development in the accompaniment.
5. Chorale canon: canonic treatment of the chorale.
6. Chorale fantasia: free treatment.
7. Ornamented chorale: decorated cantus firmus in the soprano.
8. Chorale partita: a *group* of variations, in the manner of a suite.

Bukofzer[3] lists the three manners of chorale arrangement described by the German composer and theorist Michael Praetorius (1571–1621), who died before the style had reached full flower.

1. Motet style: chorale-based imitation in all voices.
2. Madrigal style: *concertato* style dialog, using fragments of the chorale.
3. Cantus firmus style: the cantus firmus in counterpoint with an accompaniment which uses chorale-derived motives.

Bukofzer finds there are four types.[4]

1. Chorale partita or variations: a variation suite, similar to the dance suite.
2. Chorale fantasy: a virtuoso piece in rhapsodic style, using only fragments of the chorale.
3. Chorale fugue: the chorale is superimposed on either (a) a fugue whose subject is derived from the first phrase of the chorale, or (b) a chain of fughettas in motet style based on the successive phrases of the chorale.
4. Chorale prelude: the plain or ornamented chorale in the soprano is accompanied by figurative harmony or counterpoint with independent rhythms and motives.

Kennan[5] mentions seven types, some of which correspond to those listed by Apel and Bukofzer. Many of the types described by Apel, Bukofzer, and Kennan overlap, or are concerned with different levels of organization. Thus the following additional classification is offered for simplification and clarification of the subject.

Cantus firmus (C.F.) treatment: with respect to decoration, the C.F. may be plain (that is, unembellished) or embellished; with respect to continuity, it may be continuous and uninterrupted, or broken up into separate phrases between which there are mediating interludes. The polyphony may be imitative or nonimitative; if imitative, the style may be canon, invention, motet, fugue, or fantasia.

From the standpoint of this classification, a large number of combinations and permutations may be derived. For example, a given work may have an embellished C.F., with the phrases separated by interludes; and imitative polyphony in the style of a canon at the fifth.

Before considering the procedures in detail, the chief characteristics of a chorale or chorale-type melody should be noted. The note values are usually of the same

---

[3] Manfred Bukofzer, *Music in the Baroque Era* (New York: W. W. Norton, 1947) pp. 79–87, 105–07, 266–67, 282–85, 292–94, 299.

[4] Bukofzer, *Baroque Era*, pp. 266–67.

[5] Kent Kennan, *Counterpoint* (Englewood Cliffs, N. J.: Prentice-Hall, 1959) chapters 10 and 14.

length, a feature which derives from the characteristic syllabic setting of the text. In a chorale variation that utilizes the complete melody, the chorale is readily identified by its long, even rhythmic values which are in marked contrast to the variable and/or shorter rhythmic values of the accompanying part(s). The phrases are well defined and close on long notes. The fermata (⌢) found at each cadence of the chorale is not observed in the performance of the variation if the accompaniment continues without interruption.

CANTUS FIRMUS TREATMENT

Unembellished Cantus Firmus

Chorale variations may use the original chorale without embellishment or alteration, in long notes, usually either in the bass or in the soprano line and *without any separation of the phrases*. The accompanying voices use shorter values. The opening two measures and the diagram illustrate the procedure.

Example 20.1   Bach, "Puer Natus in Bethlehem" from *Orgelbüchlein,* mm. 1–2, and diagram of the complete work.

(a) Mm. 1–2.

(b) Diagram of complete work.

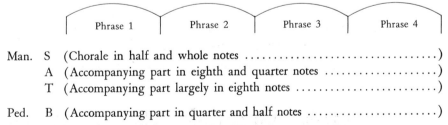

Man. S (Chorale in half and whole notes ....)
      A (Accompanying part in eighth and quarter notes ....)
      T (Accompanying part largely in eighth notes ....)

Ped. B (Accompanying part in quarter and half notes ....)

Similar procedure is used in the two chorale variations Bach composed on the melody "Komm, Gott, Schöpfer, heiliger Geist." The first of these (in *Orgelbüchlein*) treats the melody once through in the soprano. The second version (in the *Eighteen Large Chorales*), composed at a later date, is more extended: following the completion of the four-phrase melody in the soprano, there is a four-measure interlude and a second statement of the complete melody, this time in the organ pedals with the accompaniment in the upper voices.

Example 20.2   Bach, "Komm, Gott, Schöpfer, heiliger Geist," second version, from *Eighteen Large Chorales*.

		First statement						Second statement			
		Phrase 1	2	3	4			1	2	3	4

Man. S (Chorale ....)   (Accompanying voice ....)
          A (Accompanying voice ....)   (Accompanying voice ....)
          T (Accompanying voice ....)   (Accompanying voice ....)

Ped. B (Accompanying voice ....)   (Chorale ....)

(Interlude)

The phrases of the chorale may be *separated by interludes*. In this procedure, the material of the interludes is consistent throughout the variation; in addition, it usually appears in an introductory phrase before the first phrase of the chorale and again in a codetta or postcadential extension following the last phrase of the chorale. The chorale is thus superimposed as a foreground on the accompanimental background. The listener's attention shifts back and forth, as if between near and distant focus, in rondo-like alternation between the exposed accompaniment and the enrobing phrases of the chorale. This typically baroque conception is not altogether unlike the alternation of solo and tutti in the concerto grosso.

In contrast to the preludes in Bach's *Orgelbüchlein*, none of which utilize interludes, all of the *Six Schübler Chorales* of Bach do utilize interludes. Perhaps the most remarkable of these is Bach's transcription of one movement from his cantata *Wachet auf*, with which a useful comparison may be made. The nine phrases of the chorale are grouped by threes (3 + 3 + 3). The first group of three phrases, plus preceding introduction, is formally repeated. The three groups are separated by interludes and the last phrase is followed by a postlude or codetta. Not the least astonishing aspect of the work is that it would have made a satisfactory composition even without the superimposed chorale. *With* it, there is a sense of contrapuntal luxury and abundance—yet there are only three melodic lines. Example 20.3 illustrates the point of entry of the first phrase of the chorale, the four motivic components of the accompanying obbligato, and a diagram of the complete work.

Example 20.3   Bach, "Wachet Auf," from *Six Schübler Chorales*, mm. 12–16, the motivic components, and a diagram of the complete work.

(a)   Mm. 12–16, showing motive *a* and the first phrase of the chorale.

(b) Motivic components *b*, *c*, and *d*.

(c) Diagram of the complete work.

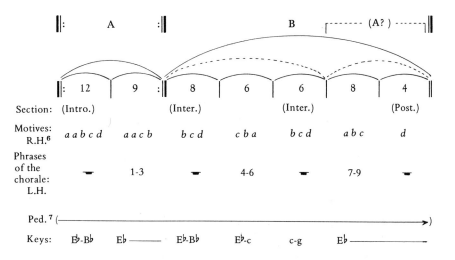

The opening chorus of Bach's *The Passion According to St. Matthew* is an even more extended example of the interlude type. The widely separated phrases of the chorale "O Lamm Gottes, unschuldig" in the soprano are superimposed on a rich, massive texture made up of a double mixed chorus and large orchestra.

The melody "Ach Gott, vom Himmel sieh' darein," used by Bach in three of his cantatas, is employed by Mozart in the finale of Act 2 of his opera *The Magic Flute,* but not with the original text. The slightly separated phrases are sung in octaves by two solo male voices against a polyphonic orchestral accompaniment.

Another example of the use of chorale variation technique in a secular dramatic work may be found in the final act of *The Damnation of Faust* by Berlioz. In the next

[6] R.H.: Continuous melody in the style of an aria. Each section uses a different combination of the motives.

[7] Ped.: Free bass line in quarters and eighths.

to last scene, Faust and Mephistopheles ride to the underworld on two black horses to the accompaniment of a quite realistic, galloping figure in the orchestra, and the intermittent phrases of "Sancta Maria, ora pro nobis" sung by a chorus of peasant women kneeling before a rustic cross. The dramatic contrast between the demonic and the devout is hair-raising.

One does not expect to find chorale variation in a mid-twentieth century piano concerto, but Bartók manages to find refreshing new possibilities for this procedure in his *Concerto no. 3 for Piano and Orchestra.* The second movement is a large ternary form ($A^1B\ A^2$). Chorale variation technique is used in both *A* parts. In A^1 the orchestral strings provide the "background" while the solo piano plays the newly composed, chorale-like melody and its harmonization. In A^2 the wind instruments of the orchestra play the chorale and harmonization against the piano's rather Bachian counterpoint. At the cadences there are *fermate* for the orchestra and florid, quasi-improvised cadenzas with more than a little Hungarian flavor in the solo instrument.

Embellished Cantus Firmus

An *unembellished* cantus firmus may be treated as a continuous melody, or its component phrases may be separated by interludes. An *embellished* cantus firmus may also be treated in either fashion.

Perhaps the most deeply expressive and almost romantic of Bach's chorale settings is the variation on "O Mensch, bewein' dein' Sünde gross." The *continuous* chorale is embellished throughout by neighboring and passing tones, trills, and the like.[8] The third phrase of the nine-phrase melody is shown below, both in its original form, and as it appears in the soprano line of the chorale variation.

Example 20.4   Bach, "O Mensch, bewein' dein' Sünde gross," from *Orgelbüchlein,* third phrase. Original and varied forms compared.

Bach composed two settings of the melody "Allein Gott in der Höh' sei Ehr'," in both of which the phrases of the embellished chorale are *separated by interludes.* (A third setting is in trio sonata style.)[9] The first setting, in A major, is rather similar in style to "O Mensch," described above. In the second setting in G major, occasional imitation of fragments of the chorale, much of it canonic, appears in the accompanying voices. The main statements of the chorale proper appear in the tenor voice, in mm. 16–24, 27–34, 45–53, 57–66, and 73–94. (The measure numbers provide an indication of the extent to which the interludes separate the phrases of the chorale.) To

[8] Similar treatment in a contemporary harmonic idiom may be found in Kohs's chorale variation on "Yigdal," No. 1 of *Three Chorale Variations on Hebrew Hymns,* Mercury Music Corp., New York, 1953.

[9] See *Eighteen Large Chorales.*

appreciate fully the procedures used, the two works should be examined and compared in their entirety. The first phrase of the chorale in its original or simple form and as it appears in each of the chorale variations is shown below.

Example 20.5   Bach, "Allein Gott in der Höh' sei Ehr',"[10] the first phrase. Original and two variants compared.

An introductory phrase, interludes between the phrases, and a postlude or codetta are in both versions. The overall structures are similar to the one shown in the diagram of Example 20.3.

POLYPHONIC STYLE

Nonimitative Polyphony

Not all polyphony is imitative. Sometimes each voice or melodic line has a style and character of its own. Thematic interchange among the several voices is not necessary. For an example of *nonimitative polyphony* see the chorale variation on "Ich ruf' zu dir, Herr Jesu Christ" in *Orgelbüchlein*. The chorale, largely in quarter notes, appears in the soprano line. The middle voice is in continuous sixteenths, the bass in eighths. The three melodic levels have lives of their own, bound together only by common

10 See *Eighteen Large Chorales*.

harmony and form. The complete work consists of seven phrases without intervening interludes. The closing phrase appears in Example 20.6.

Example 20.6   Bach, "Ich ruf' zu dir, Herr Jesu Christ" from *Orgelbüchlein,* the last phrase.

In the same collection of variations there is a setting of "Vom Himmel kam der Engel Schar," in which the polyphonic texture is made up of four lines. The soprano has the chorale in whole and half notes, the alto has a variety of rhythmic values, the tenor is in sixteenths, while the bass is in quarter notes.

Imitative Polyphony

Imitation in some form appears in most chorale variations. It may be confined to the accompanying lines, but it may also include the line that carries the chorale. Following are some of the ways in which *imitative polyphony* may be organized.

Eight of the forty-five chorale variations in Bach's *Orgelbüchlein* are *canonic* in style. Four of these are canons at the octave, two are at the fifth, one is at the fourth, and one is at the twelfth. In all, it is the unembellished chorale that is treated canonically. In four instances the canon involves the soprano and pedal lines, twice it is in the soprano and alto, and there are single instances of bass-alto and tenor-soprano coupling.

One of the eight, "In dulci jubilo," is a double canon. The canonically related soprano and pedal lines which carry the chorale are accompanied by two other lines that make up a second canon in shorter note values. Both canons are at the octave after one measure. In Example 20.7 note that the tenor line written for the organ pedals sounds higher than the bass part, which is given to the left hand. (In some works, the pedals play the chorale on a four-foot stop which sounds an octave higher than the written notes.) Since characteristically the chorale is in long notes, such procedure lends itself well to the comparatively limited pedals, freeing the manuals for the more active decorative accompanying material.

Example 20.7   Bach, "In dulci jubilo" from *Orgelbüchlein,* opening measures.

Kohs's chorale variation on "Rock of Ages" utilizes canonic procedure in the third of its three sections.

Example 20.8   Kohs, *Chorale Variation on "Rock of Ages,"*[11] third section, opening measures.[12]

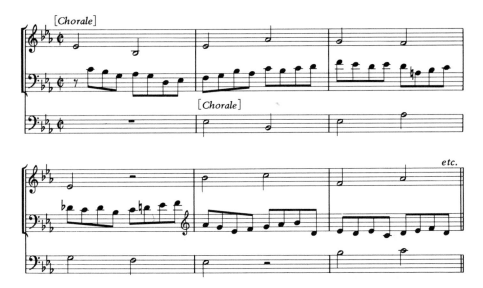

The style known as *invention* is occasionally used in works that are primarily in another form. It was noted in Chapter 18 that some of Bach's preludes (in BWTC), and sonata and partita movements use essentially the same technique. Chorale variation too may borrow from the style of the invention. Bach wrote several variations of this type, in which the continuous motivic imitation serves as background for the superimposed chorale.

For example, in "Jesus Christus, unser Heiland," the continuous chorale appears in the soprano. The three lower voices enter one at a time in imitation, and continue in the style of an invention. In the illustration which follows, the motive is indicated by a bracket.

Example 20.9   Bach, "Jesus Christus, unser Heiland" from *Orgelbüchlein,* mm. 1–3.

[11] From *Three Chorale Variations on Hebrew Hymns* by Ellis B. Kohs, © Copyright 1953, Merrymount Music, Inc. Used by permission.

[12] No. 2 of *Three Chorale Variations on Hebrew Hymns.* No. 3, not illustrated here, is also canonic, but the treatment is such that the first phrase is in canon with the second, and so forth.

The *Eighteen Large Chorales* include two rather extended compositions based on the melody "Komm, heiliger Geist, Herre Gott." The first (in F major) is in invention style. The three upper voices could well form a complete composition in themselves. The intermittent chorale phrases are in the organ pedals. Except for a few short episodes, the invention motive is used imitatively throughout. The motive makes its initial entry on the dominant note (C).

The second and third entries begin on the tonic (F).

Chorale variations in fugal and *motet* style are regarded by some theorists as variants of a single type. The chief difference between them is that motet style chorale variation uses *several* subjects, one for each section or phrase of the chorale, each having its own exposition; whereas fugal style variation is based on a *single* subject.

The difference between motet and fugal style chorale variation is evident in Bach's two settings of the melody "Wenn wir höchsten Nöten sein." The earlier setting in *Orgelbüchlein* suggests fugal procedure. The opening motive,

derived from the beginning of the first phrase of the chorale, is used in *all* the fugal expositions. The later version (*no. 18* in *Eighteen Large Chorales,* and the composer's last completed work) is in motet style. Here, each of the four phrases of the chorale is given a *separate* exposition. The chorale appears in the soprano in augmentation: the rhythmic values of the preceding entries are doubled. Added interest is provided by the use of inversion (each of the second entries), stretto, and elements of earlier phrases as counterpoints for later phrases. The rather complex design is handled with disarming ease, and gives more evidence of the composer's full creative power than it does of a man on the very threshold of death.

Bach composed a second version of the previously mentioned melody "Komm, heiliger Geist, Herre Gott" in G major which is a lucid illustration of motet style chorale variation. The techniques shown in the first three phrases (see the following diagram) are used in all nine. Following the last phrase of the chorale there is a thirteen-measure coda.

Example 20.10   Bach, "Komm heiliger Geist, Herre Gott," second version, G major, from *Eighteen Large Chorales*. Diagram of opening sections.

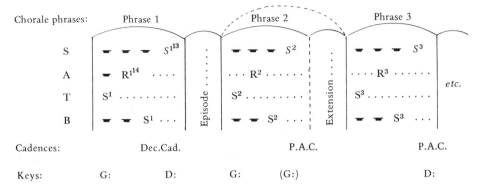

Fugal procedures are found in many chorale variations. In one subtype (see Examples 20.11 and 20.12) the complete chorale, with or without interludes, is superimposed on a background that constitutes a fugue in itself. In a second subtype the cantus firmus as a whole never appears and the relationship to the chorale is established only by means of the chorale-derived motives. The two types are further distinguishable by the fact that in the first subtype the fugue subject need not be related to the chorale. Only the first type will be considered here, leaving the discussion of the second for later, because of its great likeness to the fantasia type.

An example of the fugal type in which the fugue subject is *not* related to the chorale is found in the variation on "Meine Seele erhebt den Herren." The two phrases of the chorale are superimposed on a three-voice fugue. The chorale and the very different fugue subject may be seen in Example 20.11.

Example 20.11   Bach, "Meine Seele erhebt den Herren," from *Six Schübler Chorales*. Chorale and fugue subject contrasted.

(a) Chorale

(b) Fugue subject

The fugue subject is based on the opening notes of the chorale in Bach's variation on "Kyrie, Gott Vater in Ewigkeit" *(Clavierübung,* Part 3). The treatment given the first, second, and fourth phrases of the chorale is shown below, along with the original first two phrases.

[13] Italics indicate definitive statement.
[14] Dotted line indicates free melodic continuation.

Example 20.12   Bach, "Kyrie, Gott Vater in Ewigkeit," from *Clavierübung,* Part 3.

(a) Original first two phrases.

(b) Fugal entries, mm. 1–16.

(c) Continuation of the fugue in counterpoint with the fourth phrase of the chorale, mm. 24–32.

A number of Bach's chorale variations in fugal style are called *fantasia,* a term which suggests a free and improvisatory manner. The fantasia may be regarded as less "strict" than the fugue, much as the early baroque fantasia was freer than the strictly contrapuntal and learned ricercare. The second subtype of chorale variation employing fugal procedure may be included in this group. All compositions of this type are distinguished by the absence of the complete chorale. Fragments of the melody are used; or there may be just a suggestion of thematic derivation. Not all chorale fantasies are labeled as such, just as pieces in rondo form are not necessarily so titled.

One of the most interesting of the quasi-fugal types is the so-called "Giant Fugue," "Wir glauben all' an einen Gott" (*Clavierübung,* Part 3). The opening phrase of the chorale is suggested by the subject which is given quasi-fugal treatment in the upper voices (manuals). The organ pedals are devoted exclusively to a completely different idea, a magnificent motive that strides up and down the scale six times in different keys in widely separated entrances. This remarkable procedure, so clear in utterance and grand in effect, might have prompted a lesser composer to repeat his success. Bach, however, never at a loss for ideas, did not again use this particular formula.

In the chorale variation on "In dir ist Freude" (*Orgelbüchlein*), the pedals participate with the upper voices in free, nonfugal imitation of chorale-derived motives. In addition, the pedals have a recurring, refrain-like phrase which suggests the plan used in "Wir glauben all' an einen Gott."

Additional types of chorale variation should be noted: the *chorale partita,* the *chorale cantata,* the *trio sonata* type, the *chorale with freely motivic accompaniment.* These are largely compound forms, or are related to the types discussed above.

The *chorale partita* is a suite of variations (*partite*) on the chorale, not infrequently a dance suite. There are extant several early works of Bach in this style, as well as compositions by Pachelbel, Buxtehude, and, in the twentieth century, Ernst Krenek. In Bach's chorale partita on "Vom Himmel hoch da komm' ich her," the variations are canonic at various intervals and suggest the more elaborate series in the *Goldberg Variations* discussed in Chapter 17.

The *chorale cantata* is a composition for solo voice(s) and/or chorus and orchestra (or simply continuo), consisting of several movements or sections, one or more of which uses chorale variation procedure. Distinction must be made between a *chorale* cantata (a cantata based on a chorale) and a *choral* cantata (for chorus, in contrast to the cantata for solo voice).

Some variations resemble the *trio sonata.* In this style, two upper voices engage in free imitation over a continuo-type bass. Part of the chorale is usually introduced toward the end of the composition. Two examples by Bach (both in *Eighteen Large Chorales*) are the variations on "Herr Jesu Christ, dich zu uns wend' " and his third setting of "Allein Gott in der Höh' sei Ehr'."

Freely motivic imitation accompanying the complete chorale melody (sometimes called *figured chorale*) is found with some frequency. The cantus firmus generally is in the soprano, the accompanying voices are below it. The imitation is not organized as rigorously as in an invention, which it may seem to resemble in some ways. There is free but fairly consistent use of one figure throughout, hence the name figured chorale. In the illustration which follows, the motive is indicated in brackets; the chorale is in the soprano.

Example 20.13   Bach, "Christ lag in Todesbanden," from *Orgelbüchlein*, opening measures.

No discussion of chorale variation would be complete without mention of the remarkable use of the chorale "Es ist genug" in Alban Berg's *Concerto for Violin and Orchestra*. The composer quotes not only the melody but also Bach's four-voice harmonization intact; and he relates its tonal, diatonic material to his own atonal, chromatic, and serially organized music in very expressive and dramatic fashion.

SUGGESTED EXERCISES

1. Compare the four settings of "Vater unser in Himmelreich" by Scheidt, Buxtehude, Pachelbel, and Bach, no. 190 in the *Historical Anthology of Music*.[15]

2. Compare Bach's three settings of "Nun komm, der Heiden Heiland" in the *Eighteen Large Chorales* with the single setting of the same melody in *Orgelbüchlein*. Accompany your short essay with brief diagrams and musical quotations.

3. Identify and quote the opening measures of three chorale variations in which the cantus firmus is subject to embellishment. Describe other distinctive characteristics of each work.

4. Compare two motet style chorale variations. Discuss their similarities and differences in terms of the handling of the cantus firmus, order of entries, episodes, textures, cadences, and so forth.

5. Write a short essay on the history of chorale variation before Bach.

6. Write a short essay on the use of chorale variation in the compositions by Mozart, Berlioz, Bartók, and Berg cited in this chapter.

7. Compare the manner of treatment of the chorale "Ein feste Burg ist unser Gott" in Bach's organ chorale setting, Mendelssohn's *Reformation Symphony,* and the second movement of Debussy's two-piano composition *En blanc et noir*.

8. Compare two settings of the same chorale: Bach's "Wenn wir in höchsten Nöthen sein" (in *Orgelbüchlein*) and "Vor deinen Thron tret' ich hiermit" (*Eighteen Large chorales, no. 18*). Discuss in some detail the procedures used in each, noting separately the similarities and the differences.

9. Compose a chorale variation on the melody "Kyrie, Gott Vater in Ewigkeit" (see Example 20.12) or on "Meine Seele erhebt den Herren" (see complete melody in Example 20.11a). Use one of the imitative styles: canon, invention, motet, fugue. In a short accompanying essay, discuss the procedures and techniques you have employed.

[15] *Historical Anthology of Music,* edited by Archibald T. Davidson and Willi Apel (Cambridge: Harvard University Press, 1950).

10. Compose a chorale variation for organ or for small chamber ensemble in which the cantus firmus is treated in decorative style. Use one of the melodies mentioned in Exercise 9. If the "Kyrie" is used, do not employ interludes between the phrases. If "Meine Seele" is chosen, the two phrases should be preceded by an introduction, separated by an interlude, and followed by a postlude (coda), all of which should use the same motivic materials.

The three-part homophonic forms considered in Chapters 12 and 14 are based on the principle of statement-departure-return (A^1BA^2): there is a *single* departure or episode, and *one* return. The *rondo* forms are based on the principle of *multiple* departure and return. If three-part form may be compared to a circle, then rondo should be compared to a spiral.

Three rondo-like forms flourished in the monophonic secular vocal music of the late Middle Ages; *rondeau, virelai,* and *ballade.* The basic *rondeau* form was (AB) *aA ab AB.*[1] In the *virelai,* the two-phrase refrain *AB* always appeared both at the beginning and at the end. The central portion consisted of a repeated new musical phrase and text (*c*) followed by the music of the refrain sung to new text, thus: *AB cc ab AB.* There were several types of *ballade,* one of which follows.

(Large outline):	*A*	b b c a	*A*
(Detail):	*AB*	cd cd e ab	*AB*
	(Choral refrain)	(Solo, using continually new text)	(Choral refrain)

These forms were carried over into the secular polyphonic music of the fourteenth century by both Machaut and Landino, the chief representatives of the French and the Italian *ars nova,* respectively. Landino wrote at least one hundred forty-one examples of the *ballata,* the polyphonic equivalent of the monophonic virelai. In this form which is an instrumentally accompanied solo song, the design is *AbbaA,*[2] which is related to the virelai as indicated:

(Monophonic virelai):	*A*	*bb*	*a*	*A*
(Polyphonic ballata):	*AB*	*cc*	*ab*	*AB*
(or, if *AB = A*):	*A*	*bb*	*a*	*A*

[1] Parentheses indicate optional element. Capital letters refer to the chorus, which sings a textual refrain; lower case to solo voice, which goes on with new text. Letter repetitions designate the pattern of musical repetition. See further: Gustave Reese, *Music in the Middle Ages* (New York: W. W. Norton, 1940), p. 222.

[2] Reese, *Middle Ages,* page 336. Capital letter indicates text repetition, as a refrain; lower case, fresh text. Letter repetition stands for musical repetition.

Reese[3] mentions a considerably lengthened polyphonic rondeau by Machaut with the following form:

ABCD   abAB   abcd   ABCD

The frame-like textual refrain suggests a large ternary design (*ABA*) for all these forms, but the multiple musical departures and returns relate them unmistakably to the rondo of the baroque and classic eras. The poetic form and the musical form, although closely related, part company in these works, as the craving for new experience in words considerably exceeds the demand for new tonal experiences.

The French rondeau of the baroque era, *ABACAD . . . A,* is an instrumental dance, sometimes stylized, having a notably simpler scheme of repetitions than the above-mentioned vocal forms. It was much imitated abroad by composers of instrumental suites and partitas (see Example 21.1). The *ritornello* of the baroque concerto grosso, in which the orchestral tutti serves as a sort of refrain in alternation with the continually new material or procedure in the solo (or soli) instrument(s), is strongly reminiscent of the medieval vocal forms described above. (See, for example, the first movement of Bach's *Brandenburg Concerto no. 5 in D major.*) The fugue, the crowning achievement of the baroque era, characteristically displays statements of the subject in alternation with contrasting episodes—a further adaptation of the rondo idea.

In the rondo of the classic era (with which Chapters 21 and 22 are concerned), one may find *small* rondo forms in which the component parts or sections are no larger than a phrase, phrase group, or period, or extension of any of these. *Large* rondos have subdivisions that may consist of small part forms or small rondo forms. In the following hypothetical example, the capital letters outline a large five-part *ABABA*-type rondo, while the letters in lower case show the component subdivisions which are either small ternary or small rondo form.

A^1	B^1	A^2	B^2	A^3
ababa	*cdc*	*aba*	*cdc*	*ababa*

Thus, a rondo form may be a complete movement, or it may be only a part of a movement. In the following analyses capital letters are used for the large divisions and lower case for the small sections, in the manner just illustrated.

In the French rondeau of the late baroque and early classic eras, contrasting episodes alternate with the recurring, refrain-like principal thematic idea. Each section usually closes with a full cadence. The contrasting sections are mostly in contrasting keys. The recurring *A* sections normally are all in the tonic, and in many works are written out only at the beginning. Thus, a rondeau written as *ABCD* (with the indication "da capo" at the end of *B, C,* and *D*) is performed *ABACADA.*

During the classic era a more sophisticated kind of rondo developed in which each of the recurring *A* sections is prepared by a retransition. This retransition usually modulates and terminates on the dominant chord of the key to follow. (Compare the similar procedure in *ABA* form.) These works are "more sophisticated" because the composer is playing on the listener's expectation of the return of *A*—expectation that frequently is heightened by a prolonged dominant extension or a dominant pedal point, and sometimes frustrated by a "false" return followed in time by a redeeming

[3] Gustave Reese, *Music in the Renaissance* (New York: W. W. Norton, 1954) page 14.

"correct" restatement. The contrasting sections (B, C) thus dissolve rather than end on full cadences.

The most familiar rondo forms of the middle and late classic era are *ABABA, ABACA*, and *ABACABA*.[4] The latter may sometimes appear to be an expansion of ternary form, thus: *ABA-C-ABA*, especially if C is much larger than B, or if it tends to balance *ABA* in length and structural significance. If C is developmental in character, relating to the materials in A or B or both, then the overall design is a mixture of rondo and sonata form[5] and designated sonata-rondo.[6] There are many kinds of extensions and variants of the rondo principle, and one should be prepared to encounter them. One of the more common of these procedures is Mozart's frequent practice of almost completely suppressing the final A section by shortening it and combining its function with that of the coda.

RONDEAU

In Example 21.1 four different contrasting episodes separate the five statements of the main idea, A. The latter, in its first appearance, is given a double statement. The subsequent statements are not so repeated, but otherwise recur exactly without the slightest change. They are in E major throughout, and close with strong perfect authentic cadences.

Section B modulates at once to the relative key (c♯) and utilizes material not far removed from that of A. C is considerably longer, has more subdivisions, is more contrasting in materials except for the closing phrase which contains elements of A, and modulates in its course from E to B major (the dominant key). The material in

---

[4] Some theorists refer to *ABA* as "first rondo," the five-part *ABABA* and *ABACA* as "second rondo," and the seven-part *ABACABA* as "third rondo." There is no historical or logical justification for calling *ABA* a rondo, except in the case of

$$A^1B^1A^2 \quad C \quad A^3B^2A^4$$
$$A^1 \qquad\;\; B \quad A^2$$

where *ABA* can be reduced to A, and C to B (discussed further in this chapter).

Apel (*Harvard Dictionary*) claims that *ABABA* and *ABACA* are expanded three-part designs rather than true rondo forms because they did not develop out of the French rondeau. However, it is hardly possible to view $A^1B^1A^2B^2A^3$ and $A^1BA^2CA^3$ as expanded three-part designs unless B^2 is an exact or slightly varied repetition of B^1 (in the former), or C but a variation of B (in the latter). Furthermore, it must be pointed out that many movements with *ABABA* and *ABACA* design are specifically marked "Rondo" by the composer. See, for example, the following movements in *ABABA* form: Haydn, *String Quartet in C major*, 33/3, iv (marked "Rondo. Presto"); Mozart, *Piano Quartet in G minor*, K. 478, iii (marked "Rondo"), and BS, 49/1, ii (marked "Rondo. Allegro"). See the following movements in *ABACA* form: Haydn, *Piano Trio in G major*, 75/1, iii (marked "Rondo all, Ongarese. Presto"); Mozart, *Piano. Trio in B♭ major*, K. 254, iii (marked "Rondo: Tempo di Menuetto"); and MS, K. 545, iii (marked "Rondo"). For examples of *ABACABA* that are marked "Rondo" (or "Rondeau") by the composer, see Examples 21.6 and 21.7, and BS, 7, iv.

It should be observed that although only fast final movements appear to have been especially identified as being in rondo form, the same designs appear in slow middle movements as well. Thus, in MS, K. 545, both the second and third movements are in *ABACA* form, but only the fast final movement is designated as rondo; the second movement is marked "Andante."

[5] See Chapter 23.

[6] See Chapter 24.

section *D* is even more contrasting, and is in the relatively remote supertonic key (f♯). Longest of all, *E* touches on a number of keys, but is largely in g♯ (the mediant).

Each contrasting section begins in E major and continues the key of the preceding *A* section for a short time; the modulation takes place en route. Each section closes with a perfect authentic cadence in a contrasting key. The order of contrasting keys is noteworthy: first the relative minor, then the dominant; then *their* dominants in reverse order (f♯ being V of B; and g♯, V of c♯).

Example 21.1   Typical late baroque rondeau. Bach, *Partita no. 3 in E major for Unaccompanied Violin*, iii (Gavotte en Rondeau).

*A*¹ (8 mm. repeated)

B (8 mm.)

*A*² (8 mm.)
(Exact restatement, without repetition)

C (16 mm.)

*A*³ (8 mm.)
(Exact restatement, without repetition)

D (16 mm.)

*A*⁴ (8 mm.)
(Exact restatement, without repetition)

E (20 mm.)

*A*⁵ (8 mm.)
(Exact restatement, without repetition)

ABABA-TYPE RONDO

The following examples illustrate the *ABABA-* or *ababa-*type rondo. The first example shows rondo form as part of a movement, where the need for modulation found in a complete movement is abandoned in favor of sectional key unity. The second illustration shows a complete movement in which *B* sections are in the same contrasting key. In the third, also a complete movement, *B* sections are in different contrasting keys. Example 21.2 constitutes the middle (*B*) section of a large ternary design, and in form is a small rondo, $a^1b^1a^2b^2a^3$. Each of the recurring *a* sections is varied in a different way. The *b* sections show variation technique in the latter portion of their first and second halves; in addition, b^2 is a variant of b^1. Because of the small proportions, there are no modulations. The entire rondo is in Ab, the relative major of the prevailing key of the movement (f).

Example 21.2   Small rondo: *ababa*. BS, 2/1, iv, mm. 59–109.

a^1 (20 mm.)

b^2 (8 mm.)

Repeated phrase (4 + 4)   (I.A.C.)

a^3 (7 mm.)

Coll' 8va

Single phrase   (P.A.C.)

Rondo form in the classic era is found most frequently in fast, final movements of sonatas, chamber works, symphonies, and concertos. But it appears also in slow middle movements such as the one diagramed in Example 21.3.

The $A^1B^1A^2B^2A^3$ form here is expanded by the extensions within A^1, a repeated double period (that is, a period twice doubled). Both B sections are extended periods. A^2 is a single two-phrase period, one-fourth the length of A^1. A^3 is a three-phrase period with a post-cadential extension which also serves as codetta. When it is viewed spatially, the overall shape resembles that of an hourglass.

Example 21.3   *ABABA,* diagram. MS, K. 309, ii.

A^1 (32 mm.)

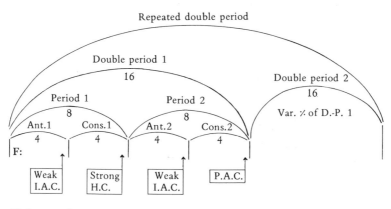

B^1 (12 mm.)

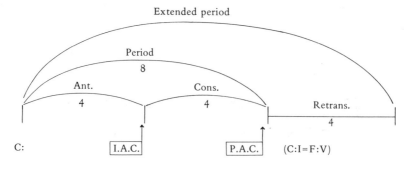

A² (8 mm.)

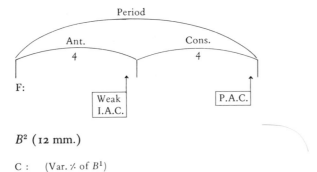

B² (12 mm.)

C :   (Var. ⸎ of *B¹*)

A³ (15 mm.)

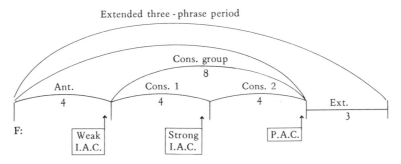

In Example 21.4 the two *B* sections are in different contrasting keys. *B¹* is in the relative major (E♭). *B²* is in another third-related key, the submediant (A♭).

The three *A* sections are in the tonic key. They end on strong cadences, except for *A³* which elides with the coda. The elision effectively removes nearly all sense of cadence, but the coda with its alternations of V–I serves as a substitute for the cadence since it provides insistence on I and the attendant feeling of harmonic repose.

In contrast to the *A* sections, *B¹* and *B²* have internal cadences only; they end in modulating dissolutions or retransitions. Thus, unlike the contrasting episodes in Example 21.1, the *B* sections are dependent rather than independent structural units.

Example 21.4   *ABABA*. Mendelssohn, *Songs without Words, no. 14, 38/2.*

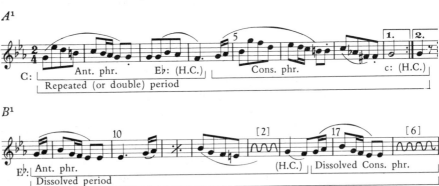

A²

B²

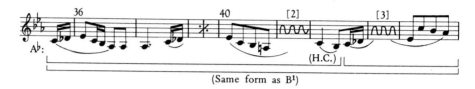

(Same form as B¹)

A³

Coda

ABACA-TYPE RONDO

The slow movement of Example 21.5 is a very clear illustration of *ABACA*-type rondo, which differs from *ABABA* in having contrasting sections that differ from each other in material and key.

The outer *A* sections (*A¹* and *A³*) correspond in length; the middle return is shorter. (Compare the similar procedure in Example 21.3.) Episodes *B* and *C* are in different keys than the *A* sections; they are modulatory and tonally unstable. (Compare the similar treatment in Example 21.1.) The design of *C* is particularly interesting because it includes modulation to a remote key by means of enharmonic change. Furthermore, the sixteenth note triplets that are introduced in *C* continue in the following *A³* and even into the coda; this particular variation treatment in *A³* not only adds contrast with *A¹*, but also creates a closer relationship between the (dependent) *C* and the (independent) *A³* sections. Observe the sense of dramatic climax in *C*, an element usually lacking in rondo forms written prior to the late classic and early romantic eras.

Example 21.5   *ABACA.* BS, 13, ii.

A¹ (mm. 1–16)

25

A² (mm. 29–36)

29

33

C (mm. 37–50)

37

40

43

A^3 (mm. 51–66)

John Dewey Library
Johnson State College
Johnson, Vermont 05656

Coda (mm. 66–73)

A¹ (16 mm.)

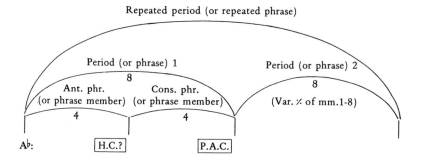

B (12 mm.)

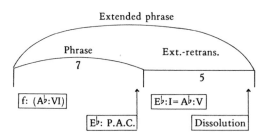

A^2 (8 mm.)

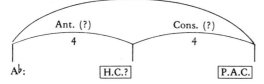

Period (or phrase)   (corresponds to half of A^1)

Ant. (?)   Cons. (?)

4   4

A♭:   H.C.?   P.A.C.

C (14 mm.)

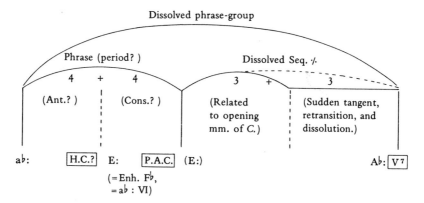

Dissolved phrase-group

Phrase (period?)   Dissolved Seq. ∕.

4   +   4   3   +   3

(Ant.?)   (Cons.?)   (Related to opening mm. of C.)   (Sudden tangent, retransition, and dissolution.)

a♭:   H.C.?   E: P.A.C.   (E:)   A♭: V⁷

(=Enh. F♭, =a♭ : VI)

A^3 (16 mm.) Varied repetition of A^1. Continued use of sixteenth note triplets from C section.

Coda (7 mm.)

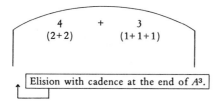

4   +   3
(2+2)   (1+1+1)

Elision with cadence at the end of A^3.

ABACABA-TYPE RONDO

Examples 21.6 and 21.7 illustrate *ABACABA*-type rondo, which has seven rather than five sections. It contains elements of both *ABABA* (recurring B section) and *ABACA* (different contrasting episodes).

In this type, *C* may have about the same weight, length, and structural significance as *B*; perhaps it will explore a somewhat more remote key (see Example 21.7).

If *C* is a small two- or three-part form (see BS, 2/2, iv, and op. 7, iv), the overall design may seem to approach that of compound ternary song form; however, the two should not be confused. Although in many ways the *B* sections in the cited movements are similar, in some ways (particularly key) they are not. In compound ternary form, A^2 (the repetition of the initial a^1ba^2 which made up A^1) is an exact restatement of A^1 except for omitted repetitions of a^1 and ba^2.

If *C*, in *ABA–C–ABA,* assumes the role of development rather than new thematic exposition, the form is properly designated sonata-rondo (see the discussion of this form in Chapter 24).

In the first illustration (Example 21.6), a cadenza at the end of *C* helps to set it off as an important section in the overall ternary design. The cadenza also suggests concerto style—one wonders if Mozart may have intended this work, in his first sketches, as a concerto for piano and orchestra. The label "Rondeau" indicates its French derivation. The Beethoven example (21.7) has no hint of ternary design. Unlike Example 21.6, in which the *C* section is somewhat larger than *B*, here *B* and *C* are almost identical length.

Example 21.6   *ABACABA.* MS, K. 311, iii.

A^1 (mm. 1–40)	B^1 (mm. 41–86)	A^2 (mm. 87–118)	C (mm. 119–73)	A^3 (mm. 174–205)	B^2 (mm. 206–48)	A^4 (mm. 249–69)
Double period (mm. 1–16) D:	Double period (mm. 41–56) A:	Double period (mm. 87–102) D:	Chain of phrases (mm. 119–54) (20 + 16) b:—G:	Double period (mm. 174–89) D:	Double period (mm. 206–21) D:	Single period (mm. 249–56) D:
Extension (mm. 16–24) D:	Phrase group (mm. 56–79) (8 + 11 + 4) A:	Extension (mm. 102–10) D:—G:	Retransition (mm. 154–73) G:—D:V⁷ (Cadenza in m. 173)	(Extension omitted)	Phrase group (mm. 221–44) D:	Extension and Codetta (8 + 5) (mm. 257–69) D:
Transition group (mm. 25–40) D:—A:	Retransition (mm. 79–86) A:I = D:V⁷	Transition group (mm. 111–18) G:—b:V		Transition group (mm. 190–205) D:	Retransition (mm. 244–48) D: (Cadential extension; rep. of V–I)	

In Example 21.6, B^2 is in the prevailing key rather than in a contrasting one. This not uncommon feature further tends to unify $A^3B^2A^4$ and add to the sense of overall ternary design. In Example 21.7, on the contrary, there is contrast of *mode* in B^2, but no change of tonal center. This provides a compromise between the need for tonal contrast and the desire for tonic stability in closing sections.

All the A sections are in the tonic key. In substance, only A^2 corresponds exactly to A^1. A^3 and A^4 are variants. B^1 and B^2 are in different keys, as indicated above: B^1 is in E♭ (the relative major), a third-related key; B^2 is in the parallel major (C). The C section is in A♭ (the submediant), another third-related key.

The precise and tightly knit *A* sections are in period form. The *B* sections are complexes of several rather disparate elements. There is consistent and striking use of variation technique in *C* (see Example 15.3).

A coda based on elements derived from *A* follows *A*⁴ at the point where correspondence with *A*¹ ceases. The tangential episode in A♭, eight measures from the end of the movement, is really an elaboration of c:VI. It is related to the *C* section of this movement and to the previous slow movement by its pensive mood and the key of A♭, in striking contrast to the passionate mood and C minor tonality of the sonata as a whole.

Example 21.7   *ABACABA.* BS, 13, iii.

*A*¹ (mm. 1–17)

*B*¹ (mm. 18–61)[7]

---

[7] This includes the seven-measure transition, mm. 18–24.

A^2 (mm. 62–78)

C (mm. 79–120)

A^3 (mm. 121–34)

B^2 (mm. 134–70)

A^4 (mm. 171–82)

Coda (mm. 182–210)

SUGGESTED EXERCISES

1. The final movement of MS, K. 309 is marked "Rondeau." Diagram the music showing overall form, large divisions, key areas, cadences, and so forth. Which of the several rondo forms does it most closely resemble? Describe any unusual features.

2. MS, K. 310, iii may be viewed either as a large ternary form, or as a modified *ABACA*. Diagram the movement and indicate appropriate evidence for both points of view. State the reasons for your final choice, if there is one.

3. Diagram the last movement of MS, K. 533 and 494,[8] marked "Rondo." How many large divisions are there? Do any of the contrasting sections employ material derived from *A*? If, *so,* what are the formal implications? In what respect is the last *A* section unconventional? Is the form expanded by any interpolations?

4. MS, K. 545, ii is a slow movement in rondo form. Make a diagram showing the large formal divisions. Indicate all thematic interrelationships.

5. Diagram MS, K. 311, ii. Discuss the relationship of the contrasting episodes to the first section.

6. Diagram BW, 79/1. If there are several ways to interpret the form, show the solutions on different levels in your analysis.

7. Diagram Example 21.7. For diagram procedure models, see Examples 21.5 and 21.6.

8. Diagram BW, 118/3. Is this work an example of rondo or ternary form? Outline the basis for both considerations. State the reasons for your choice.

9. MS, K. 281, iii (marked Rondeau: Allegro) is a highly irregular, yet unmistakable rondo form. In two columns list those factors that correspond to the norms discussed in this chapter, and those factors that deviate from reasonable expectation.

10. Make two or three diagrams of hypothetical rondo forms, other than those discussed in this chapter. Include appropriate detail as needed.

11. Using the *A* section of any of the works discussed in this chapter, compose a new continuation so as to arrive at a different overall form.

---

[8] The *Sonata in F major* consists of a rondo finale (K. 494, composed on June 10, 1786) preceded by an allegro and andante (K. 533, dated January 3, 1788), hence the two Köchel numbers.

12. Using any of the diagrams in this chapter as a point of departure, compose a rondo form with original material. Try to adhere to the details as well as to the overall design, small differences excepted. The music may be for piano or for a small instrumental ensemble drawn from class members. Following approval of the score by the instructor, parts should be copied in a clear hand, and the music performed in class. Subsequent discussion will be useful for student composers, and should be an opportunity for articulate criticism by the class as a whole.

Altered Rondo Forms 22

There are several means by which a rondo form may be extended, compressed, or otherwise altered. The combination of sonata and rondo is discussed in Chapter 24. This chapter is concerned with a few of the many other procedural possibilities.

In Example 22.1, an interpolated development section *between* A^2 and B^2 and another developmental insertion *within* A^3 expand an otherwise "normal" *ABABA*-type rondo. An interpolation in fugal style may be observed in Example 22.2. In Example 22.3, a rondo with four contrasting episodes is compressed by means of the shortening of A^2, A^4, and B^2. B^2 and C^2 are combined in the penultimate section of Example 22.4, which also has elements of variation form.

EXTENDED RONDO

The overall form of Example 22.1 is $A^1B^1A^2CB^2A^3$. This may be viewed as (a) $A^1B^1A^2B^2A^3$ with an interpolated development section between A^2 and B^2; (b) $A^1BA^2CA^3$ with an extra B section thrown in for good measure; (c) $A^1B^1A^2C$-$A^3B^2A^4$ but with the suppression of A^3, or (d) as a kind of sonata-rondo (see Chapter 24).

Example 22.1   Beethoven, *String Quartet in E minor,* 59/2, iv. Diagram showing chief thematic materials and formal divisions.

A^1 (mm. 1–69). Section of four phrases plus transition.
    (mm. 1–9) (E minor) Phrase 1.

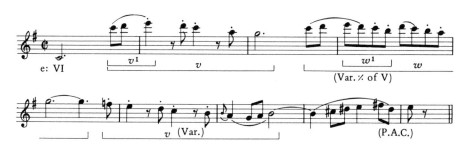

(mm. 10–22) Phrase 2. Varied repetition of Phrase 1, with the following extension which contains materials subsequently in C.

(mm. 25–35) Phrase 3. Varied repetition of Phrase 2, with the same extension.
(mm. 36–56) Phrase 4. Varied repetition of Phrase 3, with a long and new extension.
(mm. 56–69) Transition based on v^1.

B^1 (mm. 70–106). Section of two phrases plus extension and retransition.
  (mm. 70–77) (B minor) Phrase 1.

(mm. 78–85) Phrase 2. Varied repetition of Phrase 1.
(mm: 85–89) Extension. Imitative treatment of v^1.

(mm. 89–106) Modulating retransition. Further use of v^1 in imitation. Thinner texture.

A^2 (mm. 107–45) (E minor). Repetition of A^1, except for the shortened fourth phrase which dissolves into the interpolated development section.

C Interpolated development section (mm. 146–215). Two phrase groups. Group 1 develops motive w^1 and xx, a new figure derived from x.[1] Group 2 develops a variant of w^1 in augmentation.

Group 1 (mm. 146–77). Motive w^1 in counterpoint with xx.

[1] Derivation of xx from x:

(mm. 146–50) (C major) Phrase 1 (nonmodulating).

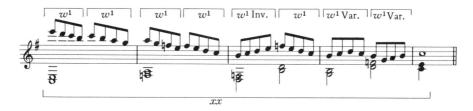

(mm. 150–54) Phrase 2. Var. ˙/ . , modulating to A minor.
(mm. 154–58) (A minor) Phrase 3. Var. ˙/ . (nonmodulating).
(mm. 158–70) Phrase 4. Var. ˙/ . , considerably extended, modulating to B♭ major.
(mm. 170–77) (B♭ major) Cadential extension, using the "head" of the *A* theme. B♭:I becomes d:VI.

Group 2 (mm. 178–215). Tonally unstable group. Continuous modulation.
(mm. 178–82) Phrase 1. Sequential development of w^1 varied and in augmentation.

(mm. 182–86) Phrase 2. Varied repetition.
(mm. 186–90) Phrase 3. Varied repetition.
(mm. 190–94) Phrase 4. Related to materials and procedures of mm. 9–10.
(mm. 194–215) Retransition. Related to the materials of the transition at the end of A^1 (mm. 56–58).

B^2 (mm. 216–74) (E minor). Extended repetition of B^1.

A^3 and *Coda* (mm. 275–409) (E minor). An extended interpolated development replaces the suppressed Phrase 3. Materials derive from both *A* and *C*. In addition, there is a short coda (in faster tempo) which grows out of the materials of Phrase 4.

(mm. 275–300) Section corresponds to Phrases 1 and 2 of A^1.
(mm. 300–71) Extended development (*D*?) with several subdivisions takes the place of Phrase 3. Materials are derived from the rhythm of motive *v* and the variant of w^1 used in m. 178.[2]
(mm. 372–84) Section corresponds to Phrase 4 of A^1.
(mm. 384–409) Coda (più presto). A closing group, further developing the rhythmic idea derived from *v*. The quasi-statement of *A* is in E minor, with tonic harmony, unlike the previous statements of *A* which were associated with the

[2] If its length is considered, one may view the interpolation as a (separate) *D* section. The surrounding *A* statements would then be seen as foreshortened, with the resultant overall form (the incomplete sections showing as lower case): *ABACBaDa* (coda). Since *D* uses materials from *C*, and like *C* is developmental in style, it might be considered C^2.

C major chord (e:VI). The treatment in the coda serves to resolve the ambiguity (e:VI vs. C:I) in favor of explicit E minor tonality.[3]

As in Example 22.1, interpolation is used to expand the form in Example 22.2. Each of the three *A* sections has a different structure: in *A*¹ there is a double statement (violin, then piano); the two statements in *A*² are separated by an interpolated fugato; *A*³ consists of a single statement; a coda utilizing *A*-derived material in diminution and stretto takes the place of the omitted second statement. Double statements characterize the *B* sections too. In *B*¹ the violin is answered by the piano; in *B*² the order is reversed.

Example 22.2   Walter Piston, *Sonata for Violin and Piano* (1939), iii.[4] Diagram showing chief thematic materials and formal divisions.

*A*¹ (mm. 1–47)

(mm. 1–19) (F Dorian). First statement (violin).

(mm. 20–37) Second statement (same key) begins in the piano, transfers to the violin at m. 29, then dissolves.

(mm. 38–47) Transition, based on a motive derived from m. 15.

*B*¹ (mm. 48–99)

(mm. 48–62) (A Aeolian) First statement (violin).

(mm. 63–77) Second (inverted) statement (violin).

---

[3] Compare the similar ambiguity at the beginning of Beethoven's *Concerto no. 4 in G major for Piano and Orchestra,* iii, (G:IV vs. C:I), and the similar "resolution" or "dénouement" in the closing statement.

[4] Copyright 1940 by Arrow Music Press, New York. Used by permission of Associated Music Publishers, Inc.

(mm. 78–99) Retransition. Materials derive from mm. 1–3. In the violin, *x* in diminution; the piano imitates, with the figure inverted.

A² (mm. 100–91)

    (mm. 100–25) (C Dorian). First statement (violin). Corresponds to mm. 1–19, but slightly extended.
    (mm. 126–63) Interpolated fugato.
Fugue subject (S):

    (mm. 126–32) S in piano (high). Key: C♯.
    (mm. 133–40) R (tonal response) in violin. Key: G♯.
    (mm. 141–46) S in Piano (low). Key: C♯.
    (mm. 147–50) Short extension based on ♩♪♪♩ rhythm.
    (mm. 151–63) Episode employing double counterpoint, based on elements derived from S. Grouping: 3 + 3 + 3 + 4.
(mm. 164–81) *A²* resumes, with the second statement (piano) an octave lower than in *A¹*. New accompaniment. The violin at first uses material from the fugato (creating a formal elision). Correspondence to *A¹* is closer after m. 173.
(mm. 182–91) Transition. Corresponds to mm. 38–47, but is transposed.

B² (mm. 192–237)
    (mm. 192–206) (B Aeolian) First statement (piano). Corresponds to mm. 48–62. However, violin and piano have exchanged parts.
    (mm. 207–21) Second statement (violin). Corresponds to mm. 63–77. Repetition is in inversion, as in *B¹*. Exchange of material continues.
    (mm. 222–37) Retransition. Corresponds to mm. 78–99, but is somewhat extended.

A³ (mm. 238–55) (F Dorian) Foreshortened section. Single (not double) statement. Corresponds to mm. 1–19.

Coda (mm. 256–91). This section is a substitute for the missing second statement in *A³*, and may be grouped with the above torso to make up a larger unit. Motive *x* is treated in diminution and stretto. The 2/4 grouping in the violin is in counterpoint with an implied 5/8 in the piano caused by the interpolated low F which serves as a tonic pedal point, thus:

COMPRESSED RONDO

In Example 22.3, a rondo with four contrasting episodes ($A^1B^1A^2CA^3DA^4B^2A^5$) is compressed by abbreviation of three of the sections. If the latter are indicated in lower case, the overall form may be more clearly viewed as *ABaCADabA*.

Example 22.3   MS, K. 281, iii.

Form:

A^1	$(a + b + c)$	mm. 1–17	B♭ major
B^1	$(d + e + f + g + h$ plus cadenza)[5]	mm. 18–43	B♭ to F major
A^2	(a)	mm. 44–51	B♭ major
C	$(i + j$ plus retransition)	mm. 52–71	G minor
A^3	$(a + b + c)$	mm. 72–89	B♭ major
D	$(k + l$ plus retransition)	mm. 90–114	E♭ to B♭ major
A^4	$(a$ varied)	mm. 115–23	B♭ major
B^2	$(f + g + h$ without cadenza)	mm. 124–42	B♭ major
A^5	$(a + b + c)$	mm. 143–60	B♭ major

Thematic elements:

[5] Subsections *d* and *e* serve also as modulating transition.

The penultimate section of Example 22.4 utilizes material derived from both B and C. The overall form may be described as:

$$A^1 \quad B^1 \quad A^2 \quad C^1 \quad A^3 \quad \frac{C^2}{B^2} \quad A^4 \quad \text{(Coda)}$$

Each A section is given somewhat different treatment. Only the outer A sections correspond in key. Since A^2, A^3, and A^4 are variants of A^1, there is a suggestion of variation form in addition to that of rondo. A short introduction, which connects this movement with the previous slow movement, contains a foreshadowing of the opening motive of A^1 and is a thematic source for the coda with which it provides a sort of frame for the main body of the movement. The filled-in interval of a third is the basic motive for both A and B sections.[6] C, in contrast, emphasizes the perfect fourth (or its inversion, the perfect fifth) in association wtih a major second (see Example 22.4).

A word about the variations of A^1. In A^2 the original key (A) is changed to G, a step below; the melody in the clarinet has the same rhythm as the original line, but the pitches form a new contour. In A^3 the key is F, an additional step down; the melody is simply a transposition of the original, but there is a new accompaniment texture in the piano. The original key and harmonic structure are restored in A^4, but both melody and accompaniment are varied.

In the sixth section, B^2 and C^2 are combined. The C theme in the clarinet is accompanied by B material in the piano. This section, too, may be viewed as a type of variation.

Despite the apparent absence of tonally related harmonies caused by the prevailing chromaticism, each section is organized around a specific tonal center, as follows:

Sections:	A^1	B^1	A^2	C^1	A^3	$\dfrac{C^2}{B^2}$	A^4	*(Coda)*
Keys:								
A sections:	A	—	G	—	F	—	A	A
Non-A sections:		G♯	—	F♯	—	E		
Overall:	A	G♯	G	F♯	F	E	A	A

The order of keys of the A sections (A–G–F–A) and of the non-A sections (G♯–F♯–E) constitute filled-in thirds. In addition, there is an overall tonal progression which outlines a perfect fourth (A to E and return). The intervals which are used for the small building blocks thus reappear in the large design.

Example 22.4   Kohs, *Sonata for Clarinet and Piano,* iv.[7] Diagram showing chief thematic materials and formal divisions.

Introduction (mm. 1–9). Serves as transitional link between the third and fourth movements.

[6] Typical filled-in thirds:

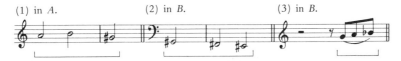

(1) in A.   (2) in B.   (3) in B.

[7] *Sonata for Clarinet in A and Piano* by Ellis B. Kohs, © Copyright 1956, Merrymount Music, Inc. Used by permission.

A^1 (mm. 10–25) (Key: A). Brackets show third-related motives.

B^1 (mm. 26–46) (Key: G♯). Brackets show third-related motives.

A^2 (mm. 47–62) (Key: G). Corresponds to mm. 10–25. The rhythm of the theme is retained, the pitch contour is changed.

C^1 (mm. 63–86) (Key: F♯). Brackets show the chief motive, a perfect fourth (or fifth) in association with a second.

A^3 (mm. 87–102) (Key: F). The theme is in the clarinet as before, but transposed down a third. The accompaniment texture contains broken rather than sustained chords.

B^2/C^2 (mm. 103–29) (Key: E). B in the piano appears simultaneously with C in the clarinet. The section is extended to provide a strong retransition to the final statement of *A*. The rhythm of the *C* melody is unaltered, the pitch contour is changed (same type of variation as in *A²*).

A⁴ (mm. 130–46) (Key: A). Ornamented version of theme. (Piano accompaniment is also varied).

Coda (mm. 147–62). Materials are derived from the introduction, mm. 1–9.

RONDEAU AND RONDO IN CONCERTO MOVEMENTS

Examples 22.5, 22.6, and 22.7 illustrate a few of the ways in which the rondo principle lends itself to the special needs and characteristics of the concerto for one or more solo instruments and orchestra. The alternation of principal and subordinate sections is in many ways analogous to the alternation of solo (usually with light orchestral accompaniment) and tutti (full orchestra, usually without the solo instrument). These examples should not be regarded as typical, but as a demonstration of a few possibilities.

Example 22.5 is a rondeau in which the *A* sections serve as a refrain played by the full orchestra (tutti), and the four contrasting episodes *B, C, D,* and *E* are played by the solo instrument, the orchestra accompanying.

In Example 22.6, solo and tutti alternate within each of the main divisions of an *ABACA*-type rondo. The solo instrument, over a light accompaniment, introduces the thematic material of each division; a full orchestral tutti, usually a modified repetition, follows. The *C* materials derive from the previous movement, and the concerto as a whole is thus an example of *cyclic form*.[8]

The diagram in Example 22.7 illustrates not only the solo-followed-by-tutti schema found in Example 22.6, but also a form that may be viewed both as *A¹BA²* (exposition-development-recapitulation in sonata form)[9] and *A¹B¹A²CA³B²A⁴* (a rondo form,

[8] For further discussion of cyclic form, see Chapter 25.

[9] See Chapter 23.

with an expanded C which is a development of A, rather than a statement of new material). This combination of sonata form and rondo form is called *sonata-rondo*.[10]

Example 22.5   Bach, *Concerto No. 2 in E major for Violin and Orchestra*, iii.

A^1 (Tutti) (mm. 1–16).

B (Solo) (mm. 17–32).

A^2 (Tutti) (mm. 33–48) Exact repetition of A^1.

C (Solo) (mm. 49–64).

A^3 (Tutti) (mm. 65–80) Exact repetition of A^1.

D (Solo) (mm. 81–96).

A^4 (Tutti) (mm. 97–112) Exact repetition of A^1.

E (Solo) (mm. 113–45).

A^5 (Tutti) (mm. 146–60). Exact repetition of A^1.

[10] See Chapter 24 for an extended treatment of sonata-rondo, and Example 24.7 for an illustration of sonatina-rondo in a concerto movement.

Example 22.6   Mozart, *Concerto No. 3 in E♭ major for French Horn and Orchestra*, K. 447, iii.

A^1 (mm. 1–33). Extended period, E♭ major.

    (mm. 1–8) Solo. Antecedent phrase of period.
    (mm. 9–16) Tutti. Consequent phrase of period.
    (mm. 16–33) Tutti, solo, alternately. Extension.

B (mm. 34–76). Period, E♭ major, extended by closing group and retransition (modulation to B♭ major, dissolution on E♭:V).

    (mm. 34–41) Solo. Antecedent phrase.
    (mm. 42–51) Tutti, then solo. Consequent phrase.
    (mm. 51–76) Tutti, solo, alternately. Closing group and retransition.

A^2 (mm. 77–97). Period, E♭ major, followed by extension-transition (modulation to A♭ major).

    (mm. 77–84) Solo. Antecedent phrase, as in A^1.
    (mm. 85–92) Tutti. Consequent phrase, as in A^1.
    (mm. 93–97) Tutti. Extension-transition, modulating to A♭ major.

C (mm. 98–154). Group of two periods, A♭ major, followed by closing group (A♭ to E♭:V) and retransition (E♭:V). The *C* theme is derived from the second movement. The closing group materials are taken from mm. 51ff of *B*.

    (mm. 98–113) Solo, tutti, alternately. Period I.
    (mm. 114–29) Solo, tutti, alternately. Period II.
    (mm. 129–41) Tutti, then solo. Closing group.
    (mm. 141–54) Solo, tutti, alternately. Retransition.

A^3 (mm. 155–90). Period, E♭ major, followed by closing group (in which the materials are similar to mm. 51–76 of *B* and mm. 129–41 of *C*).

    (mm. 155–70) Solo, then tutti. Period, as in A^1.
    (mm. 170–90) Solo. Closing group. Ends on strong E♭: P.A.C.

Coda (mm. 190–208). Materials derive from the extension (mm. 16–33) of the period in A^1.

Example 22.7   Beethoven, *Concerto no. 5 in E♭ major for Piano and Orchestra, 73,* iii. Diagram.

Sections:	A^1						B					A^2				
	(Exposition)						(Development)					(Recapitulation)				
	(a^1	b^1	a^2		c							a^3	b^2	a^4)		
	a^{1*}	b^1	a^{2**}	a^{3**}	a^{4***}	a^{5**}						a^{6*}	b^2	a^{7***}		*Coda*
Tonality:	E♭	E♭ to B♭	E♭	C	A♭	E(♮)						E♭	E♭	A♭ to E♭		E♭

* Solo is followed by tutti.

** Solo, without a following tutti.

*** Solo and orchestra in dialog in A♭, followed by tutti in E♭.

SUGGESTED EXERCISES

1. Analyze the final movements of Beethoven's *Piano Concerto no. 1 in C major,* and *no. 3 in C minor,* each an example of rondo form. Make a list of the regular features. Note any unusual or unorthodox features.

2. Identify the procedures which enlarge, compress, or make irregular the following rondo forms.

    Beethoven, *String Quartet in B♭ major,* 18/6, iv
    MS, K. 333, iii
    MS, K. 310, iii
    MS, K. 309, iii

3. Diagram and compare the following rondo movements in Brahms's *Sonatas for Violin and Piano.*

    no. 1, ii
    no. 1, iii
    no. 2, ii
    no. 2, iii

4. In which movement(s) of Stravinsky's *Octet for Wind Instruments* is there evidence of rondo form? Describe, taking note of any unusual features.

5. Chopin's ballades are more extended than most of his one movement works—the preludes, waltzes, and mazurkas, for example. Are any of the four ballades in rondo form? If so, identify and discusss in some detail.

6. Diagram several hypothetical rondo forms. Extensions or other modifications should be clearly identified.

7. Compose a work in rondo form using original materials. The general structure should be based on the outline of one of the forms discussed in this chapter, or it may combine elements drawn from two or more illustrations, or the form may be derived from one of the works listed under Exercises 2 or 3. Such details as key, instrumentation, proportions, length, and so forth, may be changed. The overall design should be approved before work is begun, and all modifications of the original intentions should be checked before the work is completed.

Sonata Form   23

One of the most widely used musical forms has no universally accepted name: *sonata form,* only one of many similarly worded terms, may describe the structure of a movement in a symphony, concerto, sonata, chamber work, or other multimovement composition; it may denote a single-movement sonata, symphony, or overture. It does *not* refer to the form of an entire multimovement sonata.[1]

Since the design appears so frequently in first movements, the term *first-movement form* has gained a certain currency. This is a misnomer, for the exact same design is used for some second, third, and fourth movements.[2]

Another popular term, *sonata-allegro,* is equally inappropriate, for it is unsuitable as a description of the slow movements in which the form not infrequently appears.

As fugal procedure pervades polyphonic music of the baroque era, so sonata form appears frequently in the homophonically oriented single movements of sonatas, trios, quartets, symphonies, concertos, and (one-movement) overtures since the classic era.[3] It gradually incorporated and assimilated other elements such as rondo and fugue, and had a tremendous influence on the music dramas of Richard Wagner and the symphonic poems of Franz Liszt and Richard Strauss.

The history of sonata form will not be reviewed here; and examples in every possible medium cannot practically be considered. This chapter will concentrate on sonata form: a structure that is essentially the same regardless of performance medium; and a form which in practice is treated with considerable freedom and flexibility, despite a number of seemingly limiting common denominators.

In large outline, the form comprises: (a) an *exposition* section, customarily repeated, in which the thematic ideas are set forth in contrasting but closely related keys; (b) a *development* section characterized by one or more of the following—modulation to more remote key area(s), comparative instability of the tonal center(s), fragmentation, sequence, and imitation of elements derived from the exposition; (c) a *recapitulation* or restatement of the materials of the exposition—usually in the original order,

---

[1] For forms of sonatas and other works comprising several movements see Chapter 26. (The one-movement sonata in sonata form is exceptional.)

[2] See MS, K. 279 and 280 (three sonata form movements in each), and Beethoven, *String Quartet in F major,* 59/1 (each of the four movements is in sonata form).

[3] *Harvard Dictionary of Music* edited by Willi Apel, (Cambridge: Harvard Univ. Press, 1970) article on sonata form.

possibly with different transitions between the subsections—but with greater emphasis on the tonic key.[4]

The overall structure should be viewed as a large ternary design, *ABA* or *AABA*. Some theorists, however, maintain that the form is better considered as binary because of a presumed balance between *AA* and *BA*.[5] This scheme may be expanded to include: a slow *introduction* for a fast movement, preceding the exposition; and a *coda*, occasionally in faster tempo, following the recapitulation.

Although exposition and recapitulation are similar and often parallel in thematic material, dramatically they are quite different. The conflicts of key in the exposition generate tensions which are resolved only through the tonal reconciliation and key unity in the recapitulation. Similarly, the tonally unstable development is unlike the tonally stable (even if thematically parallel) coda. The musico-dramatic structure of sonata form, considerably oversimplified, may be observed in Table 23.1.

Table 23.1   Musico-dramatic structure of sonata form.

Section:	Introduction[6]	Exposition		Development	Recapitulation		Coda[6]
Thematic element:	Free	P.T.[7]	S.T.[7, 8]	Thematic fragmentation, etc.	P.T.	S.T.[8]	Free
Key:	Tonic or parallel **minor, V** emphasis at close	Tonic	Dominant or other related key	Modulations, tonal instability	Tonic	Tonic	Tonic
Dramatic element:	Exploration, uncertainty	From stability to "challenge"		Conflict, instability	Resolution, "reconciliation," stability		Stability confirmed

INTRODUCTION[9]

An introduction, if present, appears most frequently in a first movement. See, for example, Beethoven's symphonies *nos. 1, 2, 4,* and *7*; and the last six symphonies by Mozart, of which three have a first movement with slow introduction. None of the

---

[4] The combined development-recapitulation may be repeated.

[5] See the relevant discussion in Chapters 11 and 13; William S. Newman, *The Sonata in the Classic Era* (Chapel Hill: Univ. of North Carolina Press, 1963) pp. 143–47; and Grosvenor W. Cooper and Leonard B. Meyer, *The Rhythmic Structure of Music* (Chicago: Univ. of Chicago Press, 1960) pp. 83–87.

[6] Optional element.

[7] P.T.: principal theme; S.T.: second theme.

[8] S.T. may be followed by a third theme (T.T.), closing section (C.S.), and/or codetta (C[tta]). If they appear, they do so in the order as given.

[9] Optional element.

first movements in Mozart's piano sonatas has a slow introduction. Only four of Beethoven's thirty-two piano sonatas (op. 13, 78, 81a and 111) open with a slow introduction.[10]

The materials of the introduction seldom reappear in the main body of the movement. Interesting rare cases in which they do recur may be observed in BS, 13, i, where elements of the introduction appear in both the development and the coda (Example 23.3); Beethoven's *Leonore Overture no. 3*, where a melodic idea from the introduction recurs, somewhat transformed, as the second theme in both exposition and recapitulation; and Beethoven's *String Quartet in F major, 135*, iv, in which the three-note motto of the slow introduction is inverted in the subsequent exposition of the principal theme.

The key is almost certainly the tonic. If the movement is in a major key, the introduction may be in the parallel minor mode. The introduction may terminate on the dominant chord (possibly a half cadence), or end with a cadential dissolution. An authentic cadence is unlikely.

Introductions in concertos are rare. One well-known instance is the brilliant cadenza for piano accompanied by a few supporting chords in the orchestra that opens Beethoven's *Concerto no. 5 in E♭ major for Piano and Orchestra* ("Emperor").[11] Another is the introduction of the first movement of Tchaikovsky's *Concerto in B♭ minor for Piano and Orchestra*, which precedes the main thematic exposition.

Slow movements, whatever their form, do not usually have introductions. A short transitional or bridge-like introduction may prepare for a changed mood or a remote key (see Dvořák's *Symphony in E minor*, "From the New World," and Mendelssohn's *Concerto in E minor for Violin and Orchestra*).

Introductions to final movements are present in three of Beethoven's nine symphonies: *no. 1*, iv; *no. 3*, iv; and *no. 9*, iv. The latter movement, which is quite extended and includes the famous and unprecedented use of chorus and vocal soloists, has an introduction with several tempo changes, brief reminiscences of the prior movements, and anticipations of the main theme. The finale of the first of the three cited works is the only one in sonata form; the other two are free variation forms. (See also the introduction to Beethoven's *String Quartet in F major, 135*, iv.)

EXPOSITION

The exposition section is largely binary in structure no matter how many subdivisions it may have. The opening portion, variously called principal theme, first theme, principal group, and principal theme group, is essentially tonic in orientation. Everything that follows is unified by the fact that it is nontonic.

The exposition as a whole is usually repeated. The repeat sign, sometimes associated

[10] The two-measure *Largo* in BS, 31/2, i, mm. 1–2, is part of the principal theme of the exposition. The four-measure introduction of BS, 110, i, in the prevailing tempo, recurs later, and is better viewed as part of the exposition.

[11] An almost identical cadenza appears immediately prior to the recapitulation.

with separate first and second endings, is the usual mark indicating the end of the exposition. Formal repetition is sometimes omitted in works of the nineteenth and twentieth centuries.

Concerto first movements normally have a double rather than a repeated exposition;[12] characteristically, the solo instrument makes its first appearance in the second exposition. Beethoven again provides two interesting exceptions: in the first movement of his fourth piano concerto the piano plays a few measures of the main theme unaccompanied, and then remains silent until the second exposition; his fifth piano concerto opens with a piano cadenza, following which the piano is not heard from until the close of the first exposition.

The opening portion of the exposition, the *principal theme, group,* or *section,* is normally in the tonic key. It may be a phrase group or several groups; it is seldom one of the period forms. It either closes on a cadence, authentic or half, in the original or a related key; or it dissolves into the[13]

Transition: a modulating connective passage of one or more parts which is designed to prepare the listener for the new key and, probably, for new thematic material. It may begin with material derived from the principal theme and end with material anticipating the second theme. There may be a thematic group, or there may be neutral material such as scales and arpeggios. The texture generally is different from that of the surrounding principal and second sections. In most cases, the transition closes on the dominant of the new key, perhaps on a half cadence; it may however dissolve without cadence. In a diagram, principal theme and transition are customarily grouped together under one arch since the latter is heard as an outgrowth of the former.

The most essential trait of the *second theme, group,* or *section* is its *contrasting key.* Thus a transition or transition theme which begins in the tonic key should never be mistaken for a second theme. Contrasting *material* is customary but not absolutely essential. There are examples of Haydn symphonies in which a "second theme" is nothing more than the first theme in a different key and with new treatment. (This peculiarity is found chiefly in works of the early classic era, and undoubtedly derives from the thematically more unified sonata of the baroque era.) The second theme of Haydn's *String Quartet in Bb major, 76/4,* is but the inversion of the first theme, in the dominant key.

The second theme is usually more lyrical than the first; consequently, it is likely to show period structure. A carefully prepared terminal cadence is characteristic, in order to help establish the new key. However, the expectation of a cadence may be frustrated by tactics of evasion or deception; then the desired cadential fulfillment is provided in the next following section.

If a *closing (or third) theme, group,* or *section*[14] is present, this portion of the exposition may be in the same contrasting key as the second theme, or in a different one. The following chart illustrates a few of the many possible effective key relationships for principal theme (P.T.), second theme (S.T.), and closing theme (C.T.). (See also the exposition columns in Tables 23.4 and 23.5.)

---

[12] See Example 23.6.

[13] The dissolution of this sentence is a verbal homologue of the procedure in music.

[14] Optional element.

Table 23.2   Some effective key relationships in sonata form exposition sections.[15]

	P.T.	S.T.	C.T.	Comment
Major keys:	I	V	V	S.T. and C.T. in same contrasting key.
	I	vi	vi	
	I	vi	V	S.T. and C.T. in different contrasting keys.
	I	iii	V	
Minor keys:	i	III	III	S.T. and C.T. in same contrasting key.
	i	v	v	
	i	v	III	S.T. and C.T. in different contrasting keys.
	i	♭VII	III	

If the thematic material of this third section is strikingly new and fairly extended, *and* in a new contrasting key (as is often the case in Schubert, Brahms, Bruckner, and Mahler), then the term *third theme* is more appropriate. The closing section and/or codetta then follows the third theme rather than the second, and confirms the third key rather than the second key.

Material that is motivically related to the principal theme may appear in the closing section. Such similarity is never more than slight and is not necessary. It can be helpful in preparing the ear for the principal theme which is heard in the repeated exposition. In this respect it may convey a certain sense of retransition. Like the second theme, and perhaps even more regularly, the closing theme or section usually terminates on a well-defined authentic cadence.

The *codetta*[16] is a short extension designed to bring the exposition to a satisfactory close. It should not be confused with the coda, a section which ends the whole movement. It is usually very stable in tonality, and may be little more than an expression of the cadential formula (for example, I–VI–IV–I₆–V–I). It may dissolve into a modulating transition to the repeated exposition and/or the development section.

DEVELOPMENT

The central development section is usually, but not necessarily, shorter than the exposition and is composed of several subdivisions. The first of these is often quite short, perhaps an outgrowth of the last part of the codetta. It is a sort of "maneuver for position" before the "serious business" that follows.

The many techniques of development include thematic fragmentation, sequence, imitation, textural thickening, and series of modulations, all of which assist in achieving increased dramatic intensity and climax. The materials may derive from the principal theme (most common), second theme, closing section, codetta, or even transitional passages. There may be new material as well. Each subsection within the development is usually identified with one or more themes and/or techniques, used with

[15] Major keys in capitals, minor keys in lower case.
[16] Optional element.

some consistency, and should be quite distinguishable from its neighboring subsections which use different materials and/or techniques.

The closing portion of the development section, the *retransition,* can be the climax of the whole movement and may be marked by an extended dominant pedal point[17] Sometimes there are anticipatory fragments of the principal theme which if sufficiently extended may be heard as a "false recapitulation." This strategic portion of the movement may arouse such tonal tensions that it will require most or all of the following recapitulation to provide adequate resolution and fulfillment.

RECAPITULATION

The recapitulation is a modified restatement of the exposition. In contrast to the tonal dichotomy of the exposition (tonic-nontonic), the emphasis in this section is on tonal unity (tonic-tonic). Themes usually return in their original order, but sometimes certain elements are omitted, shortened, extended, transplanted, or varied. Previously separated themes or motives may appear simultaneously. An unexpected key may be used for added variety and interest, or other reason; if this is the case, the reason and a tonal counterbalance elsewhere in the movement, should be sought.

It is a rare recapitulation indeed that does not begin with the *principal theme, group,* or *section* in the tonic key. Among the exceptional specimans are MS, K. 545, i, m. 42, where the principal theme is in the subdominant key. In the first movement of Stravinsky's *Sonata for Two Pianos* (Example 23.5), both statements of the main theme (mm. 53 and 63) are in the dominant. In Beethoven's *Leonore Overture no. 3,* the first statement of the principal theme in the recapitulation is in the key of the dominant, but the second statement is in the expected tonic key. In Example 23.6 the principal theme is omitted completely.

The texture and—in a work for more than one instrument—the distribution among the instruments may or may not be the same in the recapitulation as they are in the exposition. In Beethoven's *Symphony no. 8 in F major,* i, the development spills over into the recapitulation in a formal elision during which the principal theme appears *below* the accompanying harmonies, rather than *above* them as it does in the exposition.

The *transition* is the one portion of the recapitulation most likely to be altered. This is because it is here that the greatest probability of a departure from the key scheme of the exposition exists. If the second theme *is* in the tonic, the transition which leads to it may be omitted since no modulation is needed, or it may be redirected so as to proceed away from the tonic and back to it again—a sort of refreshening process. If the second theme *is not* in the tonic it will be in a *different* contrasting key than the one of the second theme of the exposition section; there may be a new transition altogether, or the old transition may be revamped to fit the new conditions.

The key of the *second theme, group,* or *section* of the recapitulation is usually the tonic, since the end of the movement requires tonal stability. However, *should* there

---

[17] The tonic which follows such an extended dominant should not be confused with a V–I cadential progression. Cadences include uninterrupted harmonic motion up to the point of harmonic resolution. A retransition which emphasizes the dominant chord effectively postpones the tonic and establishes *nontonic* harmony as the terminus, not the tonic. The purpose of the interruption is to make possible the accumulation of harmonic tension rather than permit it to be dissipated by immediate resolution.

be a third theme, the tonic key may be reserved for *that* section and, in order to avoid overusing the tonic, another key may be used for the second theme. In the latter event, the same relationship between second and third themes normally appears in both exposition and recapitulation. Thus, in mathematical terms, the relationship "exposition S.T. is to T.T. as recapitulation S.T. is to T.T." may be expressed as "exposition (S.T. : T.T.) : : recapitulation (S.T. : T.T.)." In the chart which follows, the principle is applied in hypothetical cases.

Table 23.3   Some typical second and third theme key relationships: exposition and recapitulation compared.[18]

| | Exposition | | | Recapitulation | | | Relationship of |
	P.T.	S.T.	T.T.	P.T.	S.T.	T.T.	S.T. to T.T.
Major keys:	I	V	V	I	I	I	V:V: :I:I
	I	vi	V	I	ii	I	vi:V: :ii:I
	I	iii	V	I	vi	I	iii:V: :vi:I
Minor keys:	i	III	III	i	I	i	III:III: :i:i
	i	III	iii	i	i	i	III:iii: :I:i
	i	bVII	III	i	V	I	bVII:III : :V:I

See further Table 23.5 which demonstrates the key structure in the first movements of the four symphonies by Brahms. In each of these late romantic works there is a distinct third theme which is in a different key or mode than the preceding second theme.

In the classic era there is usually only one key for the second and for the optional closing themes; and, as shown in Table 23.4, key relationships display considerable uniformity.

Thirty-three of the fifty-seven movements in Mozart's nineteen piano sonatas (each has three movements) are either in fully developed sonata, diminutive sonata, sonatina, or sonata-rondo[19] form. Twenty-five of these have the key structure: exposition, I–V; recapitulation, I–I. Each of the others is a different and most interesting exceptional design.

The probability that the substance of the optional *closing (or third) theme, group,* or *section* of the recapitulation will closely match that of the corresponding section of the exposition is considerable—a *higher* probability than can be expected in the previous sections. The possible use of minor mode for materials which in the exposition had been in the major mode is of particular interest; in Mozart's *Symphony no. 40 in G minor,* i, the S.T.–C.T. groups are in Bb *major* in the exposition but in G *minor* in the recapitulation. Not all thematic and harmonic materials lend themselves so effectively to treatment in both modes. (See further the minor mode examples cited in Table 23.4 and Examples 23.1 and 23.3.)

Parallelism with the exposition normally continues in the *codetta*. This short section may be suppressed or modified or replaced by the coda, with which it should not be confused.

[18] Major keys in capitals, minor keys in lower case.
[19] See Chapter 24.

Table 23.4   Exposition-recapitulation key schemes in the thirty-three sonata-form movements of Mozart's *Piano Sonatas*.[20]

Number of Examples	Keys	Exposition P.T.	S.T.	(C.T.)	Recapitulation P.T.	S.T.	(C.T.)	Source
25	*Major*	I	V ---------		I	I ---------		
1		I	v	V	I	i	I	K. 332, iii
1		I	V --------		I	V–I	I	K. 330, i
1		I	V --------		IV	I --------		K. 545, i
1		I	{ Trans. { S.T. { IV { V		I	{ Trans. { S.T. { IV { I		K. 570, i
1		I	V --------		S.T. I (themes appear in reverse order)	P.T. I --------		K. 311, i
1	*Minor*	i	III -------		i	i ---------		K. 310, i
1		i	III -------		v–i	i ---------		K. 280, ii
1		i	III -------		i	i --------- (second half of S.T. only)		K. 457, i

CODA[21]

A coda usually begins at the point where parallelism between recapitulation and exposition ceases. The end of the recapitulation may not be immediately apparent, however, if the codetta is altered. In the *Sonata no. 3 in D minor for Violin and Piano,* i, by Brahms, there is an interpolated restatement of the principal theme at the end of the recapitulation;[22] the coda, strikingly similar to the development, follows this interpolation and does not include it.

The thematic parallelism of coda and development sections, if sufficiently extended, may suggest an incipient second development, as in the opening movement of Beethoven's *Symphony no. 3 in E♭ major* ("Eroica").

The coda generally is not this long; in fact, it is usually much shorter than any of the previous sections. Since its primary purpose is to provide additional tonal stability, there are few if any departures from the tonic key. Phrases and measure groups tend to be progressively shorter; tonic cadences recur with increasing frequency.

An increase in intensity may be achieved by a change to faster tempo. This can be particularly effective if the movement begins with an inversely matching slow introduction.

[20] Major keys in capitals, minor keys in lower case.

[21] Optional element.

[22] Unlike the previous statements, which are marked *piano* and modulate from tonic to dominant, this statement is *forte* and remains in the tonic key.

Return to material of the introduction is unusual. See, however, Example 23.3, and the close of Schubert's *Symphony in C major* (1828), i, in which the quiet and meditative horn theme of the slow introduction becomes a triumphant peroration for full orchestra.[23]

Another rarity is the coda which dissolves into a transition leading to a slow second movement. (See Mozart's *Symphony in Eb major*, K. 184, i.)

SOME EXAMPLES OF SONATA FORM

Six examples of sonata form follow. These represent a variety of historical periods, styles, and performance media. Although not absolutely necessary, it would be helpful to have the score of each work at hand.

Example 23.1   Haydn, *String Quartet in G minor*, 74/3, i.

Exposition (mm. 1–78), G minor to Bb major.
Principal Theme Group (mm. 1–54), G minor to Bb major.
Principal theme (mm. 1–20), phrase group, G minor.

First phrase (mm. 1–10).

Reduction:

Second phrase (mm. 11–20).

The second phrase, apparently contrasting, is in fact based on two motives which derive from phrase 1. As indicated above, G–Bb–D in mm. 1–3 and Eb–C♯–D with its associated rhythm are the sources of the ascending triad *b* and the melodic-rhythmic shape *c¹*. Imitation at such an early stage suggests there may be further polyphonic activity in the development section, a not altogether unwarranted assumption.

[23] Some conductors do broaden the tempo here, to match the slower pace of the introduction, but there is no evidence in the score to justify this practice.

Transition (mm. 21–54), phrase group, G minor to B♭ major. The developmental transition, somewhat longer than the principal theme, is subdivided as indicated below. Materials include the new motive *d* along with c^1 or its variant, c^2. The overlapping of *c* derivatives and *d* in the opening twelve measures of the transition provides an elision with the principal theme proper. Although the tonality shifts to B♭ around m. 28, the tonic chord in root position is largely avoided until the final cadence. Brackets on the diagram show alternative groupings of the four- and five-measure phrase elements.

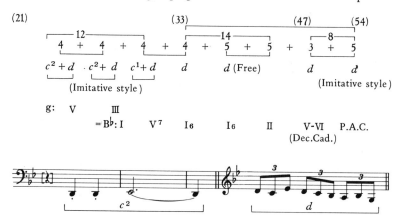

Second Theme Group (mm. 55–70), repeated period, B♭ major.
First statement, in Violin I.

Second statement, in Violin II, accompanied by sequences of d^1 (a varient of *d*) in Violin I.

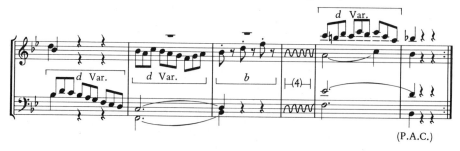

Codetta (mm. 70–78), B♭ major. A cadential extension, the codetta combines further variants of *d* with the previously neglected *b* motive of the principal theme.

Development (mm. 79–127), C minor–E♭ major–C minor–A♭ major (= c:VI or g:N6) – G minor (g:₀V⁹).

Part One (mm. 79–96), c:–E♭–c:V. Imitative style. The materials include variants of *d* plus an occasional *b* and *a*. The varied repetition of the closing measures of the exposition creates a sense of elision with the codetta.

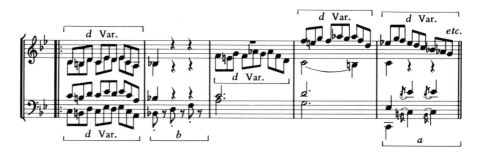

Part Two (mm. 96–107). Largely a prolongation of c:V. Imitation of a figure that combines *c²* with *d*.

Part Three (mm. 107–14). Violin I and cello discourse briefly on the second theme (not previously used in the development section). There is a modulation from c:V to A♭:I. Part Four (mm. 114–27). Retransition. Motive *c¹* is used in close imitation. The development section dissolves without cadence following g: ₀V⁹.

Recapitulation (mm. 128–97), eight measures shorter than the exposition, G minor to G major.

Principal Theme Group (mm. 128–68), thirteen measures shorter than the corresponding group in the exposition.

Principal theme (mm. 128–37). The first phrase is omitted. As a result, the P.T. is half the original length.

Transition (mm. 138–68). The transition is completely reworked, yet it follows the exposition in substance and in style of treatment. Instead of modulating to the relative major (B♭) as before, it proceeds to the parallel major (G).

Second Theme Group (mm. 169–84). Substantially an exact restatement except for the key (G) and small changes in instrumentation.

Codetta (mm. 185–97). Like the second theme, the codetta is substantially unchanged. Following a three-measure extension of the final cadence, the combined development and recapitulation are repeated.

Overall Form of the Movement

Exposition	Development	Recapitulation
‖:I Tr II C^tta	:‖ : 4 sections.	I Tr II C^tta :‖ or ‖: A¹ :‖ :B A² :‖
g: - - - B♭: - - -	Largely c:,	g: - - G: - - - I–III–IV–V–I
	ends on g:V	

Example 23.2   MS, K. 279, ii. Diminutive sonata form in a slow movement.

Exposition[24] (mm. 1–28), F major to C major.
Principal Theme Group (mm. 1–10), extended phrase.
Principal theme (mm. 1–6), F major.

Transition (mm. 7–10), F major to C major.

Second Theme Group (mm. 11–28), extended chain phrase, C major throughout.
Second theme (mm. 11–17).

Closing section (mm. 17–26).

Codetta (mm. 26–28).

[24] The exposition is repeated.

Development (mm. 29–42), largely C major (or F:V). Chief tonal areas: C–d–g–F:V (or F:V–VI–II–V).

Part One, C to d:V, or F:V to V–of–VI.   Part Two,

d to g, or F:VI–II.

Part Three, g, or F:II to F:V⁷.   Part Four,

retransition, F:V⁷.

Recapitulation[25] (mm. 43–74), F major throughout.
Principal Theme Group (mm. 43–50), single phrase.
                        Principal theme (mm. 43–47). (Dissolution and new

transition)

Second Theme Group (mm. 51–74), extended chain phrase.
Second theme (mm. 51–57).

[25] The combined development and recapitulation are repeated.

Closing section (mm. 57–68), lengthened.

Codetta (mm. 68–74), lengthened.

Cadential extension 1, derived from omitted transition

(mm.6-9)   Cadential extension 2, corresponds to mm.26-28

Example 23.3   BS, 13, i.

Introduction (slow) (mm. 1–10), C minor. Two phrases. Phrase 1 modulates from C minor to the relative major (E♭), where it closes on a P.A.C. Thematically related phrase 2 returns to C minor, dissolves on c:V⁹.

Phrase 1   Phrase 2

Exposition (Allegro) (mm. 11–132), C minor to E♭ major.
Principal Theme Group (mm. 11–50), C minor to e♭:V.
Principal theme (mm. 11–35), C minor. Following two statements of the P.T., of which the first ends on a P.A.C., the second on an H.C., there is a cadential extension of the dominant chord (c:V). A tremolo accompaniment is a significant feature of the main portion of the theme. In the postcadential extension, there is anticipatory use of an accompaniment figure that appears throughout the subsequent second theme.

First statement (beginning)   Second statement (close)

Extension.

Transition (mm. 35–50). A series of sequences leading from c:V to eb:V. The tremolo accompaniment returns. Thematic material, based on a two-note motive, derives from the similar principal theme.

Second Theme (mm. 51–88). Proceeds from Eb minor ("wrong" mode) to Eb, the relative major. The extended phrase group dissolves without cadence. An accompaniment motive, derived from a portion of the P.T. cadential extension, is used throughout.

Closing Section (mm. 89–113). Establishes Eb major. Two statements: in the first there is an evaded cadence, in the second, a P.A.C. New texture.

Codetta (mm. 113–32). Part one (113–21), largely cadential in character, further establishes the new key. The bass line is 1–6–4–5–1, repeated. The accompaniment motive derives from that of the second theme. Part two (121–32) is a *retransition* to the repeated exposition[26] (first ending), or a *transition* to the development section (second ending). The newly established tonality is weakened to permit a close on c:V⁷ (first ending) or g:V₆⁵ (second ending). Thus the exposition ends with a dissolution instead of a cadence. The materials of the (re)transition derive from the principal theme.

[26] According to the earliest editions, the repetition does *not* include the slow introduction. Some later editions and recent concert and recorded performances do.

Development (mm. 133–94), G minor to C minor.

Part One (mm. 133–36), G minor to e:V⁷. The material and the slow tempo derive from the introduction. These measures, which dissolve without cadence, serve as a bridge to the chief portion of the development, part two.

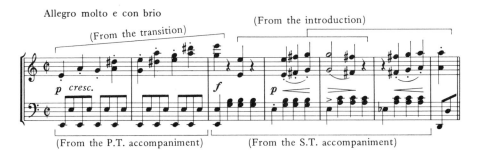

Part Two (mm. 137–66). Return of fast tempo. There is a remarkable synthesis of the following previously separated elements: (a) the tremolo from the P.T. accompaniment; (b) the accompaniment figure associated with the S.T.; (c) the rising melodic line derived from the transition at the close of the P.T. group; and (d) a motive derived from the slow introduction. A six-measure excerpt (mm. 137–42) illustrates the manner in which these elements are combined.

The measure groupings in part two are as follows: 137–48 (6 + 6, in sequence), 149–56 (4 + 4, another sequential group), 157–66 (2 + 4 + 4, which grows out of the previous 4 + 4).

Part Three (mm. 167–94), largely an extended c:V; the retransition contains some new materials, none of great thematic significance. There are occasional references to the transition portion of the P.T. group. Two groups: mm. 167–87 (8 + 12, the 12 being an extended repetition of the 8), and mm. 187–94 (thin texture; an unaccompanied stream of eighth notes descends from high F to low C). Dissolution on c:V⁷.

Recapitulation (mm. 195–294), C minor–F minor–C minor.

Principal Theme Group (mm. 195–220), C minor to f:V. Fourteen measures shorter than the corresponding section of the exposition.

Principal theme (mm. 195–207), C minor. At m. 207 the shortened second statement dissolves into the new transition.

Transition (mm. 207–20), c:I to f:V. Perhaps because the transition material derived from the exposition had been exploited in the development section, Beethoven may have felt it necessary to use different material at this point in the recapitulation. The prominent feature is a threefold series of descending half-note chords which derive from the close of the P.T. phrases. A tremolo accompaniment unifies the entire P.T. group. The close, on f:V, is in the "wrong" key (the subdominant), an "error" that is "corrected" in the course of the second theme.

Second Theme (mm. 221–52), F minor to C minor. Although six measures shorter and with a different harmonic direction than the corresponding section in the exposition, this section retains the thematic substance and overall style of the second theme. As in the exposition, the section dissolves on V without cadence.

Closing Section (mm. 253–77), C minor. Except for the change of key, this section corresponds exactly to the closing section of the exposition.

Codetta (mm. 277–94), C minor. Part one (277–85) corresponds to the codetta of the exposition except for the change of key. Part two (285–94) is a transition to the coda. As in the exposition, there is harmonic motion away from the tonic. This time the transition closes on c: $_0$V^9 of V.

Coda (mm. 295–310). The coda resembles the beginning of the development section. Part one moves to c:V^7 rather than to a remote key as in the development, but the means are much the same. Part two, related to mm. 137–39, uses material derived from the principal theme rather than from the transition to the S.T. It is an expanded I–IV–V–I progression. A strong P.A.C. brings the movement to a decisive close.

Overall Form of Movement

Introduction	Exposition				Development Parts			Recapitulation				Coda Parts	
	I	II	CS	C^{tta}	1	2	3	I	II	CS	C^{tta}	1	2
‖ c–E♭–c:V ‖ :	c–	e♭	–E♭ - -	c:V :	|g –	e –	c:V	c–	f	–c - - - - - - - - - - - - -‖			
		to		or					to					
		E♭		g:V					c					

Before turning to the first movement of Brahms's *Symphony no. 2 in D major,* analyzed in Example 23.4, the exposition-recapitulation key schemes of the first movements in each of Brahms's four symphonies should be considered for a sense of the wide range of possibilities. Note that two of the movements are in major (*no. 2,* i; *no. 3,* i), and two are in minor (*no. 1,* i; *no. 4,* i).

Table 23.5 Exposition-recapitulation key schemes in the first movements of Brahms's four symphonies.

	Introduction	Exposition			Recapitulation			Coda
		P.T.	*S.T.*	*T.T.*	*P.T.*	*S.T.*	*T.T.*	
no. 1 in C minor	i (ends on c:V)	i	III	iii	i	I	i	i
no. 2 in D major	(none)	I	iii	V	I	vi	I	I
no. 3 in F major	(none)	I	III	iii	I	VI	vi	I
no. 4 in E minor	(none)	i	v	V	i	i	I	i

All four have fully developed third themes of striking character. These expand the form much more than the analogous closing sections found in symphonies of the classical era.

The most important similarity in the four otherwise different schemes is that the tonal relationship of S.T. to T.T. in the exposition is preserved in the recapitulation. In all but *no. 2*, the adjacent S.T. and T.T. have the same tonal center but contrasting modes. A marked irregularity in *no. 3* is the close in D minor (F:VI) in the recapitulation, the tonic having been reserved for the consequently necessary coda. Only *no. 1* has a slow introduction.

One of the two symphonies in minor keys uses the *mediant* (the relative major) and its parallel minor as the areas of key contrast; the other uses the *dominant* (both major and minor). One of the two symphonies in major uses *two different* keys for S.T. and T.T.; the other employs a *single* tonal center but modal contrast.

Example 23.4 Brahms, *Symphony no. 2 in D major,* op. 73, i.

Exposition (mm. 1–183), D major to A major.
Principal Theme Group (mm. 1–81), D major to f♯:V.
Principal theme (mm. 1–44), D major. The important *a* and *b* motives, which pervade the entire movement in numerous guises and disguises, appear at once in the opening measures.

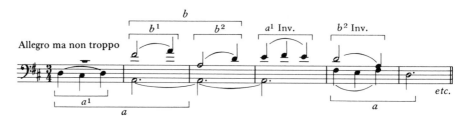

Transition (mm. 44–81), D major to f♯:V.
   Part one (mm. 44–58). An apparently new theme, but still in D major and motivically related to the principal theme proper.

Part two (mm. 59–66). Contrapuntal development of motive *a* and a derivative of *b*.

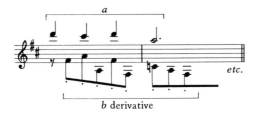

Part three (mm. 66–81). Further development of *a*¹ (now in diminution) and the *b* derivative.

Second Theme (mm. 82–118), F♯ minor. There are two statements. The second, which is differently orchestrated, dissolves into the third theme.

Third Theme Group (mm. 118–55), A major.
Part one (mm. 118–36). Dotted rhythm prevails.

Part two (mm. 136–55). Quasi-canonic, stretto-like imitation of a four-note motive derived from *a*.

Closing Section (mm. 156–83), A major. It seems appropriate to call these measures closing section rather than codetta because of the substance and treatment of the thematic material which is derived from the S.T. The first ending (mm. 179–86) is a retransition leading to a repeat of the exposition. The covered P.A.C. in m. 179, second ending, is followed by a postcadential extension which dissolves in m. 183 as a result of the change of function of A (from the root of A:I to the third of F:I₆).

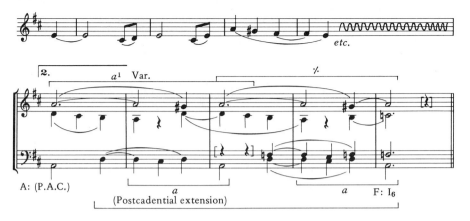

A: (P.A.C.)

a
(Postcadential extension)

a   F: I₆

Development (mm. 183–301), F–c–E–e–G–F (d:III?)–D:V.

Part One (mm. 183–205), F major to C minor. Sequential treatment of elements derived from motives *a* and *b* (P.T.), largely homophonic in style. The last two measures overlap with the beginning of part two (elision).

Part Two (mm. 204–24), C minor to E major (A:V?). Polyphonic (quasi-fugal) development of the second phrase member of the P.T. (mm. 6–8). A counterpoint (quasi-countersubject) in eighth notes is used with considerable consistency.

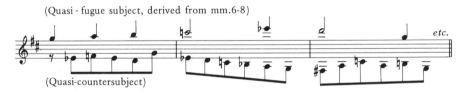

(Quasi-fugue subject, derived from mm.6-8)

(Quasi-countersubject)

Part Three (mm. 224–46), E minor to G major (C:V?). Imitative and sequential treatment of motive *a¹*, which appears both in the original values (quarter notes) and in diminution (eighth notes).

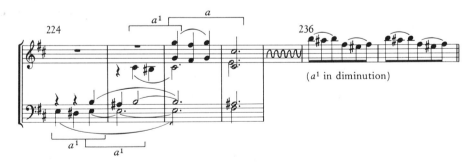

(*a¹* in diminution)

Part Four (mm. 246–81), G major (C:V?) to F major (d:III?). The materials derive from several sources: (a) the ascending third (from m. 2) in association with the neighboring tone motive (from m. 1); (b) the transition theme (mm. 44–46, primarily); (c) a pattern used in mm. 187–90, earlier in the development section (see lower portion of following diagram). The harmonies shift in continuous tonal flux (see harmonic reduction). The phrases are made up of four-measure units. The overall design includes two overlapping 24-measure groups. Group 1 (mm. 246–69) is composed of two parts, mm. 246–57 and 258–69, which correspond thematically and texturally. Group 2 (mm. 269–81) has two similarly related parts, mm. 262–69 and 270–81. The diagram shows harmonic structure, chief tonal centers, and materials used.

Harmonic Structure

Chief Tonal Centers (ascending fifths).

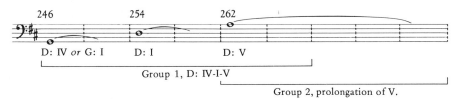

Materials Used. (Measure numbers indicate first appearance in part four [mm. 246–81].)

Motive a^1 (in diminution) combined with b^1.

Figure derived from the transition theme.

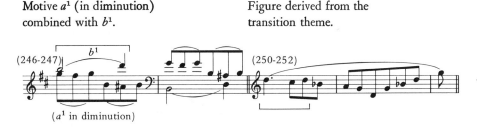

Four-measure pattern using a^1 in sequences, derived from mm. 187–90.

Part Five (mm. 282–301), largely D:V. Retransition. Materials and treatment are similar to those in part four; thus the two parts should be associated to form a group within the development section. There are five four-measure units grouped 8 + 8 + 4. The first eight are devoted to motive b^1. In the next eight there is a blend of a^1

(augmented), the transition theme, and motive *b*. The density of the texture and the intensity of the polyphony help to make these measures the dramatic climax of the movement.

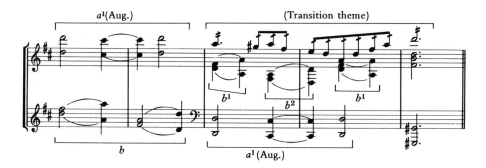

The final four measures of part five which bring the development section to a close constitute a chromatically altered II⁷ instead of the customary V. This supports greater augmentation of motive *a*. The harmonic resolution to I$_6^4$ at the beginning of the recapitulation (followed later by V⁷–I) ensures an elision at this structural joint.

Recapitulation (mm. 302–446), D major–B minor–D major.

Principal Theme Group (mm. 302–49), D major to b:V. The principal theme and the transition are compressed into a single section. The transition theme, instead of following the principal theme, is heard in counterpoint with it.

The drastic curtailment of the important principal theme group may be attributed to the extended use of the P.T. in the development section and the consequent wish to avoid overusing it. This abbreviation is combined with the alteration needed in order to redirect the harmony to B minor.

Second Theme (mm. 350–86), B minor. The same as the corresponding portion of the exposition, except for the key and details of orchestration.

Third Theme (mm. 386–423), D major. Related to the exposition in the same manner as the second theme.

Closing Section (mm. 424–46), D major. Corresponds to the exposition (in the same manner) until the end, where instead of a P.A.C. there is a deceptive cadence. This helps to maintain the forward momentum required for the rather extended coda which follows.

Coda (mm. 447–523), D major throughout.

Part One (mm. 447–77). The deceptive cadence is followed by a short bridge; this leads to an extended horn solo based on motive a^1 (inverted). Although the motive is familiar, the treatment is quite novel, and as satisfying as it is unexpected.

Part Two (mm. 477–96). Strings and horns further develop principal theme elements.

Part Three (mm. 497–513). Material from the abbreviated transition is introduced and given new treatment in the woodwinds, the strings accompanying pizzicato.[27]

Part Four (mm. 513–23). The accompaniment texture from part three continues; the last echoes of motive *b* can be heard over it. The movement ends quietly, as it began.

Example 23.5   Stravinsky, *Sonata for Two Pianos,* i.[28]

Exposition. Principal Theme.

(First statement, mm. 1–9 . . . .

. . . .) (Second statement, mm.

10–13 . . . .) (Dissolving

(Modulation to C)

---

[27] This procedure counterbalances the compression of the transition already noted in the analysis of the P.T. in the recapitulation.

[28] Copyright 1945 by Schott and Company, Ltd. Used by permission of Belwin-Mills Publishing Corp., Melville, N.Y. Condensed score shows chief thematic lines only.

transition, mm. 14–16 ....) Second Theme.
(First statement, mm.

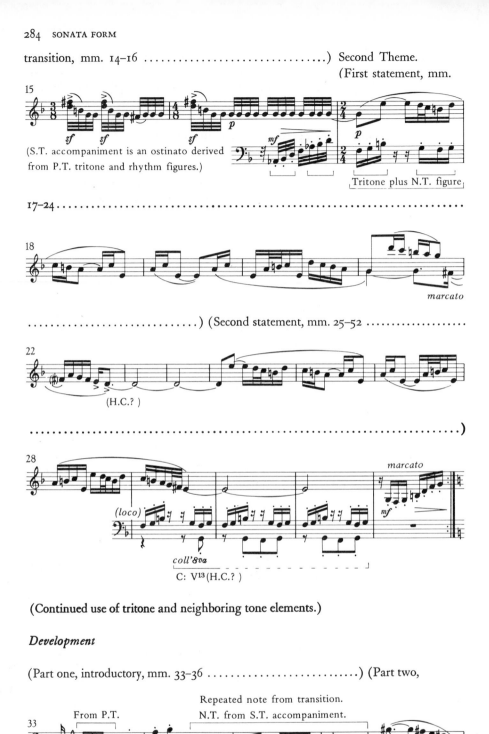

(S.T. accompaniment is an ostinato derived
from P.T. tritone and rhythm figures.)

Tritone plus N.T. figure

17–24 ....

marcato

.............................) (Second statement, mm. 25–52 ....

(H.C.?)

....)

marcato

(loco)

coll'8va

C: V¹³ (H.C.?)

(Continued use of tritone and neighboring tone elements.)

Development

(Part one, introductory, mm. 33–36 ....) (Part two,

Repeated note from transition.
From P.T.   N.T. from S.T. accompaniment.

e: *sf marc. sforzato*   *p subito*   E: *p dolce*

synthesis of P.T. and S.T. elements, mm. 37–40 . . . .)(Part three,

varied repetition of part two, mm. 41–46 . . . .

. . . .) (Part four, retransition, mm. 47–52. . . . .
(A♭ [dominant] pedal point in upper register . . . .

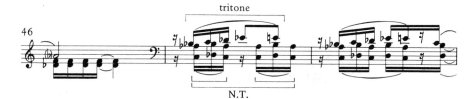

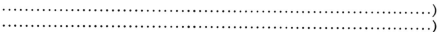

. . . .)
. . . .)

Recapitulation. Principal Theme.

(First statement, mm. 53–62 . . . .

. . . .)

(Second statement, mm. 63–69 . . . .

. . . .) Dissolving transition, mm. 70–72. . . . .

. . . .) Second theme.

(Two statements compressed, mm. 73–86 . . . . . .

. . . .) Coda, mm 87–94 . . . .

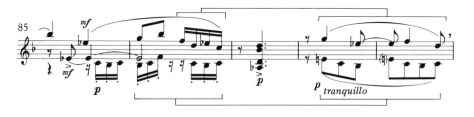

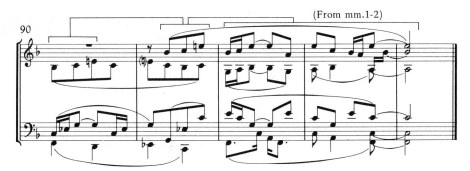

Tenor line: c minor triad.
Bass line derives from mm.88-89. $F:\frac{V^7}{I}$ (P.A.C.[?] with "unresolved appoggiatura chord")

Tenor: V outline. Bass: I outline.

The movement illustrated in Example 23.6 differs from the preceding examples of sonata form in having a double exposition rather than a repeated exposition. This particular procedure is characteristic of first-movement sonata forms in concertos of the classic era, and in late romantic concertos such as those by Brahms. A notable example of a single exposition in a concerto of the romantic era is found in the first movement of Mendelssohn's *Concerto in E minor for Violin and Orchestra*.

By placing this illustration at the end of the chapter instead of in its proper chronological sequence, the distinctive qualities of the double exposition are stressed and comparison with the rondo form and sonatina form concerto movements (discussed at the ends of Chapters 22 and 24) is facilitated.

The alternation of solo and tutti sections in all concerto movements is a significant element in the larger formal design. In Example 23.6 there are a number of radical differences between Exposition 1 and Exposition 2. The greater emphasis on the tonic in Exposition 1 is not unusual, nor is the drawing upon both exposition sections in the recapitulation. The absence of the solo instrument in Exposition 1 is characteristic of the form. The many redistributed elements and the omission of the opening and main portion of the principal theme are of particular interest in the recapitulation.

Example 23.6   Sonata form with double exposition in a concerto first movement. Mozart, *Concerto no. 4 in D major for Violin and Orchestra*, K. 218, i.

Exposition 1 (mm. 1–41). D major and tutti throughout.
Principal Theme Group and Transition (mm. 1–18).

Second Theme Group (mm. 18–41).

Second theme (mm. 18–26).

Closing group (mm. 26–34).

Codetta (mm. 34–41).

Exposition 2 (mm. 42–116), D major to A major.
Principal Theme and New Transition Group (mm. 42–86).
Principal theme (mm. 42–57), D major, solo.
New transition group (mm. 58–86), D major to A major, solo.
　Part one (mm. 58–65), D major to D:V (= A:I), solo.

　Part two (mm. 66–86), A major, solo.

Second Theme Group (mm. 87–116), A major throughout.
Second theme (mm. 87–94), solo.
Closing group (mm. 95–109), solo.
Codetta (mm. 109–16), tutti. (mm. 115–16 elide with part one of the development section.)

Development (mm. 117–45), B minor to D:V, solo throughout.
Part One (mm. 117–25), B minor.
Part Two (mm. 126–45), B minor to D:V.

Recapitulation (mm. 146–212), D major throughout.
Principal Theme and Transition Group (mm. 146–80).
(Principal theme omitted.)

Transition group. Part one (mm. 146–53), solo (derived from transition group part one of Exposition 2). Part two (mm. 153–56), tutti, then solo (fragment of the suppressed principal theme, from mm. 8–12 of Exposition I, here used as a connecting link between parts one and three). Part three (mm. 157–77), solo (derived from the transition group part two of Exposition 2). Part four (mm. 177–80), tutti (fragment derived from mm. 30–33, part of the closing group of the second theme group of Exposition I, used here as a connecting link to the second theme).

Second Theme Group (mm. 181–212).
Second theme (mm. 181–88), solo (as in Exposition 2).
Closing group (mm. 188–200), solo (as in Exposition 2).

Codetta (mm. 200–212), solo, then tutti (new codetta based on the dotted rhythm motive of the principal theme, perhaps in compensation for the suppression of the principal theme at the beginning of the recapitulation). Closes on I_6^4, the traditional chord of preparation for the cadenza that follows.

Cadenza, supposedly improvised unaccompanied solo, ending on an understood V which leads directly to the I in the coda that follows.[29]

Coda (mm. 213–20), D major, tutti. (Identical with the codetta of Exposition I.)

SUGGESTED EXERCISES

1. Compare Examples 23.1, 23.2, 23.3, 23.4, and 23.5. Discuss their similarities and their differences in terms of all pertinent features, for example, the relative proportions of the comparable sections, P.T.-S.T. relationships in key and length, the source and treatment of materials in the transitions, development procedures, irregular features, overall key scheme.

2. Analyze Mozart's *String Quartet in G major*, K. 387, iv, which unites fugal procedure and sonata form.

3. Compare another Beethoven sonata (or string quartet, or symphony) first movement with the one analyzed in Example 23.3.

4. Diagram a sonata form movement of a Mozart or Beethoven sonata, chamber work, symphony, or concerto; or an overture. Indicate the chief thematic and motivic materials. Accompany your diagram with pertinent commentary.

5. Write an essay comparing small three-part form and sonata form. Consider separately the similarities and the differences.

6. Compare first and second expositions and recapitulation in the first movement of any Mozart concerto. To what extent do first and second expositions differ? Is the recapitulation related more closely to the first or to the second exposition?

[29] The optional but very commonly found cadenza in the sonata form first movement of a concerto appears most frequently between recapitulation and coda sections, but sometimes between development and recapitulation sections.

7. Using the form of any of the compositions analyzed above as a general outline, write a movement using original materials.

8. Using the form and material of one of the Mozart or Haydn movements analyzed in this chapter, rewrite the development section completely, and change the key scheme and necessary transitions of the recapitulation. The exposition should be retained without alteration.

SONATINA

The term *sonatina* denotes a miniature sonata; one with simpler structure, smaller proportions, and fewer technical demands on the performer. As with the term *sonata,* a work of several movements is implied. Like the corresponding term sonata form, *sonatina form* denotes the structure or design of a single movement, not the from of the multimovement work as a whole. Thus, it is possible that the first movement of a sonatina may be in sonata form (see BS, 79, i), and the first movement of a sonata may be in sonatina form (as in Example 24.2).

In sonatina form there is an exposition and a recapitulation, but there is no central development section; this is the chief distinction between it and sonata form. Thus, it is clearly binary rather than ternary in design. In some respects it is similar to the binary forms discussed in Chapter 11. In fact, sonatina form and sonata form are related in much the same fashion as small two-part and small three-part song forms. The latter, of course, do not possess the P.T.-S.T. dichotomy that clearly distinguishes the former. The closing section (or codetta) of the exposition may dissolve into a retransition which leads directly to the recapitulation. See, for example, the Overture to *The Marriage of Figaro* by Mozart; and MS, K. 332, ii (Example 24.1).

Example 24.1   MS, K. 332, ii.

Part One (no formal repetition), (mm. 1–20). *Exposition,* B♭ major to F major.
Principal Theme (mm. 1–8), period, B♭ major to F minor. The final measures serve as transition, (f:I#3 = F:I).

Second Theme (mm. 9–19), extended period, F major. (For details, see Example 8.6.)

Extension and Retransition (mm. 19-20), F:I = B♭:V.

Part Two (mm. 21–40): *Recapitulation,* Bb major.
Principal Theme (mm. 21–28), Bb major to F minor, (f:I#³ = Bb:V).
Second Theme (mm. 29–39), Bb major.
Extension (now as Codetta), (mm. 39–40), Bb:I.

A brief retransitional episode may appear immediately after the double bar at the close of the exposition. If it is quite short and lacking in such procedures as sequence, imitation, and fragmentation, it cannot properly be regarded as a development section. Examples of this structural type are MS, K. 282, i; and K. 281, ii (see Examples 24.2 and 24.3 which follow).

Example 24.2   MS, K. 282, i.

Part One (repeated), (mm. 1–15): *Exposition,* Eb major to Bb major.
Principal Theme (mm. 1–8), two phrases (not a period), Eb major to Bb minor (bb:V). Phrase 1 culminates (m. 4) in an I.A.C. and elides at that point with phrase 2. The latter, which also serves as transition, closes on a slightly extended H.C. in the parallel minor mode of the (major) dominant key which follows in the next section.

Second Theme (mm. 9–15), chain phrase, Bb major.

Part Two (repeated), (mm. 16–33).
Episode (mm. 16–21). The tonally roving and harmonically unstable episode finally reaches Eb:V, where it dissolves in retransition. Materials are distantly related to both P.T. and S.T.

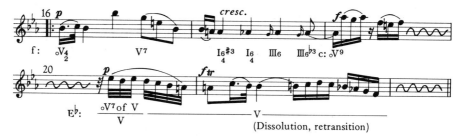

Recapitulation (mm. 22–33), E♭ major-minor-major.

Principal theme (mm. 22–26), E♭ major to E♭ minor. One phrase instead of two. The opening measures of the P.T. are omitted. The remainder, a considerably varied restatement, closes on e♭:V.

Second theme (mm. 27–33), E♭ major. Like the corresponding measures of the exposition, except for the key.

Coda (mm. 34–36). The coda is separated from the repeated recapitulation by an intervening double bar. Its presence may be viewed as compensation for the omitted measures of the P.T. at the beginning of the recapitulation, the material of which now makes a belated appearance.

Example 24.3   MS, K. 281, ii.

Part One (repeated), (mm. 1–46): *Exposition,* E♭ major to B♭ major.
Principal Theme Group (mm. 1–27), E♭ major to B♭:V.
Principal theme (mm. 1–15), E♭ major. (Period form questionable. See Example 7.11.)

Transition (mm. 16–27), E♭ major to B♭:V.

Second Theme Group (mm. 28–46), B♭ major.
Second theme (mm. 28–43), a chain phrase with three extensions, mm. 36–38, 39–40, and 41–42. There is a deceptive cadence at m. 35. Cadences are evaded at mm. 39 and 41. The P.A.C. in m. 43, which ends the phrase, elides with the four-measure codetta.

Codetta (mm. 43–46). The materials of this brief cadential extension derive from the accompaniment of the S.T. (sixteenth note triplets). The repeated chord at the close recalls the similar procedure at the end of the P.T. (mm. 14–15).

Part Two (repeated), (mm. 47–106).

Episode (mm. 47–58), largely over B♭ pedal point. S.T. materials are used. There is again a repeated chord (compare mm. 15–16 and 45–46). B♭:I becomes E♭:V.

Recapitulation (mm. 59–106), E♭ major.
Principal theme group (mm. 59–87), E♭ major–A♭ major–E♭ major.
  Principal theme (mm. 59–73), E♭ major to A♭:V. The theme is embellished by six-teenth note triplets designed to continue the previously established momentum, but otherwise is the same. The repeated chord at the end now serves as a modulatory agent (E♭:I = A♭:V).
  Transition (mm. 74–87), A♭ major to E♭:V. The key scheme is analogous to that of the exposition. Removal from the tonic key helps to refresh the central tonality for the subsequent section.
Second theme group (mm. 88–106), E♭ major.
  Second theme (mm. 88–103). The same as the corresponding portion of the exposition, except for a few small changes.
  Codetta (mm. 103–06). Corresponds to the codetta of the exposition.

In sonatina form, the recapitulation may be expanded by the inclusion of developmental procedures. Development and recapitulation are thus compressed into a single section which does double duty. Examples may be found in Beethoven's *String Quartet in D major,* 18/3, ii (see Example 24.4, which follows), BS, 49/2, i, and the finale of Brahms's *Symphony no. 1 in C minor.* In the latter example, the form is additionally expanded by a slow introduction and a coda. The designation sonatina form clearly refers to the lack of a separate and central development section here, and does not imply modest proportions and technical demands. The following analysis illustrates the procedure. It would be advantageous to have a copy of the score at hand.

Example 24.4   Beethoven, *String Quartet in D major,* 18/3, ii. Outline of chief thematic materials and formal divisions.

Part One (no formal repetition), (mm. 1–46): *Exposition,* B♭ major to F major.
Principal Theme Group (mm. 1–22), B♭ major to F:V.

Principal theme (mm. 1–12), period, B♭ major. In the antecedent phrase the melody is given to the second violin. In the consequent phrase the melody is transferred to the first violin. The phrases are in asymmetrical balance, 4 + 8.

Transition (mm. 13–22), B♭ major to F:V. The one cadence (F:H.C.) is in m. 17. The remaining measures constitute a postcadential extension and dissolution.

Bb:

Second Theme Group (mm. 23–46), F major (with a passing suggestion of F minor). At the close, F:I = Bb:V.

Second theme (mm. 23–37), chain phrase, F major–minor–major. A deceptive cadence in m. 30 is followed by phrase extension in the minor mode. The P.A.C. in major elides with the closing section.

F:

Closing section (mm. 37–46), essentially a prolongation of the cadence and F:I (note tonic pedal point). Materials derive from the P.T. A variation of the chief motive of the P.T. (see viola part) appears in simultaneous contrary motion with the unvaried motive (see Violin II part). The measures are grouped 4 + 4 + 2, of which the second four is a varied repetition of the first four. The section dissolves without cadence.

F:

Part Two (mm. 47–151): *Recapitulation* (which includes interpolated passages of developmental character), Bb major with occasional transient modulations in the developmental interpolations.

Principal Theme Group (mm. 47–96), Bb major.

Principal theme (mm. 47–58). Corresponds to mm. 1–12 of the exposition. The theme is in the first violin throughout.

Transition (mm. 59–95). This portion of the recapitulation begins like the corresponding section of the exposition, but at m. 63 it veers off on a modulatory and developmental tangent. After nine measures of mostly new material, the chief P.T. motive appears in contrary motion against itself, at first in the remote key of Db major

Db:

and then in m. 80 (at the P.A.C.) in F minor. Further development of the P.T. motive, with a new countermotive in thirty-second notes and considerable imitation of both figures, leads to a Phrygian-type H.C. in Bb minor (mm. 80–90).

The measures that follow constitute a return from the tangential interpolation. Thus, mm. 90–95 correspond in material and function to mm. 17–22 in the exposition. There is in both an extended dominant pedal point assisting the transition to the next following section.

Second Theme Group (mm. 96–151), B♭ major.

Second theme (mm. 96–110). Corresponds to mm. 23–27 of the exposition. An expected cadence on the first beat of m. 110 is weakened by elision with the next section and absence of the chord root in the bass.

Closing section (mm. 110–39). The opening ten measures (mm. 110–23) are much the same as the corresponding portion of the exposition, but there is an interpolation of new material (chords in sixteenth note sextuplets with marked accents on the beat) which extends the ten to fourteen measures (4 + 6 + 4). The measures which follow (124–34) are a varied repetition of the preceding group. A short third group (mm. 135–39) further develops the P.T. in B♭ minor and closes on a P.A.C.

Codetta (mm. 139–51). There is no corresponding section in the exposition. Because of its brevity (it is largely an expansion of the cadence in m. 139) it seems best to consider the section as part of the recapitulation, rather than as a coda following the recapitulation. The motive from m. 1 is treated further in imitation and sequence.

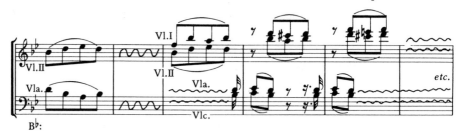

SONATA-RONDO

Composers frequently combine two or more kinds of musical form. One of the more familiar of these combinations is sonata-rondo. Here the large ternary design of sonata form is blended with the principle of multiple departure and return that is an earmark of rondo form.

Movements in which developmental interpolations expanded otherwise regular rondo forms were encountered in Chapter 22. Since a development section is one of the distinctive features of sonata form, such movements are in fact a mixture of sonata and rondo forms. It is useful to distinguish between that procedure, in which development is added to the design as a decoration, and the one in which the development section is essential and necessary to the formal balance. The former creates asymmetry; the latter, symmetry. In the present discussion, use of the term sonata-rondo will be limited to the second of these types.

The first two illustrations show how *ABABA* may be combined with sonata form. The scheme in BS, 31/2, iii is:

$$\left|\left|: A^1\text{--}B^1 :\right|\right| \; Devt. \; \text{--}A^2\text{--}B^2\text{--}A^3 \; \left|\left|.^1\right.\right.$$
$$\text{of } A$$

The three *A* sections and B^2 are in D minor, B^1 is in A minor, and the development section is tonally unstable. A^1–B^1 correspond to P.T.-S.T. in a sonata form exposition, a resemblance which is enhanced by the formal repetition. A^2–B^2 correspond to the recapitulation, and A^3 serves as coda.

The mixture is more complex in MS, K. 576, iii. Considering the symbol D^a as indication of a development section based on *A*, the form may be represented as follows:[2]

	A^1	D^{a1}	B^1	A^2	D^{a2}	D^{a3}	B^2	A^3
or	A^1	....	B^1	A^2	....		B^2	A^3
or	P.S.	S.S.	C.S.				C.S.	P.S.
							(reverse order)	
i.e.:	(Exposition)			(Development)			(Recapitulation)	
keys:	D	A	A	D	F	D	D	D

A second *section* (S.S.) based on the principal section (P.S.), instead of a new, contrasting second *theme* is rather unusual for Mozart. Thus, S.S. shares material with P.S. but tonality with C.S., and in this sense is a large formal elision.

A second contrasting section (*C*) may be a development of *A* or *B* materials, or both, rather than a new and independent theme. In an *ABACA*-type rondo, for example, the design may be altered to *A-B-A*-Development-*A* (Example 24.5).[3] In *ABACABA* a centrally located development (*C*) would contribute to a sense of large ternary design, thus: *ABA*-Development-*ABA* (Example 24.6).

Example 24.5   MS, K. 545, iii. Diagram showing chief thematic materials and formal divisions.

A^1 (mm. 1–8).

Period with parallel construction, C major (repeated).

---

[1] See Example 22.7.

[2] D^{a2} is a second development; D^{a3} is closely related to D^{a1}.

[3] The same music, with a few small changes and in a different key, forms the second movement of MS, K. 547a.

B (mm. 9–20).

A group of three phrases, G major. Phrase 1 contains new material. Phrase 2 is related to *A*. Phrase 3 is a retransition over an extended dominant (G:I = C:V).

A² (mm. 21–28). Restatement of *A¹* in the original key, but without repetition.

C (Development section) (mm. 29–52).

Imitative treatment of *A*-derived material. The prevailing key is A minor. Twenty-four measures are grouped in a diminishing arithmetic progression, 12 + 8 + 4. (Mm. 29–32 are illustrated below.) The middle group of 8 elides with the final group of 4, a modulating retransition.

A³ (mm. 53–60). Restatement of *A¹* in the original key, without repetition.

Coda (mm. 61–73). Thirteen measures (8 + 6 with one measure elision). The opening eight is 4 + ·/. ; the six consists of a repeated 2, plus a two-measure extension. Materials derive from the cadential portion of *A*.

Example 24.6 Beethoven, *String Quartet in F major,* 18/1, iv. Diagram showing chief thematic materials and formal divisions.

A¹ or *Principal Theme Group* (mm. 1–43).

A¹ has two subdivisions. Part one (mm. 1–18) is a statement in the tonic key (F major) closing with a P.A.C. Part two, which is transitional, leads to the "wrong" key of G major which, in retrospect, turns out to be C:V. Measures 1–4 are cited.

B^1 (Section 1) or *Second Theme Group* (mm. 43–79).

B^1, after eight measures on the "wrong" tonal foot (G major), modulates to the "correct" key of C major (the dominant of F). At the close there is an unexpected shift to C minor. The section is composed of two large parts, mm. 43–58 and 59–78, which are subdivided 8 + 8 (= 16) and 12 + 8 (= 20) respectively. The main material and its initial treatment is indicated.

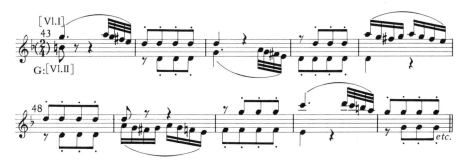

B^1 (Section 2) or *Closing Section* or *Retransition* (mm. 79–90). Twelve measures which prepare for the return of *A* by means of the quasi-pedal point on C (F:V). New material, a figure composed of a dotted quarter and an eighth note, is combined with hints of the returning *A* motive (triplet sixteenths). The grouping is 4 + 4 + 4, evenly divided between C minor, C major and F:V, a notable illustration of gradual change of mood and function.

This marks the end of the exposition (in sonata form). The development follows. However, the latter may be viewed as beginning at m. 102, the beginning of the *C* section (in rondo form).

A^2 or *Development Section* (introductory portion) (mm. 91–102). A restatement of the opening twelve measures of the movement, original key, leads directly to the main body of the development which follows.

C or *Development Section* (main portion). This very large section (nearly half again as long as the entire exposition) consists of six well-defined subdivisions, as follows:

mm. 102–15. Very close, stretto-like imitation of material from *A* (P.T.), chiefly the motive from mm. 1–2.

mm. 116–33. Polyphonic treatment of material from both *A* (P.T.) and *B* (S.T.).
mm. 133–59. Relatively homophonic working out of material from the closing section (retransition).

mm. 159–85. Similar to mm. 116–33. Quasi-fugal development of *A* and *B* materials.

mm. 185–219. Similar to mm. 133–59. Material derived from closing section (retransition).

mm. 219–34. Similar to mm. 102–15, but less imitative. Head of P.T. helps prepare for its return. Emphasis on F:V.

The section is quite symmetrical in construction, as the brackets indicate. Chief keys of the six subdivisions are: d; d–g–c–f; Db–C; c–f–Db–C; D–Eb; C (= F:V). Ascending half-step D–Eb in part five is the inverted counterpart of descending half-step Db–C in thematically corresponding part three.

A^3 or *Principal Theme Group* (beginning of the recapitulation in sonata form) (mm. 235–78). Corresponds to A^1 in key (F), length, and substance. The final (transition) portion, is tonally adjusted to effect a modulation to C major (F:V). The use of dominant instead of "normal" tonic is analogous to the use of supertonic (V of V) instead of the dominant in the corresponding portion of the exposition.

B^2 (Section 1) or *Second Theme Group* (mm. 279–315). Corresponds to B^1, section 1, except for the key, which begins as C but shortly changes to the expected tonic (F).

B^2 (Section 2) or *Closing Section* or *Transition* (mm. 315–26). Restatement of corresponding section (mm. 79–90). As a prolonged C became F:V in the previous statement, so the F, which should remain tonic at this point, now changes to B♭:V. This marks the end of the recapitulation in sonata form.

A^4 or *Coda* (mm. 327–81). After a few measures in the subdominant key (B♭) the tonic returns and remains to the end. The several subdivisions resemble the development section in their use of imitation and quasi-fugue. There are three groups: mm. 327–45 (which resembles mm. 91–108), mm. 346–65 (which combines *A* and closing section materials), and mm. 365–81 (a cadential extension based on the head of *A*).

SONATINA-RONDO IN A CONCERTO LAST MOVEMENT

Example 24.7 is offered more as a further example of mixed types than as a new formal category. The materials of the movement, the key scheme, and the proportions strongly indicate sonatina form in which developmental procedures expand the recapitulation section. The developmental techniques suggest sonata form. The use of principal theme materials in the extended coda that follows the cadenza may suggest to some the final return of *A* in a rondo form; careful consideration, however, makes it evident that the very brief suggestion of *A* cannot realistically be considered a restatement. It should be observed further that unlike the sonata form first movement of a concerto—in which there is a double exposition—there is only a single exposition.

Example 24.7 Sonatina-rondo in a concerto last movement. Mozart, *Concerto in D minor for Piano and Orchestra,* K. 466, iii.

Part One: *Exposition* (mm. 1–167).
Principal Theme Group (mm. 1–92), D minor to F:V.
Principal theme (mm. 1–63), D minor, ends on d: P.A.C.

Part one (mm. 1–31), solo statement (mm. 1–14);

tutti statement (mm. 15–31).

Part two (mm. 31–63), tutti throughout; expansion of d:V–I (mm. 31–52), dissolving in a deceptive cadence; cadential extension (mm. 52–63), to strong P.A.C.

Transition theme (mm. 64–92), d:I to F:V, solo.

Second Theme Group (mm. 93–139), F minor to F major, solo throughout.

Closing Theme Group (mm. 140–67), F major, dissolving to d:V.
Closing theme (mm. 140–55), F major, tutti, then solo.

Cadential extension, followed by retransition (mm. 155–67), F:I to d:V, solo.

Part Two: *Recapitulation* (mm. 168–346).
Principal Theme Group (mm. 168–271), D minor, A minor, G minor, to d:V.
Principal theme (mm. 168–96), solo and tutti statements of the P.T. corresponding to those in the exposition, mm. 1–31.

Development of transition theme (mm. 197–230), A minor to g:V; unaccompanied solo. This is followed by a polyphonic development of the head of the principal theme in solo piano and woodwinds.

A second development of the transition theme (mm. 231–71), G minor to d:V, this time somewhat more extended in treatment; solo piano and woodwinds without strings.

Second Theme Group (mm. 272–302), D minor and solo throughout.
Closing Theme Group (mm. 303–38), D minor and solo throughout. The carefully prepared cadence dissolves with evasion to d:VI.

Codetta (mm. 338–46), tutti. This preparation for the cadenza has no counterpart at the end of the exposition. The materials derive from the cadential extension (mm. 52–63) of the principal theme group of the exposition.
Cadenza (improvised solo).

Coda (mm. 347–429).

Part One (mm. 347–54), d:I to $_0V^9$ of D:V, a short-lived reminiscence of the P.T., which is put aside in favor of the subsequently developed closing theme materials. These measures serve as a connecting link between the (unwritten) cadenza and the coda proper, which is in D major from mm. 355 to the end.

Part Two (mm. 355–71), based on the closing theme; tutti, then solo.

Part Three (mm. 371–95), twenty-four measures (12 + ·/.), somewhat related to mm. 31–52 of the principal theme group in the exposition; tutti-solo-tutti-solo.

Part Four (mm. 396–429), like part two above, based on the closing theme. Melodic material is in the orchestra, while the piano plays accompanying broken chords and scale passages.

SUGGESTED EXERCISES

1. Diagram one or two of the movements discussed in this chapter. Use the diagram procedure employed in Example 21.5. Show the alternative interpretations.

2. Analyze and diagram the overture to Mozart's *The Marriage of Figaro*. Identify the transitions and extensions as well as the larger structural features.

3. Write a short essay on the use of developmental procedures in the recapitulation section of Brahms's *Symphony no. 1 in C minor*, iv.

4. Prepare a detailed analysis of MS, K. 576, iii. Show clearly the alternative interpretations.

5. Diagram the finale of the *Concerto no. 5 in E♭ major for Piano and Orchestra* by Beethoven. Comment briefly on significant regular and irregular features.

6. Analyze the last movement of the *Sonata no. 3 in D minor for Violin and Piano* by Brahms. Is it in sonata, rondo, rondo with interpolated development section, or sonata-rondo form? Provide appropriate reasons to support your conclusions.

7. Analyze BS, 49/2, i, and 31/2, iii. Discuss separately, then compare.

8. Identify the chief structural features of the first movement of Ravel's *Sonatine* for piano.

9. Draw diagrams showing three or four hypothetical sonatina and sonata-rondo forms. Show all essential elements. Discuss any unusual or irregular features and their implications.

10. Using one of the movements analyzed in this chapter as a model, or (if approved by the instructor) one of the hypothetical structures submitted in connection with Exercise 9 above, compose an original work in a style of your own choice.

Vocal Forms

The forms that appear in vocal and instrumental music tend to be different, but they are not mutually exclusive. A more important distinction is the fact that vocal and instrumental compositions must be approached from different points of view. A composition for one or more voices is usually a textual setting. Thus the relationship between text and music is an important factor to be considered in examining a work's form and style. Analysis of vocal music should attempt to deal with the possible interrelationships of three components: the text, the vocal line(s), and the accompaniment.

The composer of instrumental music has had to develop a large repertory of forms because such music does not have the supporting structure and extramusical associations which a text can provide. The composer of vocal music may use the form and the imagery suggested by a text as the basis for his choice of musical structure and style. The design of a musical setting that is compatible with the words may be influenced by such factors as metrical elements, rhyme scheme, stanza structure, pictorial allusions, and dramatic contrasts.

A text that incorporates dialogue, such as that by Goethe in Schubert's *Der Erlkönig* ("The Erlking"), suggested to the composer the need for changes of key, mode, vocal tessitura, and accompaniment style, to project the changes of mood and the contrasting personalities engaged in the discourse (see Example 25.12). The different ways in which music and words unfold sometimes make it necessary for the text to be repeated while the music continues. The variety of ways in which words and music may interact is enormous and beyond the scope of the limited study in this chapter. The examples which follow distinguish between style and form using just a few representative works for solo voice with piano or orchestral accompaniment.

RECITATIVE

Recitative (*recitativo* in Italian) is a style in which a prose text is set to music in a manner that approximates the tempo and inflections of speech. Words assume greater importance than the music, which is usually an association of loosely related phrase members. The harmonic and rhythmic balances characteristic of a song or an aria are notably lacking in recitative.

There are three types: (a) *recitativo secco* (dry recitative), in which the accompaniment is quite spare, little more than a series of occasional and widely separated chords, normally written for a keyboard instrument (in the baroque era, keyboard and low register stringed instrument) without the orchestra; (b) *recitativo accompagnato* or *stromentato* (accompanied or instrumented recitative), where an accompaniment of changing or sustained chords is played by the orchestra; and (c) *arioso* (song-like recitative), a mixture of recitative and aria elements in which the vocal style is like that of recitative while the accompaniment is rather active and sustained and often motivically developmental.

The three styles are demonstrated in Examples 25.1, 25.2, and 25.3. Example 25.4 is a hypothetical illustration in which the vocal arioso of Example 25.3 is changed to *recitativo secco* (25.4a) and *accompagnato* (25.4b).

Example 25.1   Recitativo secco. From *The Passion According to St. Matthew* by Bach.

Example 25.2   Recitativo accompagnato. From *The Passion According to St. Matthew* by Bach.

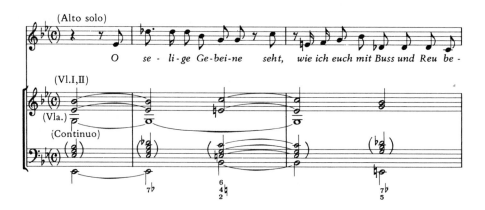

Example 25.3   Arioso, "Ach Golgatha." From *The Passion According to St. Matthew* by Bach.

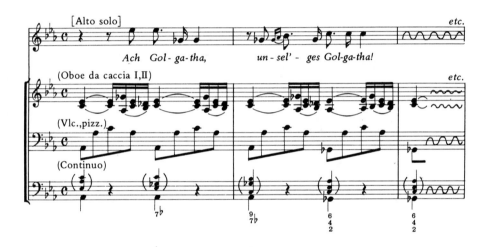

Example 25.4 The vocal line of "Ach Golgatha" treated as recitativo secco, and as recitativo accompagnato.

(*a*) As recitativo secco.

(*b*) As recitativo accompagnato.

ARIAS AND ART SONGS

In contrast to recitatives, which are rather amorphous, arias and art songs are usually in some definable form. The following illustrations show a few of the more commonly found types.

Examples 25.5 and 25.6 are in binary form, but the treatment of the form is rather different in each. In the Mozart aria (Example 25.5) there is *very little* contrast between the two sections. The measures immediately preceding the cadences closely correspond. The two parts begin differently, and have different key directions: part one modulates from the tonic to the dominant key, part two is unstable at first but closes in the tonic key.

In the song by Schubert (Example 25.6) there is *very great* contrast between the two parts. There is little to hold them together, except for the key, the meter, and the continuity provided by the text. The dualism of mood and style may have been intended to symbolize the irreconcilable dualism of life and death, with death having the last word. The balancing introduction and coda help to provide a containing frame.

Example 25.5   Sarastro's aria, "O Isis and Osiris," from Act 2 of Mozart's opera *The Magic Flute;* the vocal line.

Example 25.6   Schubert, *Der Tod und das Mädchen* ("Death and the Maiden").

The aria "Agnus Dei" in Bach's *Mass in B minor* is as remarkable for its capacity to arouse the most profound emotions as it is for its musical design. As in Examples 25.5 and 25.6, the two parts of a binary form are separated by a brief interlude, and the main body is surrounded by an introduction and a coda. There is a suggestion of rounded binary form in the Bach illustration because of the parallelism of phrases 2–3 of part 2 (mm. 31–37) with phrases 1–2 of part 1 (mm. 9–17). Introduction, interlude, and coda are related in an interesting and unusual manner: the introduction consists of two phrases, of which the first (transposed to the dominant) is used as the interlude, while the second (in the tonic key) is used as the coda.

Example 25.7   Bach, "Agnus Dei," aria from the *Mass in B minor;* the continuo part is omitted.

In bar form, another adaptation of binary design, there are three sections; the first two (A^1A^2) are very closely related (the second being an exact or slightly modified repetition of the first), the third (B) is different in substance but related in mood and style. It is the chief design of the songs of the German *Minnesinger* and *Meistersinger,* and it is customary to use the German words *Stollen* for the two stanzas (A^1A^2) and *Abgesang* for the aftersong (B). Wagner provides a modern model in Act 3 of his opera *Die Meistersinger,* where Hans Sachs instructs Walther in the art of song composition.

Example 25.8   Bar form aria. From Wagner, *Die Meistersinger von Nürnberg*, Act 3, scene 2; vocal line (text omitted).

Ternary form is illustrated in Examples 25.9 and 25.10. The first of these examples is a *da capo* aria, a form which appears in many operas, oratorios, and cantatas of the baroque and early classic eras. Here, part 3 of a three-part design is not written out, but is a repetition of part 1. The procedure is specified by the indication "da capo" which is placed at the end of part 2. The outer parts of this *ABA* form begin and end in the tonic key, and may include a passing modulation to a closely related key. The *B* part usually emphasizes the dominant key, and it too may include a passing modulation. Each part closes with a strong authentic cadence. There are no connecting transition passages between the parts. In the Bach aria illustrated, the *A* parts modulate to the comparatively rare subdominant key, and return to the tonic. The key scheme of the aria as a whole is f♯: i–iv–i, i–♭VII–v, i–iv–i. ♭VII or f♯ is E, which is the relative major of c♯, the minor dominant of f♯.

The second example, although *ABA*, is not a da capo form. A^2 is set to different text than A^1, and there are different final cadences in the two *A* parts. *B* lacks a strong terminal cadence, and dissolves into an orchestral retransition. The symmetrical four-measure phrase structure—which is broken only by the orchestral extensions, the introduction, and the coda—and the repetitions within *A* and *B* provide a considerable degree of thematic unity and formal balance.

Example 25.9   Da capo aria. Bach, "Buss und Reu," from *The Passion According to St. Matthew.*

Example 25.10   Prokofiev, "The Field of the Dead," aria from the cantata *Alexander Nevsky*[1] for chorus and orchestra.

[1] *Alexander Nevsky*, Op. 78 by Sergei Prokofieff, © Copyright 1945, 1949, 1966 by MCA Music, A Division of MCA, Inc., 445 Park Avenue, New York, N.Y. 10022. All rights reserved. Used by permission.

For an additional example of ternary design, see Example 13.9 (Wolf, *Das verlassene Mägdlein*). In this song, the middle section of an essentially *ABA* design has been expanded so that the overall form is more accurately rendered *ABCA*. Only the *A* sections have cadences; *B* and *C* dissolve into the ensuing piano interludes. *A¹* closes with a half cadence. *A²* ends on a perfect authentic cadence in the piano part, but the lack of voice participation (perhaps to suggest the unrequited love and the continuing, unending grief of the forsaken maiden) helps to weaken the cadence which elides with the coda.

Strophic form is a pattern in which two or more stanzas of metrical poetry are set to exact repetitions of the music. Thus, a four-stanza poem (*ABCD*) may be set to four statements of a single musical design (*AAAA*). This form appears frequently in hymns, anthems, solo songs, and operatic arias. It is particularly well suited for texts that deal with simple rather than complex or powerful emotions, and static rather than developing moods and situations. It also may be used as a means of securing unity in a ballad or long narrative poem. In Example 25.11, Marguerite's aria "The King of Thule," from Berlioz's dramatic legend, *The Damnation of Faust,* there are three strophes with intervening interludes. An introduction in the orchestra and a coda in which solo voice and orchestra exchange material serve as an enclosing frame. Each of the three identical musical strophes consists of four phrases; the first two have a close relationship which suggests period form. The key scheme within the strophe (F–B♭–A♭–F) is rather unconventional, but its very unorthodoxy helps to make the strophic repetitions both desirable and necessary. The use of melodic fragmentation in the coda is probably a figurative allusion to the king's demise, and recalls the similar procedure at the end of the slow movement (in the style of a funeral march) in Beethoven's *Symphony no. 3 in E♭ major.*

Example 25.11   Berlioz, Marguerite's aria, "The King of Thule," from *The Damnation of Faust.*

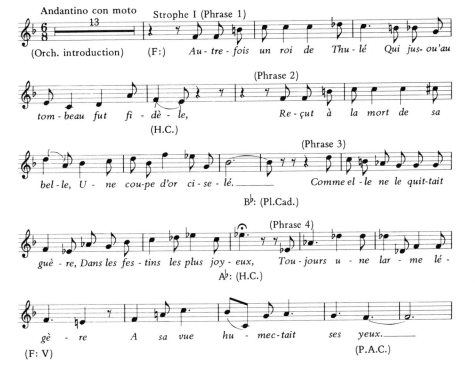

Example 25.12 is an illustration of *through-composed form*. As the term indicates, the structure is open and continuously unfolding without section repetitions. In this type, formal unity may be provided by one or more frequently recurring motives in the vocal line, in the accompaniment, or both. Occasional instances of parallelism of style or material may serve as a substitute for the formal repetitions which are found in closed forms such as *ABA* and the several types of rondo.

Through-composed form is especially appropriate for a ballad or a narrative poem with continuously advancing dramatic action; the changing tensions require corresponding changes in the musical design.

Schubert's first published work, *Der Erlkönig* ("The Erlking"), set to a text by Goethe, and one of his greatest songs, is an excellent demonstration of the application of these techniques.

Example 25.12   Schubert, *Der Erlkönig* ("The Erlking").[2]

[2] The complete song is in Charles Burkhart, *Anthology for Musical Analysis*, 2d ed. (New York: Holt, Rinehart and Winston, 1972). The familiar English title is meaningless; there is no such thing as an "erl." The English for *Erle* is "alder." The German name is also an error based on a mistranslation of the old Danish *Ellerkong* (in modern Danish, *Elverkong*), which should have been translated in German as *Elfenkönig* and into English as "King of the Elves."

war - ten schön, mei - ne Töch-ter füh-ren den nächt-lich-en Reih'n und

wie - gen und tan - zen und sin - gen dich ein sie wie-gen und tan - zen und

[Father - son dialogue 3]

sin - gen dich ein." "Mein Va - ter, mein Va - ter, und

siehst du nicht dort Erl - kö-nigs, Töch-ter am düs - tern Ort?"

"Mein Sohn, mein Sohn, ich seh' es ge - nau, es

[Interlude 2]

schei - nen die al - ten Wei - den so grau." (f)

[Erlking claims his victim]

"Ich lie - be dich, mich

reizt dei - ne schö - ne Ge - stalt; und bist du nicht wil - lig, so

brauch' ich Ge - walt." "Mein Va - ter, mein Va - ter, jetzt fasst er mich

[Postlude; "Narrator"]

an! Erl - kö - nig hat mir ein Leids ge - than!"

Dem Va - ter grau - set's er rei - tet ge - schwind, er

hält in den Ar - men das äch - zen - de Kind.

Er - reicht   den   Hof   mit   Müh'   und   Noth:

Recit.
(pp)

in sei-nen Ar - men das Kind   war todt!

f

Prelude		Interlude 1	Father-son dialogue 1		
Piano Introduction	"Narrator"		"Father"	"Son"	"Father"
mm. 1–15 g:	mm. 16–32 (Ext.)	mm. 33–36	mm. 37–41 g: to c: (=I–IV) (Father queries son)	mm. 42–51 c: to F: (F=Bb :V) (Son replies)	mm. 52–57 F: to Bb: (Father reassures son)
			(Ascending fourths, G–C–F–Bb)		
(Suggestion of the howling wind and clatter of the horse's hoofs)	(Description of father and son riding home through the night)				

	Father-son dialogue 2			
"Erlking"	"Son"		"Father"	"Erlking"
mm. 58–72 Bb:	mm. 73–80 Bb to b♮: (B=C:VII)		mm. 81–86 b: to G: (G=C:V)	mm. 87–97 C:
	(Ascending half steps, Bb–B–C)			
(Erlking portrays the joys of another world)	(Son queries father)		(Father again tries to reassure son)	(Erlking again entices the boy)

Father-son dialogue 3...................̤.............		Interlude 2
"Son"	"Father"	
mm. 98–105 C:VI to c♯:	mm. 106–12 c♯: to d:	mm. 113–16 d: (Ext.)
(Ascending half steps, C–C♯–D, compare dialogues 2 and 3)		(Compare with interlude I)
(Son again cries out to father)	(Father continues attempts to calm the boy)	

Erlking claims his victim		*Postlude*
"Erlking"	"Son"	"Narrator"
mm. 117–23	mm. 124–32	mm. 133–48
E♭: to d:	d: VI^{b3} to g:	g:
(=d: ♭II–V–I)	(d: = g: V^{b3})	(I–IV–♭II–V–I)
(Continuation of half-step motion, E♭–D)	(Ascending fourth, D–G)	
(Erlking threatens to use force)	(Son shrieks as Erlking seizes him)	(Father arrives home, his son—dead)

SUGGESTED EXERCISES

1. Compare Examples 25.5 and 25.6. Examine the full score of each work. Your discussion should include reference to elements other than those already mentioned in the text, and to the illustrations in the chapters on binary form.

2. Discuss the form of Example 25.7 with reference to motives, polyphonic devices, phrase structure, key relationships, cadences, and so forth. Identify the distinguishing differences among the similar sections, and the common elements found in the contrasting sections.

3. Compare the examples of ternary design illustrated in this chapter. Relate them to the examples cited in the chapters on ternary form.

4. Analyze three songs by Schubert and three by Wolf. Identify the form of each. Relate the musical forms to those of the texts. Compare the songs that have common characteristics.

5. Rewrite Example 25.1, first as recitativo accompagnato, then as arioso. As a preliminary step, study again Examples 25.2, 25.3, and 25.4.

6. Write a song in through-composed form for voice and piano using the text of Example 25.11.

7. Set the Goethe text in Example 25.12 as a strophic song with eight four-line stanzas. A brief introduction may serve also for the interludes and for the coda. Version 1: as a solo song with accompaniment of piano or small instrumental ensemble. Version 2: for SATB chorus, with or without accompaniment.

Works Comprising Several Movements

26

The musical elements and their combinational possibilities in one-movement works and single movements of larger compositions have been examined. Forms containing two, three, four, or more movements will now be reviewed, and the much-debated question of the larger unity displayed by such works will be considered.

A composition of several movements is like a family in many ways. As each member of a family has dissimilar functions and mutual responsibilities, so first, middle, and last movements of a musical composition play different roles in its structure. The choral movement of Beethoven's *Symphony no. 9 in D minor* is imaginable only as finale. A four-movement sonata which began with a minuet and trio and had the "heavy-weight" sonata form as its third instead of its first movement would be highly irregular. (It may be noted that in the nineteenth century there is a tendency to place the "center of gravity" in the last movement rather than in the first movement favored during the classic era.) Musical movements are analogous to the acts of a play, although they display less continuity of theme and line; musical movements are more independent, being more complete in expression and more self-contained in design.

Evidence of mutual dependency in a group of associated musical movements may vary from the flimsy to the incontrovertible. Some works may appear to be unified by tonality alone; others have a single curve and thematic basis. A random group of Brahms intermezzi or Chopin mazurkas, although they are in the same key, display less unity than the movements of a Beethoven sonata, even if one or more movements of the sonata are not in the prevailing key. In nearly any early Mozart or Haydn string quartet or symphony, another movement of the same type by the same composer could easily be substituted without noticeable damage to the work as a whole. What then distinguishes a group of movements that is *necessarily* bound together (like the members of a family or the acts of a play) from one in which the components are just loosely associated?

Motivic consistency is one means of achieving unity among movements, as it is between sections of a single movement. The well-known motive that opens Beethoven's *Symphony no. 5 in C minor* (see Example 2.1) pervades the entire work. It is heard in the first movement as the chief building block of the principal theme; in the accompaniment to the second theme; again in the third movement (see the repeated notes in the French horn near the opening); and only slightly disguised in the second theme of the second and fourth movements. Additional unity is provided by the introduction of a portion of the third movement in the course of the fourth. Third and fourth movements are further linked by a connecting transition.

Cyclic form, the name given to the practice of using the same material in two or more movements, was used with particular frequency by César Franck and his followers, including Debussy whose early *String Quartet in G minor* provides a good illustration. The *idée fixe,* a melodic idea recurring intermittently in several movements, usually associated with the music of Berlioz (see his *Fantastic Symphony, Harold in Italy,* and other works), often has extramusical associations of one kind or another. In the latter quality, the *idée fixe* is perhaps parent of the Wagnerian *leitmotiv* (leading motive). Not just one idea, but a whole battery of such recurring ideas is the rule in Wagner. The prime example of leading motives as a powerful unifying force can be seen in the four operas of the Nibelung cycle.

Rudolf Reti has made a noteworthy study of the interrelationships between contrasting themes of a single movement and between parallel themes of different movements of a given work.[1] He claims that in the music of "great" composers there are very subtle but highly significant relationships between corresponding themes in every movement, and that apparently different themes are in fact offspring of a single germinal idea. Principal and second themes, according to Reti, are "in reality ... contrasting on the surface but identical in substance."[2]

In his view, it is not only the thematic unity of the various "transformations" (he distinguishes these from simple "variations") which is of compelling significance, but also the fact of "thematic creation, in which variegated ideas and expressions converge into one architectural entity."[3] For Reti the larger significance transcends music itself.

> What Beethoven and all great composers have given us is more than the substance of their works, magnificent as it may be: it is the dynamism and mystery of the creative process through which music becomes an expression of life itself. . . . Music is created from sound as life is created from matter. In the organic sphere one cell engenders the other in its own image, yet each of the innumerable cells is different from all the others. By a magic interplay between these identical yet different cells, the higher forms of life come into existence.[4]

Whatever the merit of Reti's conclusions, his serious desire to come to grips with one of the stickier questions of musical form must be respected. The general methodology is quite sound if followed without excessive dogmatism. The fact that analysts using the same procedure may arrive at different conclusions does not impair the value of the technique. This approach to analysis deserves the careful consideration of every serious musician.

TWO-MOVEMENT WORKS

Contrasting coupled dance movements are found at least as early as the sixteenth century. Willi Apel observes that a large variety of dances occurs in the lute, keyboard, and

---

[1] Rudolf Reti, *The Thematic Process in Music* (New York: Macmillan, 1951) p. 348.

[2] Reti, *Thematic Process,* pp. 4–5.

[3] Reti, *Thematic Process,* p. 353.

[4] Reti, *Thematic Process,* p. 359.

ensemble music of the sixteenth century, usually in the paired arrangement of a slow-moving main dance followed by a lively jumping dance.[5]

Although not strictly a form, recitativo-aria in opera and oratorio constitute a similar pair of contrasting, semi-independent elements. Baroque French overture style—a slow first part with stately dotted rhythms, followed by a fast second part in fugal style, generally followed by a coda in broadened tempo—is perhaps an outgrowth of the coupled dance forms.

A keyboard fugue in the baroque era often is preceded by a prelude, fantasia, toccata, or similar loosely constructed movement. Such pairing of a quasi-extemporary first movement with a highly organized second movement is thoroughly consistent with baroque taste, which favored striking contrasts and clearly distinguishable effects.

A particularly interesting example of coupled movements in the baroque era is the celebrated organ *Passacaglia and Fugue in C minor* by Bach,[6] in which the *first half* of the passacaglia theme, far from being exhausted by its many repetitions, is used again as the principal subject of the immediately following double fugue. The accompanying second fugue subject (or countersubject) is based on a motive clearly derived from the *second half* of the passacaglia theme.

Ralph Kirkpatrick, in his eminent study of the music of Domenico Scarlatti,[7] observes that this composer's sonatas are in the large majority of instances

> conceived in pairs. One may be in minor and the other in major, but both members of a pair always have the same tonic.... Almost without exception, the pairwise arrangement of the Scarlatti sonatas has been overlooked by modern editors. [This has resulted in] the utter disruption in all modern editions of any chronological order, and hence of stylistic coherence.... The real meaning of many a Scarlatti sonata becomes much clearer once it is reassociated with its mate.
>
> The relationship between the sonatas of a pair is either one of contrast or of complement. The sonatas that bear a complementary relationship to each other may share a certain overall unity of style or of instrumental character or they may be composed in the same harmonic color ....
>
> In the contrasting pairs, a slow movement may be followed by a fast [one] ... a simple movement, generally slow, may serve as an introduction to a more elaborate [one] ... or an elaborate and concentrated movement may be followed by a simpler and lighter movement, for example a Minuet, which serves as a kind of *Nachtanz* [after-dance] ....[8]

Although frequent in pre-classical and baroque music, two-movement works in the classic era are relatively rare.[9] Schubert's *Symphony in B minor* (the "Unfin-

[5] *Harvard Dictionary of Music*, edited by Willi Apel, 3rd ed. (Cambridge: Harvard Univ. Press, 1970) p. 223.

[6] See Example 16.6.

[7] Although a contemporary of J. S. Bach (1685–1750), Scarlatti (1685–1757) is both post-baroque and pre-classical. He is "situated on the arbitrary border line between the two eras." (William S. Newman, *The Sonata in the Classic Era*, [Chapel Hill: Univ. of North Carolina Press, 1963] p. 261.)

[8] Ralph Kirkpatrick, *Domenico Scarlatti* (Princeton: Princeton University Press, 1953) p. 143.

[9] Newman points out that pre-classical Italian composers tended to favor two-movement sonatas, giving rise to the term "Italian sonata" for this type. About 20 percent of Haydn's forty-nine and Beethoven's thirty-two keyboard sonatas are in two movements. (See Newman, *The Sonata in the Classic Era*, pp. 133–34.)

ished") may be considered a torso since the two movements do not have the same tonic key (the second movement is in E major, the major subdominant of B minor).

For examples of Beethoven's two-movement piano sonatas, one may look briefly at op. 78 and op. 111. The former consists of a moderately fast first movement in sonata form followed by a very fast second movement in rondo form. Both movements are in the key of F♯ major. The fast and stormy first movement of op. 111 (in C *minor*) is in sonata form; the slow, tranquil second (in C *major*) is a theme with variations.[10]

THREE-MOVEMENT WORKS

The three-movement sonata, chamber work, or orchestral piece is an enlargement of the so-called Italian overture first introduced in the late seventeenth century by Alessandro Scarlatti. It consisted of three sections, F(ast)–S(low)–F(ast). All of Mozart's keyboard sonatas are of this type, as are three-fourths of Haydn's, and nearly half of Beethoven's.

> Haydn and Beethoven show a slight preference for a slow middle movement and Mozart for a moderate (i.e., andante) movement. Otherwise, their three-movement plans are too varied to generalize, including even the plan F–F–F (as in Beethoven's op. 10/2). Haydn uses a minuet as the middle or final movement in more than half his three-movement sonatas. Mozart uses it only twice, as the middle movement, and Beethoven not at all in his three-movement sonatas, though he does use a scherzo or quasi-scherzo in several instances, as in op. 27/2/ii. In the three-movement sonatas of all three masters, "sonata-form" or some approximation of it prevails in the first movements and rondo form in the finales....
>
> Haydn and Mozart did not use slow introductions in their keyboard sonatas, notwithstanding the use of them in their symphonies. The big Fantasy in c, K.V. 475, with which Mozart published his Sonata in c, K.V. 457, can hardly be reduced to that classification. But he did use slow introductions to the first movements in some of his sonatas for piano and violin, whether long and nearly independent (K.V. 385e) or short and unquestionably dependent (K.V. 454).[11]

A quite exceptional example is 27/2 (the "Moonlight" Sonata), in which movements i–ii–iii (S–F–F) are clearly similar in style and form to movements ii–iii–iv of Beethoven's four-movement sonatas. The composer's omission of the usual fast opening movement in sonata form is perhaps one indication of his growing romantic tendencies.

The three-movement classic-romantic concerto (F–S–F) dispenses with the minuet movement completely; a noteworthy exception is the four-movement plan (F–F–S–F) of Brahms's *Concerto no. 2 in B♭ major for Piano and Orchestra*, in which a scherzo with elements of sonata form is interpolated after the first movement. The form of a slow middle movement is somewhat less predictable than that of a fast outer move-

---

[10] A slow final movement may indicate a romantic inclination. In such late nineteenth and early twentieth century works as Mahler's *Symphony no. 4* and *no. 9*, his *Das Lied von der Erde*, and Tchaikovsky's *Symphony no. 6*, the slow finale is associated with a mood of resignation, pessimism, or despair.

[11] Newman, *The Sonata in the Classic Era*, pp. 135–36. For a description of characteristic key schemes in the classic era sonata as a whole, see Newman, p. 138.

ment; it may be a rondo, sonata form, simple or compound song form, or theme and variations. Last movements are generally rondos but may be in sonata, sonata-rondo, or variation form. First movements are the most predictable; absence of sonata form is extremely rare (see the exceptional BS, 27/2).

FOUR-MOVEMENT WORKS

The baroque suite, unless it includes one or more of the variable and optional dance movements is in four movements, *allemande-courante-sarabande-gigue*.[12]

The closely related *sonata da camera* (chamber sonata) also has four movements. See, for example, twelve such works for two violins and continuo, op. 2, by Corelli, which are mostly in such format as *preludio-allemanda-corrente* (or *sarabanda*)-*giga* (or *gavotta*).

The *sonata da chiesa* (church sonata), a contemporary of the sonata da camera, has a more serious and elevated style. It is without stylized dance movements, and generally features four movements in S–F–S–F sequence. The difference between the two types is very clear if one compares the three *camera* or suite-like partitas and the three *chiesa*-type sonatas for unaccompanied violin by Bach.

The number of movements varies considerably among works of a given composer, as well as among the works of composers writing in different countries and different styles. Thus it is not surprising to discover widely differing plans in the number and order of movements in, for example, Bach's *English Suites, French Suites,* partitas for solo clavier; sonatas and partitas for unaccompanied string instrument; sonatas for solo instrument with clavier accompaniment; and orchestral suites.

Even greater diversity of style, order, and content is found in suites of the nineteenth and twentieth centuries. They may be distinguished from contemporaneous sonatas, chamber works, and symphonies mainly by their comparative freedom from extensive elaboration and development, and a style that is more "relaxed" than "elevated."

Most symphonies and chamber works of the classic and romantic eras are in four movements rather than in three.[13] The scheme is essentially the same as that outlined for the three-movement work of this genre, but with a minuet (or scherzo) and trio appearing either before or, more commonly, after the slow movement.

WORKS OF MORE THAN FOUR MOVEMENTS

In the baroque suites, and in works of the sonata da camera type, the "standard" group is sometimes preceded by a prelude or, as in the orchestral suites of Bach, a French overture. Among the several dances or dance groups usually appearing before or after

---

[12] Apel observes (*Harvard Dictionary*, p. 815) that Froberger, generally regarded as the creator of the four-movement baroque suite, invariably ends with the (slow) sarabande rather than the later more generally preferred (fast) gigue. It was not until after his death "that the positions of the sarabande and gigue were exchanged as appears from the earliest printed edition of his suites (published posthumously in 1693) which bears the remark: 'mis en meilleur ordre' (put in better order)."

[13] See the exceptional five movements in Beethoven's *Symphony no. 6 in F major* ("Pastoral") and Berlioz's *Fantastic Symphony*. Mozart's *Symphony no. 38 in D major*, K. 504, has three.

the gigue there may be a minuet, bourrée, gavotte, passepied, rigaudon, or polonaise. Occasionally one of the first three may be augmented to form a compound ternary group (for example, Minuet I–Minuet II–Minuet I da capo).

In the early classic era the terms *divertimento, serenade,* and *cassation* were used to describe multimovement compositions in which elements of the symphony and the suite were combined. Usually at least two movements were of a dance type, the minuet being particularly favored. In these rather similarly planned works, the movements tend to be less developed, shorter, and more numerous than those of the more serious symphony of that time, befitting their usual function as entertainment pieces.

The late string quartets of Beethoven, op. 127, 130, 131, 132, 133, and 135 should be mentioned here. They are intensely personal documents, a kind of musical last testament, and show an enormous advance in style, form, and content over any previously written chamber works. Together with this composer's last keyboard sonatas and his *Symphony no. 9 in D minor,* these quartets signaled the arrival of musical romanticism more than any other instrumental works of their time. To this day they are unequaled in audacity of spirit and invention, and unparalleled in range and scope of expression.

The first and the last of the late quartets in number (but not in chronology), op. 127 and op. 135, are each in the "standard" four movements. Op. 133 (the "Great Fugue"), in one long movement, was originally planned as the last movement of op. 130. However, because of its great difficulty in performance, Beethoven was persuaded to substitute the present finale (his last completed composition), and the fugal movement was published separately with its own opus number.

Of the other quartets, op. 132 has five movements, of which the fourth is little more than an introduction to the finale;[14] op. 130 has six; and op. 131 has seven which follow one another without interruption. In the latter, the first movement is a slow fugue; sonata form is present in the second and seventh movements; the third is a recitativo-like introduction to the fourth which is a theme with variations; the fifth is a scherzo with double trio; and the sixth, like the third, serves as an introduction to the more extended movement that follows.

Among the monuments of large-scale musical forms, notable examples include Bach's *Die Kunst der Fuge* ("The Art of Fugue"), a series of fugues of diverse types all derived from a single subject; *Musikalisches Opfer* ("Musical Offering"), a number of very learned contrapuntal pieces and a trio sonata, all of which are based on a theme attributed to King Frederick the Great of Prussia; and *Das wohltemperierte Clavier* ("The Well-tempered Clavier"), two sets of preludes and fugues in all the major and minor keys.[15]

A work with text for one or more voices, with or without instrumental accompaniment, possesses an overall form that is a product of many extramusical as well as musical factors. Analysis of such compositions should reveal all the relevant factors and demonstrate the extent to which they interact with each other and with the musical elements. Sometimes one will be the central organizing principle or force, sometimes another.

[14] A similar arrangement may be observed in Mozart's *String Quintet in G minor,* K. 516.

[15] See the similarly arranged series of fugues and interludes for piano, *Ludus Tonalis,* by Paul Hindemith.

Included in this large category are song cycles, cantatas, oratorios, masses,[16] musical settings of the Passion, operas, and—as in the vast edifice of Wagner's *The Ring of the Nibelung*—opera cycles.

It is not possible to provide analyses of complete works of such magnitude here, but the studies that were undertaken should help to provide the basic skills needed for the analysis of any musical composition, regardless of its length, medium, style, or period.

SUGGESTED EXERCISES

1. Write an essay on one of the multimovement works by Bach, Beethoven, or Hindemith discussed in this chapter. Discuss the chief details and the broad formal outlines. Properly document your references to relevant literature, but for the most part base your report on original study and independent conclusions.

2. Devise diagrams of three or four large-scale works of different kinds in various media. Indicate the general outline and all essential features. Omit minor detail.

3. Using one of the diagrams prepared in Exercise 2, and after consultation with your instructor, compose an original work for one or more instruments and/or voices. Choose a practical medium that you can handle effectively and idiomatically. The finished composition should be given a public performance.

---

[16] The multimovement mass was well established as early as A.D. 500. The earliest known polyphonic setting of the Mass by a single composer was written by Guillaume de Machaut (ca. 1300–1377).

References

Bukofzer, Manfred. *Music in the Baroque Era*. New York: W. W. Norton, 1947.

Cone, Edward T. *Musical Form and Musical Performance*. New York: W. W. Norton, 1968.

Cooper, Grosvenor W., and Meyer, Leonard B. *The Rhythmic Structure of Music*. Chicago: University of Chicago Press, 1960.

Dickinson, A. E. F. *Bach's Fugal Works*. London: Pitman and Sons, 1956.

Ellinwood, Leonard. *The Works of Francesco Landini*. Cambridge: The Medieval Academy of America, 1939.

Erickson, Robert. *The Structure of Music*. 2d ed. New York: The Noonday Press, 1959.

Grove's Dictionary of Music. Edited by Eric Blom. 5th ed. New York: St. Martin's Press, 1954.

Harvard Dictionary of Music. Edited by Willi Apel. 3d ed. Cambridge: Harvard University Press, 1970.

Historical Anthology of Music. Edited by Archibald T. Davison and Willi Apel. Cambridge: Harvard University Press, 1950.

Horsley, Imogene. *Fugue, History and Practice*. New York: Free Press, 1966.

Journal of Music Theory. New Haven: Yale University Press.

Kennan, Kent. *Counterpoint*. Englewood Cliffs, N.J.: Prentice-Hall, 1959.

Kirkpatrick, Ralph. *Domenico Scarlatti*. Princeton: Princeton University Press, 1953.

Kohs, Ellis B. *Music Theory*. Vols. 1–2. New York: Oxford University Press, 1961.

LaRue, Jan. *Guidelines for Style Analysis*. New York: W. W. Norton, 1970.

Mann, Alfred. *The Study of Fugue*. New York: W. W. Norton, 1966.

Newman, William S. *The Sonata in the Baroque Era*. Rev. ed. Chapel Hill: University of North Carolina Press, 1966.

Newman, William S. *The Sonata in the Classic Era*. Chapel Hill: University of North Carolina Press, 1963.

Newman, William S. *The Sonata Since Beethoven*. 2d ed. New York: W. W. Norton, 1972.

Oldroyd, George. *The Technique and Spirit of Fugue*. London: Oxford University Press, 1948.

Parrish, Carl, and Ohl, John F. *Masterpieces of Music Before 1750*. New York: W. W. Norton, 1951.

Redlich, Hans. *Alban Berg*. New York; Abelard-Schuman, 1957.

Reese, Gustave. *Music in the Middle Ages*. New York: W. W. Norton, 1940.

Reese, Gustave. *Music in the Renaissance*. New York: W. W. Norton, 1954.

Reti, Rudolf. *The Thematic Process in Music*. New York: Macmillan, 1951.

Spitta, Philipp. *J. S. Bach*. New York: Dover Publications, 1961.

Tovey, Sir Donald Francis. *The Forms of Music*. [Articles drawn from the *Encyclopedia Britannica*.] New York: Meridian Books, 1956.

Index

Page numbers of musical examples appear in italics.

Alberti bass, *13*
Allemande, 327
Anacrusis, 7, 23, 40
Apel, Willi, 148, 219n, 261n, 324–25, 327n. *See also Harvard Dictionary of Music*
Appoggiatura chord, 28, *40*
Aria, *306–16*
Arioso, *304, 305*
Augmentation, 178, 183–84, *185, 195–98,* 210, 282

Bach, Johann Sebastian, 14, 18, 34, 89, 210
   Art of Fugue, The, 96, 188, 328
   Brandenburg Concertos, 34, 218
   chaconnes, 154–55
   chorale cantatas, 214
   chorale harmonizations, 201n
   chorale partita, "Vom Himmel hoch," 214
   chorale variations
     in *Clavierübung:* "Kyrie, Gott Vater in Ewigkeit," *212–13;* "Wir glauben all' an einen Gott," 214
     in *Eighteen Large Chorales:* "Allein Gott in der Höh' sei Ehr," *207,* 214; "Herr Jesu Christ, dich zu uns wend'," 214; "Komm, Gott, Schöpfer," *204;* "Komm, heiliger Geist, Herre Gott," 210–11; "Wenn wir in höchsten Nöten sein," 210
     in *Orgelbüchlein:* "Christ lag in Todesbanden," *215;* "Ich ruf' zu dir, Herr Jesu Christ," 208; "In dir ist Freude," *214;* "In dulci jubilo," *208;* "Jesus Christus, unser Heiland," *209;* "Komm, Gott Schöpfer," *204;* "O Mensch, bewein dein' Sünde gross," *206;* "Vom Himmel kam der Engel Schar," 208; "Wenn wir in höchsten Nöten sein," 210
     in *Six Schubler Chorales:* "Meine Seele erhebt den Herren," *211;* "Wachet auf," *204–05*
   concertos
     Brandenburg no. 3, 34; *no. 4,* 34; *no. 5,* 218; *no. 6,* 34
     in E major for Violin and Orchestra, 257, *258*
   correntes, *103. See also* Courante
   English Suites, 327
   French Suites, 327
   fugues, 96, 178–84, 187–88, 328. *See also* Bach: *Well-Tempered Clavier*
   Goldberg Variations, 163–65, 189, 214
   inventions
     Three-Voice, no. 9, 172, 173
     Two-Voice, no. 4, 169, 170
   Mass in B minor, 19, 147, *187, 188, 309–11*
   Musical Offering, 160n, 165, 177n, 186, 328

Bach, Johann Sebastian (cont.)
  partitas
    for clavier, 327; *no. 4 in D major,
      114–15; no. 5 in G major, 103*
    *for Unaccompanied Violin: no. 2
      in D minor,* 154–55; *no. 3 in E
      major,* 219, 220
    and sonatas for unaccompanied
      violin, compared, 327
  *Passacaglia and Fugue in C minor,
    148–53,* 179n, 325
  passions, 201, 205, *304–06, 313–14*
  "St. Anne" *Fugue in E♭ major,* 188
  St. John Passion, 201
  St. Matthew Passion, 201, 205,
    304–06, 313–14
  sonatas
    for Clavier and Violin, 34, 155–56,
      162, 188–89
    for unaccompanied violin, 327
  suites, for orchestra, 327
    no. 3 in D major, 102, 115–16
    See also Bach: *English Suites,
      French Suites,* partitas
  Well-Tempered Clavier, Volume 1,
    178–84
    Fugue no. 1 in C major, 178–81,
      183
    Fugue no. 2 in C minor, 179–81,
      182, 183, 187, *190–94*
    Fugue no. 7 in E♭ major, 182
    Fugue no. 8 in D♯ minor, 178–79,
      184, 187
    Fugue no. 11 in F major, 178–79,
      182, *187*
    Fugue no. 12 in F minor, 39
    Fugue no. 14 in F♯ minor, 182
    Fugue no. 16 in G minor, 37–38
    Fugue no. 22 in B♭ minor, 95
    Prelude no. 1 in C major, 12; *no.
      13 in F♯ major,* 12; *no. 14 in F♯
      minor,* 12; *no. 19 in A major,
      173, 174; no. 20 in A minor,* 12
  Well-Tempered Clavier, Volume 2,
    183, 187
    Fugue no. 2 in C minor, 187, 190,
      195–98
    Fugue no. 9 in E major, 184, *185*
    Prelude no. 22 in B♭ minor, 94
Balance, 1–3
Ballade, 217

Ballata, 217
Bar form, 311, *312*
Bartók, Béla, *11,* 43, 143, 201, 206
Basso ostinato, *see* Ground bass;
    Ostinato; Passacaglia
Beethoven, Ludwig van
  concertos, piano
    no. 4 in G major, 252n, 264
    no. 5 in E♭ major, 260, 263
  Leonore Overture, no. 3, 263, 266
  quartets, strings
    op. 18/1, *298–300*
    op. 18/3, *294–96*
    op. 18/5, *139–40*
    op. 59/1, 261n, *249–52*
    op. 127, 328
    op. 130, 328
    op. 131, 184, 328
    op. 132, 328
    op. 133, 328
    op. 135, 263, 328
  sonatas, piano, 263, 326
    op. 2/1, 10, 12, 28–29, *40–42,* 69,
      84–85, 122–23, 221–22
    op. 2/2, 29, *41,* 69, 77, 229
    op. 2/3, *31–32*
    op. 7, 29, 37, *83,* 229
    op. 10/1, 31, 132, *133*
    op. 10/2, 43, *50,* 189, 326
    op. 10/3, *45, 49, 59, 82*
    op. 13, *8, 13,* 29, *63, 224–29,
      239–46,* 263, *274–77*
    op. 14/1, *13,* 28, 56, *84, 116*
    op. 14/2, *30, 135*
    op. 22, 24, *60, 66, 112*
    op. 26, *65, 67, 100, 109, 117,* 124
    op. 27/1, 24
    op. 27/2, *30, 41,* 66, 326
    op. 28, *14, 60, 66, 113, 131*
    op. 31/2, 263n, 297
    op. 49/2, 294
    op. 78, 263, 326
    op. 79, 291
    op. 81a, 263
    op. 106, *186*
    op. 110, *185–86,* 263n
    op. 111, 263, 326
  symphonies, 262–63
    no. 3 in E♭ major, 138–39, 143,
      189, 268, 315
    no. 4 in B♭ major, 126, 262

no. 5 in C minor, 8, 43, 81
no. 6 in F major, 327n
no. 7 in A major, 126, 189, 262
no. 8 in F major, 266
no. 9 in D minor, 323, 328
Bellini, Vincenzo, 18
Berg, Alban, *117–18,* 186, 215
Berlioz, Hector, *35,* 203–04, *315–16,*
    322, 327n
Biber, Heinrich, 148n
Binary form, 69, 99–119, 291
    elements in ternary form, 107
    rounded, 69, 111–12
Bizet, Georges, 14, *144*
Bourrée, 328
Brahms, Johannes, 265, 267, 277–78,
    323
    Concerto no. 2 for Piano and
      Orchestra, 326
    intermezzi
      op. 116/2, *61*
      op. 118/5, *8,* 32
    key schemes in symphonies, first
      movements, 277–78
    rhapsodies
      op. 79/2, *12, 42*
      op. 119/4, 85, *86*
    romances, op. 118/5, 32
    Sonata no. 3 in D minor for Violin
      and Piano, 13, *14,* 82, 268
    symphonies, 277–78, 294
      no. 1 in C minor, 14, 144–45
      no. 2 in D major, 126, *278–83*
      no. 3 in F major, 275–76
      no. 4 in E minor, 157, 277–78
    Variations on a Theme by Joseph
      Haydn, 95, 146, 157
Bridge, 116n, 173, *174, 178,* 180
Bruckner, Anton, 265
Bukofzer, Manfred, 178, 202
Buxtehude, 214

Cadence, 19, 25–35
    authentic, 25, 28–31
    covered, 22n, 56n, *174*
    deceptive, 29, 49, 283
    evaded, 27, *49–50*
    extended, 28, 33, 48–49, *274, 280*
    half, 26, 32–34
    imperfect authentic, 25, 31

modal, 26, 34–35, *35*
    perfect authentic, 25–31
    Phrygian, 26, 34, 295. *See also*
      Cadence, modal
    with Picardy third, 27n, 58
    plagal, 25–26, 32–33, *314*
    rhythmic delay of, 30
    types, mixed, 32–33, *33*
    weakened by continuing motion,
      29–31
    weakened by lack of explicit
      harmony, 30, *31*
    weight, factors affecting, 26–27
Cadenza, 24, *235,* 263n, 288, 301
Cancrizans, 93, *96, 178, 186*
Canon, 159–60, *160–65, 208–09,* 214
    double, *208*
Canonic imitation, 23, 43, *44, 131–32,*
    171–72, 183
Cantata, 214, 329
Cassation, 328
Cesura, 22, 51
Chaconne, 148–49, *154–55*
Chain of phrases, 81, *82–83*
Chain phrase, 43–44, 81, *82*
Chopin, Frederic, 18
Chorale
    canonic, 202, *208–09*
    cantata, 214
    characteristics of, 201–03
    "Es ist genug" in Berg Violin
      Concerto, 215
    fantasia, 202, 214
    figured, 202, 214, *215*
    fugue, 202, *210–13*
    motet, 202, *210–11*
    ornamented, 202, *206–07*
    partita, 202, 214
    prelude, 201
    variation, *201–15*
Circle of fifths, 155n
Closed form, 177n. *See also* Open form
Closing section (theme or group), in
    sonata form, 262n, 264–65,
    267–68, 272–75, 277, 279, 283,
    287, 288. *See also* Second theme;
    Sonata form; Sonata-rondo;
    Sonatina form
Coda, 107, 109, 118, *119,* 126, 132, 139,
    198, 219, 223, 228, 229, 246, 251,
    253, 257, 259–60, 262, 268, 277,

Coda (cont.)
278, 283, 286, 289, 293, 297–98,
300, 301, 309–11, 313, 313–14,
320, 325
compared with codetta, 135n, 267
as second development in sonata
form, 268
Codetta, 8, 139, 238, 239, 265, 267,
270–72, 274–75, 277, 279,
288–89, 291–94, 296, 301
Compound song forms, 121–26
Compression
formal, 249, 254–57, 282, 286, 294
interval, 92
Concerto
first movement form, 264
rondo forms in, 257–60
sonata form in, 287–89
sonatina-rondo form in, 300–02
Contrary motion, 91
Contrast, 1–3
Cooper, Grosvenor, 262n
Corelli, Arcangelo, 327
Corrente, 103. See also Courante
Counterpoint
double (invertible), 93, 169, 170–73
triple (invertible), 172, 173
Countersubject, see Fugue
Courante, 327. See also Corrente

Da capo aria, 312, 313–14
Dance forms, 99, 103, 327. See also
Allemande; Bach: English
Suites, French Suites, partitas,
Passacaglia and Fugue in C
minor, suites; Corrente;
Courante; Divertimento;
Gavotte; Gigue; Minuet and
trio; Passacaglia; Passepied;
Rigaudon; Sarabande; Suite
Debussy, Claude, 17, 324
Development
fugal, 181–87
in sonata form, 265–88 passim
in sonata-rondo form, 296–301
in sonatina-form recapitulation,
294–95
interpolated, 249
Diagram procedure, 23–24, 39–40,
44–45, 73–76

Diminution, 81–92, 178, 184, 185–86,
279
Dissolution
compared to extension, 78
of period, 62
of phrase, 38
in rondo form, 223
in small part form, 116
in sonata-form development, 271,
276
Divertimento, 328
Double canon, 208
Double counterpoint, 169, 173
Dvořák, Antonin, 163n, 263
Dynamics, 27

Elision, 22–23, 27, 30, 39, 224,
282, 297–98
Episode
in fugato, 253
in fugue, 178, 180, 189–98
in invention, 169, 173–74
in sonatina, 294
Erickson, Robert, 165
Expansion of motive interval, 92
Exposition
double
in concerto sonata form, 287–88
in fugue, 178–81
in fugue, 178–81, 190, 195
in sonata form, 263–65, 267–88
passim
in sonata-rondo form, 296–301
passim
in sonatina form, 291–96 passim
Extension
of chain phrase, 44
confirming, compared with
dissolution, 78
in course, 47, 48, 51, 73, 76
dissolving, 78–79
of the period, 73–78
of the phrase, 23, 44, 47–52
by phrase repetition, 50
postcadential, 23, 49, 76–77, 279
precadential, 49, 51, 76, 78
preliminary, 47, 51–52, 76
of small part form, 116–19
in variation form, 140–41

Fantasia, 325
First-movement form, 261
Four-movement works, 327
Fragmentation, *10–11*, 94
French overture, 325, 327
Frere Jacques, *3*
Frescobaldi, Girolamo, *10*
Froberger, Johann Jakob, 327n
Fugato, 189, 252
Fughetta, 189
Fugue, 177–89, *188–98*
  accompanied, 177n, 188
  answer, 179–80, *190, 195*
  in Beethoven, *185–86, 328*
  bridge in, 180
  counterexposition in, 181
  countersubject in, 179–81, *190–98*
  defined, 177
  development section in, 181–87,
    190–98 passim
  double, 177n, 187–88
  episode in, 178, 180, *190–98*
  exposition section in, 178–81, *190,*
    195
  and invention compared, 169, 189
  key scheme in, 181–82
  Passacaglia and, 325
  response, 178–80, *190, 195*
  and rondo compared, 218
  style in chorale variation, 201–02,
    211–13
  subject, 177–78
    augmentation of, *184–85*
    diminution of, *184–85*
    double diminution of, *186*
    inversion of, 182n, 183, *185–86*
    modulating, 179
    order of entries, 180
    retrograde of, *186*
    stretto, *183–86, 195–98*
  triple, 177n, 188
  without episodes, 178n
  See also Fugato; Fughetta

Gavotte, *220–21, 328*
Gigue, 327
Goethe, Wolfgang von, 303, 316
Gregorian chant, 18, *19*
Ground bass, 141, *145–47*. *See also*
  Ostinato; Passacaglia

Handel, Frederic, 32
Harmony, 27
Harvard Dictionary of Music, 17n,
  148n, 165, 201n, 219n, 261n,
  325n, 327n
Haydn, Franz Joseph, 4, 86, 163, 264,
  259–72, 323, 325n, 326
Hindemith, Paul, 34, 165, 201, 328n
Historical Anthology of Music, 148n,
  215n
Homme Armé, l', 96

Idée fixe, 324
Imitation, 7, *89–90,* 299
Imitation, compared with sequence, 89
Incipient ternary form, *see* Ternary
  form, incipient
Interlude, *307–08, 309–11, 313–14,*
  315, 317–18
Interpolation, 10n, 187, 249, *250–51,*
  253, 296–97, 326
Introduction
  single phrase as, 41
  in sonata form, 262–63, *274, 276,* 326
  in sonatina form, 294
  in vocal forms, 306, *307–08,* 313
Invention, 12, 169–70, *170–74,* 201–02,
  209
  compared with fugue, 169, 189
Invention style, in chorale variation,
  209
Inversion, 8, *10–11,* 91, 170, 178, 182n,
  185–86
Italian overture, 326
Italian sonata, 325n

Kennan, Kent, 202
Key relationships in sonata form,
  265, 267
Key schemes
  in Brahms symphonies, first
    movements, 278
  in Mozart sonata-form movements,
    268
  in sonata-rondo form, 297
Kirkpatrick, Ralph, 325n
Kohs, Ellis B., *96, 171–72, 209, 255–57*
Krenek, Ernst, 214

Landino, Francesco, 217
Language, compared with music, 19–21
Leitmotiv, 324
L'homme Armé, 96
Liszt, Franz, 18

Machaut, Guillaume de, 217, 329n
Mahler, Gustav, 265, 326n
Mass, 329. *See also* Bach: *Mass in B minor*
Measure counting, 23–24
Melody, *17–24*, 27
Mendelssohn, Felix, *52,* 223–24, *263*
Meyer, Leonard B., 262n
Minuet and trio, 69, 121, *122–26 passim,* 325, 327
Mitchell, William, 33
Mode, 27
Motet style, in chorale variation, 201–02, 210
Motive, *3, 7–14,* 21
Mozart, Wolfgang Amadeus, 18, 86, 323, 326
   concertos
      no. 3 in E♭ major for Horn and Orchestra, K. 447, 259
      no. 4 in D major for Violin and Orchestra, K. 218, 287–88
      no. 20 in D minor for Piano and Orchestra, K. 466, 300–01
   Fantasy and Sonata for piano, K. 475 and 457, 326
   key schemes, in sonata-form movements, 268
   The Magic Flute, 306, 308
   The Marriage of Figaro, 291
   Quartet, String, in G major, K. 387, 189
   Quintet, String, in G minor, K. 516, *124–26,* 328n
   Sonatas for piano, 262–63, 268
      K. 279 (*in C major*), *13,* 28–29, *40–41,* 272–74
      K. 280 (*in F major*), 48
      K. 281 (*in B♭ major*), 61, *254,* 292, *293–94*
      K. 282 (*in E♭ major*), 48, 292–93
      K. 283 (*in G major*), *11,* 29, *39,* 44, *50–51,* 56, 62, 67
      K. 284 (*in D major*), 23, *41, 44, 57, 62, 135–38*
      K. 309 (*in C major*), *13, 47, 49, 61, 64, 67, 132–33*
      K. 310 (*in A minor*), 29–30, 51, *113–14*
      K. 311 (*in D major*), 29, 77, 229–30, *230–38*
      K. 330 (*in C major*), 45, *101*
      K. 331 (*in A major*), 45
      K. 332 (*in F major*), 44, 58, *78–79, 291–92*
      K. 333 (*in B♭ major*), 8, *130*
      K. 533/494 (*in F major*), 68, 108, 246n, *131–32*
      K. 545 (*in C major*), *13,* 69, 129, 266, 297–98
      K. 547 (*in F major*), 92, 297n
      K. 570 (*in B♭ major*), *101–02 108,* 126
      K. 576 (*in D major*), 58, 126, *131,* 162–63, 297
      See also Mozart: Fantasy and Sonata for piano
   sonatas for piano and violin, 326
   symphonies, 262
      K. 96 (*in C major*), *103*
      K. 133 (*in D major*), *104*
      K. 184 (*in E♭ major*), 269
      K. 504 (*no. 38, "Prague," in D major*), 327n
      K. 551 (*no. 41, "Jupiter," in C major*), 189

Newman, William S., 325n, 326n

One-part form, 99
Open form, 177n
Opera, 329. *See also* Aria; Bar form; Da capo aria; Recitative
Oratorio, 329. *See also* Bach: *St. John Passion, St. Matthew Passion*
Orchestration, 27
Ostinato, 14, 143, *144–45, 155, 156, 172,* 253

Pachelbel, Johann, 214
Paganini, Niccolò, 18

Partita, *see* Bach: partitas

Passacaglia, *148–53, 325*
   compared with chaconne, 148

Passepied, 328

Pedal point, 13, *14, 31,* 253

Period, 55–70
   contrasting construction, *60–61*
   dissolved, 62, *68*
   double, 66, *67*
   with double antecedent, *62–63*
   with double antecedent and double
      consequent, 65, *66*
   with double consequent, *63*
   extended, *73–79*
   four-phrase, 64n, *65–67*
   with mixed construction, *62*
   modulating, *58–60*
   nonmodulating, *56–67*
   nonperiod, *67–70*
   parallel construction, *56–58,* 297
   questionable, *61*
   repeated, *66*
   with repeated antecedent and
      consequent, *65*
   repeated four-phrase, 64n
   with sequential construction,
      59–60
   three-phrase, *62–64*
   two-phrase, *55–62*

Phrase, 17–24, 37–52
   antecedent, 55, *56–67*
   chain of phrases, *82–86*
   chain phrase, *43–45, 81, 82*
   consequent, 55, *56–67*
   dissolved, 38
   extension, 23, *42,* 44, *47–52*
   group, 81, *82–86*
   group, chain phrase and chain of
      phrases compared, 81
   length, 22, *39–43*
   melodic, *17–24, 37–38*
   melodic and structural compared,
      37–38
   member, *43, 51*
   nonphrase, 45, *45*
   overlapping, *37–39*
   repetition, *50*
   rhythmic structure of, *21–22*
   as structural unit, *37–38*

Picardy third, 58

Piston, Walter, *252–53*

Polonaise, 328

Polyphony, 89–96, 143–215

Postlude, 320. *See also* Coda; Codetta

Prelude, 12, *317,* 323, 327

Principal theme (group or section), in
      sonata form
   exposition, 263–64, 267–88 *passim*
   omitted from recapitulation, 266
   recapitulation, 266, 271, *273,* 277,
      282, *285,* 286
   See also Sonata-rondo; Sonatina
      form

Prokofiev, Serge, *105, 314*

Purcell, Henry, 14, 147, *147*

Quodlibet, 163

Recapitulation, 266–67, 271, 273, 277,
      282, *285,* 288
   false, 266
   themes in reverse order, 268, 297
   use of development procedures in,
      294

Recitative (recitativo), 303–04, *304–06,*
      325, 328

Reese, Gustave, 217n, 218

Register, 27

Repetition, 1–3, 11. *See also* Period,
      repeated; Phrase repetition;
      Rondo; Sonata form; Song
      forms

Reti, Rudolf, 324

Retransition, 116–17, 126, 144, 218,
      223–24, 266, 281–82, *285,*
      291–92, 298, 301. *See also*
      Transition

Retrograde, 93, *96,* 178, *186*

Rhythm, 18–19, 21–22, 26

Ricercare, 177n

Rigaudon, 328

Ritornello, 218

Rondeau
   baroque, 219–20, *220–21,* 257, *258*
   medieval, 217

Rondo, 126, 217–60
   ABABA-type, *221–24*
   ABACA-type, *224–29*
   ABACABA-type, *229–46*
   compressed, *254–57*

Rondo (cont.)
  extended, *249–53*
  as part of movement, *221–22*
  and rondeau compared, 218
  small and large compared, 218
  sonata-, 219n, 257–58, 296, *297–300*
  types of, 219
  See also Sonata-rondo
Round, 159
Rounded form, 83. *See also* Binary
  form, rounded

Sarabande, 154, 327n
Scarlatti, Alessandro, 326
Scarlatti, Domenico, 40, 99n, 325
Scherzo
  and trio, 121–22, *123–24*
  with two trios, 126
Schoenberg, Arnold, 186
Schubert, Franz, 9, 43, 265, 269, 303,
  307–08, 316–20, 325–26
Schumann, Robert, 22, 94
Second theme (group or section), in
  sonata form
  exposition, 14, 264, 267–68, 270, 272,
  275, 278, 279, *284, 287–88*
  recapitulation, 267–68, 271, 277, 282,
  286, 289
  See also Sonata-rondo; Sonatina
  form
Sequence, *42,* 89, 170, *173*
  compared with imitation, 89
Serenade, 328
Sinfonia, *see* Invention
Slow final movement, 326n
Sonata, 261, 323–27 *passim*
  -allegro, 261
  da camera, 327
  da chiesa, 327
Sonata form, 261–89, 327
  closing section, *see* Closing section
  coda, 13, 268. *See also* Coda
  development section, 8–9, 13,
  265–66, *271, 273,* 276, 277, 280,
  284, 288
  diminutive, 267, *272–74. See also*
  Sonatina form
  double-exposition, *287–89*
  exceptional procedures in design of,
  267–68

exposition section, 263–65, *269–70,*
  272, 274–75, 277–78, *279,*
  283–84, 287–88. See also
  Sonatina form
introduction, 262–63. *See also*
  Introduction
key relationships in, 264–65, 267,
  277–78
large outline of, 261–62
musico-dramatic structure of, 262
recapitulation section, 266–68, 271,
  273, 277–78, 282, *285–86,*
  288–89. See also Sonatina form
retransitions in, *see* Retransition
third theme in, 278
  See also Principal theme; Second
  theme
Sonata-rondo, 219, 257–58, 296,
  297–300
Sonatina form, 267, *291–96*
  compared with sonatina, 291
Sonatina-rondo, in concerto last
  movement, 300–02
Song cycle, 329
Song forms, 99–126. *See also*
  Vocal forms
Space, musical, 4
Stravinsky, Igor, 86, *145,* 266,
  283–86
Stretto 11, 91, 178, 183, *184–86,*
  196–97
Strophic form, 315
Structure and ornament compared, 4
Subject, fugue, *see* Fugue, subject
Suite, 99, *102,* 327n. *See also* Bach:
  partitas, suites
Suite style, in chorale variation,
  201–02
Symphony, 261–83 *passim,* 323–27
  passim. See also Beethoven:
  symphonies; Brahms:
  symphonies; Mozart:
  symphonies

Tchaikovsky, Peter I., 263, 326n
Tempo, 27
Ternary form, 69, 83, 107, *108–10,*
  121–26, 312, *313–14, 315*
  incipient, 111, *112–16*
Texture, 4, 27

Thematic transformation, 9–10, 276
Third theme (group or section), in
      sonata form, 264, *278–82*
Three-movement works, 326–27
Three-part form, *see* Ternary form
Through-composed form, 316,
      317–19
Toccata, 325
Transition, 8, 11, 116n, 126, 141, 264,
      266, 270, *272, 273, 275–76,*
      282, 283, 286, 287–88, *293–96,*
      301. *See also* Retransition
   compared with retransition and
      bridge, 116n
Trio (minuet or scherzo), defined,
      121–22
Triple counterpoint, 172, *173*
Two-movement works, 324–26
Two-part form, *see* Binary form

Variation, 1–4, 129–56, 201–15
   character, 134, *140*

chorale, *201–15*
combined with rondo form, 249, 255
continuous, 134, 141
form, 134–56, 327
free, 134, *139*
homophonic, *129–41*
polyphonic, 143, *144–56, 201–15*
procedure, compared with variation
      form, 129
in repeated or double period,
      131–32
in repeated phrase, *129–30*
sectional, 134, 141
strict, 134, 141
Vaughan Williams, Ralph, 34
Verdi, Giuseppe, 189
Virelai, 217
Vocal forms, 303, *304–20*

Wagner, Richard, 4, 7, 189, 311,
      312, 324, 329
Webern, Anton von, 4, 165
Wolf, Hugo, 118, *119,* 315

BCDEFGHIJ-H-79876

781.5 K827mc1   AAO-3237
Kohs, Ellis B.,   060101 000
Musical form : studies in anal

0 00003 01984100 0

Johnson State College

PLEASE NOTE
TO SAVE DOLLARS

No overdue notice will be sent on this material. If not returned or renewed by date on due slip, you will be billed for replacement costs. Minimum charge $10.00.

Johnson State College
Johnson, Vermont 05656